GHOSTS: AN ENEMY OF THE PEOPLE: THE WILD DUCK

GHOSTS: AN ENEMY OF THE PEOPLE: THE WILD DUCK:

BY HENRIK IBSEN.

EDITED BY

WILLIAM ARCHER

GYAN

Published by

Gyan Publishing House
5, Ansari Road
Daryaganj, New Delhi-110002
Phone: 011-47034999, 9811692060
E-mail: books@gyanbooks.com

Distribution Network
gyanbooks.com
India, USA, Canada, UK, Australia

ISBN: 978-81-212-0544-3 (HB)
First Published, 1881

2nd Impression 2024

Printed at: Gyan Press, Delhi.

GHOSTS: AN ENEMY OF THE PEOPLE: THE WILD DUCK
Author: HENRIK IBSEN, Editor: WILLIAM ARCHER

GHOSTS: AN ENEMY OF THE PEOPLE: THE WILD DUCK:

BY HENRIK IBSEN.

AUTHORISED ENGLISH EDITION.

EDITED BY

WILLIAM ARCHER.

FOURTH EDITION.

THE WALTER SCOTT PUBLISHING CO., LTD.,
PATERNOSTER SQUARE, LONDON, E.C.
CHARLES SCRIBNER'S SONS,
153–157 FIFTH AVENUE, NEW YORK.
1906.

CONTENTS.

PREFATORY NOTE.

It is impossible to find an English word which exactly represents the Norwegian *Gengangere,* the title of the first play in this volume. It means literally "Again-goers," spirits that "walk." The French word "Revenants" comes nearer the sense than the English *Ghosts,* which, however, seems to be the best available equivalent.

The three plays contained in this volume stand in a certain historic relation to each other, which I may perhaps indicate without trespassing upon criticism properly so called. The publication of *Ghosts* brought down upon Ibsen's head a perfect tempest of obloquy. Critics who had hitherto been friendly, turned round and attacked him furiously; while "the general public and its representatives in the press," says Henrik Jæger, "raised a howl of reprobation such as had not been heard since the appearance of *Love's Comedy.*" Oddly enough (for one would have imagined him prepared for an outburst of exasperation) Ibsen seems to have been astonished to find his play thus received. If not astonished, he was at any rate indignant; and in shorter time than usual he produced a new play, *An Enemy of the People.* It is impossible not to recognise the analogy between Dr. Stockmann's position and that of the poet himself. Ibsen, like Stockmann, thought to win the gratitude of his fellow-countrymen by speaking out the truth as he conceived it; Ibsen, like

Stockmann, found himself deserted by his friends, denied his right of free utterance (on the stage), and denounced as an enemy of society. It would be easy to carry this analogy too far, and nothing could be more unjust than to regard *An Enemy of the People* as a mere polemic parable; but it certainly took its rise in a mood of half-humorous indignation. Having so far unburdened his soul, the poet apparently suffered a reaction, and passed from vigorous, cheerful defiance into dejection and scepticism. This mood dominates *The Wild Duck*, the gloomiest of all Ibsen's plays, in which he seems to caricature his own motives, and scoff at his own ideals. Gregers Werle, no less than Thomas Stockmann, may be regarded as in some sense a fantastic adumbration of the poet himself. With *The Wild Duck*, however, he worked off the mingled indignation and depression begotten by the *Ghosts* incident. In his next play, *Rosmersholm*, he returns to the unqualified objectivity of his earlier manner.

The following translation of *Ghosts* is to some extent founded upon a version of that play by Miss Frances Lord, which appeared several years ago in a magazine. The Editor of the "Camelot Series" volume of Ibsen's plays, having obtained Miss Lord's consent to the republication of her version, requested me to revise it. I did so, very carefully; and I have since re-revised my revision, so that scarcely a phrase of the original translation remains unaltered. It would be equally unjust to Miss Lord and to myself to represent as hers a text for which she is in no way responsible. At the same time I have pleasure in acknowledging my indebtedness to her rendering of the play. In prose translation, the pioneer has always the hardest task. The text of *An Enemy of the People*, as it now stands, differs largely from that which appeared in the "Camelot Series" volume. For all alterations, whether for the better or for the worse, I alone am answerable. I hope, however, that the essential merits of Mrs. Marx-Aveling's spirited and ingenious rendering will be found intact. *The Wild Duck* is now for the first time translated into English. It is probably the most difficult of all Ibsen's modern plays to render satisfactorily. Gina Ekdal's speeches are especially troublesome. Her language is that of an uneducated woman of the small-shopkeeper class, full of vulgarisms and Malapropisms. Some of her Malapropisms have been reproduced; others it would have been impossible to indicate without departing altogether too widely from the sense of the original. Dr. Relling's speeches, too, are full of stumbling-blocks for the translator, who has, however, spared no effort to remove them from the reader's path.

W. A.

GHOSTS.

(1881.)

Characters.

Mrs. Alving (**Helen**), *widow of Captain Alving, late Chamberlain* to the King.*

Oswald Alving, *her son, a painter.*

Pastor Manders.

Jacob Engstrand, *a carpenter.*

Regina Engstrand, *Mrs. Alving's maid.*

The action takes place at Mrs. Alving's country-house, beside one of the large fjords in Western Norway.

* Chamberlain (Kammerherre) is the only title of honour now existing in Norway. It is a distinction conferred by the King on men of wealth and position, and is not hereditary.

GHOSTS:

A FAMILY-DRAMA IN THREE ACTS.

Act First.

(*A spacious garden-room, with one door to the left, and two doors to the right. In the middle of the room a round table, with chairs about it. On the table lie books, periodicals, and newspapers. In the foreground to the left a window, and by it a small sofa, with a work-table in front of it. In the background, the room is continued into a somewhat narrower conservatory, which is shut in by glass walls with large panes. In the right-hand wall of the conservatory is a door leading down into the garden. Through the glass wall one catches a glimpse of a gloomy fjord-landscape, veiled by steady rain.*)

(ENGSTRAND, *the carpenter, stands by the garden-door. His left leg is somewhat bent; he has a clump of wood under the sole of his boot.* REGINA, *with an empty garden syringe in her hand, hinders him from advancing.*)

REGINA (*in a low voice*). What do you want? Stop where you are. You're positively dripping.

ENGSTRAND. It's the Lord's own rain, my girl.

REGINA. It's the devil's rain, *I* say.

ENGSTRAND. Lord! how you talk, Regina. (*Limps a few steps forward into the room.*) What I wanted to say was this——

REGINA. Don't clatter so with that foot of yours, I tell you! The young master's asleep upstairs.

REGINA. Haven't you many a time sworn at me and called me a——? *Fi donc!*

ENGSTRAND. Curse me, now, if ever I used such an ugly word.

REGINA. Oh! I know quite well what word you used.

ENGSTRAND. Well, but that was only when I was a bit on, don't you know? Hm! Temptations are manifold in this world, Regina.

REGINA. Ugh!

ENGSTRAND. And besides, it was when your mother rode her high horse. I had to find something to twit her with, my child. She was always setting up for a fine lady. (*Mimics.*) "Let me go, Engstrand; let me be. Remember I've been three years in Chamberlain Alving's family at Rosenvold." (*Laughs.*) Mercy on us! She could never forget that the Captain was made a Chamberlain while she was in service here.

REGINA. Poor mother! you very soon worried her into her grave.

ENGSTRAND (*turns on his heel*). Oh, of course! I'm to be blamed for everything.

REGINA (*turns away; half aloud*). Ugh! And that leg too!

ENGSTRAND. What do you say, girl?

REGINA. *Pied de mouton.*

ENGSTRAND. Is that English, eh?

REGINA. Yes.

ENGSTRAND. Oh, ah; you've picked up some learning out here; and that may come in useful now, Regina.

REGINA (*after a short silence*). What do you want with me in town?

ENGSTRAND. Can you ask what a father wants with his only child? Am I not a lonely and forsaken widower?

REGINA. Oh! don't try on any nonsense like that! Why do you want me?

ENGSTRAND. Well, let me tell you, I've been thinking of starting a new line of business.

REGINA (*contemptuously*). You've tried that often enough, and never done any good.

ENGSTRAND. Yes, but this time you shall see, Regina! Devil take me——

REGINA (*stamps*). Don't swear!

ENGSTRAND. Hush, hush; you're right enough there, my girl. What I wanted to say was just this—I've laid by a very tidy pile from this Orphanage job.

REGINA. Have you? That's a good thing for you.

ENGSTRAND. What can a man spend his ha'pence on here in the country?

REGINA. Well, what then?

ENGSTRAND. Why, you see, I thought of putting the money into some paying speculation. I thought of a sort of sailors' tavern——

REGINA. Horrid!

ENGSTRAND. A regular high-class affair, of course; not a mere pigstye for common sailors. No! damn it! it would be for captains and mates, and—and—all those swells, you know.

REGINA. And I was to——?

ENGSTRAND. You were to help, to be sure. Only

for appearance' sake, you understand. Devil a bit of hard work shall you have, my girl. You shall do exactly what you like.

REGINA. Oh, indeed!

ENGSTRAND. But there must be a petticoat in the house; that's as clear as daylight. For I want to have it a little lively in the evenings, with singing and dancing, and so forth. You must remember they're weary wanderers on the ocean of life. (*Nearer.*) Now don't be stupid and stand in your own light, Regina. What can become of you out here? Your mistress has given you a lot of learning; but what good is it to you? You're to look after the children at the new Orphanage, I hear. Is that the sort of thing for you, eh? Are you so desperately bent upon wearing yourself out for the sake of the dirty brats?

REGINA. No; if things go as I want them to, then—well, there's no saying—there's no saying.

ENGSTRAND. What do you mean by "there's no saying"?

REGINA. Never you mind. How much money have you saved up here?

ENGSTRAND. What with one thing and another, a matter of seven or eight hundred crowns.[1]

REGINA. That's not so bad.

ENGSTRAND. It's enough to make a start with, my girl.

REGINA. Aren't you thinking of giving me any?

ENGSTRAND. No, I'm damned if I am!

REGINA. Not even of sending me a scrap of stuff for a new dress?

[1] A "krone" is equal to one shilling and three-halfpence.

ENGSTRAND. If you'll come to town with me, you can get dresses enough.

REGINA. Pooh! I can do that on my own account if I want to.

ENGSTRAND. No, a father's guiding hand is what you want, Regina. Now, I've my eye on a capital house in Little Harbour Street. It won't need much ready-money, and it could be a sort of sailors' home, you know.

REGINA. But I will *not* live with you. I have nothing whatever to do with you. Be off!

ENGSTRAND. You wouldn't remain long with me, my girl. No such luck! If you knew how to play your cards, such a fine girl as you've grown in the last year or two——

REGINA. Well?

ENGSTRAND. You'd soon get hold of some mate —or perhaps even a captain——

REGINA. I won't marry any one of that sort. Sailors have no *savoir vivre.*

ENGSTRAND. What haven't they got?

REGINA. I know what sailors are, I tell you. They're not the sort of people to marry.

ENGSTRAND. Then never mind about marrying them. You can make it pay all the same. (*More confidentially.*) He—the Englishman—the man with the yacht—he gave three hundred dollars, he did; and she wasn't a bit handsomer than you.

REGINA (*going towards him*). Out you go!

ENGSTRAND (*falling back*). Come, come! You're not going to strike me, I hope.

REGINA. Yes, if you begin to talk about

mother I shall strike you. Get away with you, I say. (*Drives him back towards the garden door.*) And don't bang the doors. Young Mr. Alving——

ENGSTRAND. He's asleep; I know. It's curious how you're taken up about young Mr. Alving—(*more softly*) Oho! it surely can't be he that——?

REGINA. Be off at once! You're crazy, I tell you! No, not that way. There comes Pastor Manders. Down the kitchen stairs with you.

ENGSTRAND (*towards the right*). Yes, yes, I'm going. But just you talk to him that's coming there. He's the man to tell you what a child owes its father. For I am your father all the same, you know. I can prove it from the church-register.

(*He goes out through the second door to the right, which* REGINA *has opened, and fastens again after him.* REGINA *glances hastily at herself in the mirror, dusts herself with her pocket handkerchief, and settles her collar; then she busies herself with the flowers.* PASTOR MANDERS, *in an overcoat, with an umbrella, and with a small travelling-bag on a strap over his shoulder, comes through the garden door into the conservatory.*)

MANDERS. Good morning, Miss Engstrand.

REGINA (*turning round, surprised and pleased*). No, really! Good morning, Pastor Manders. Is the steamer in already?

MANDERS. It's just in. (*Enters the sitting-room.*) Terrible weather we've been having lately.

REGINA (*follows him*). It's such blessed weather for the country, sir.

MANDERS. Yes, you're quite right. We townspeople think too little about that. (*He begins to take off his overcoat.*)

REGINA. Oh, mayn't I help you? There! Why, how wet it is? I'll just hang it up in the hall. And your umbrella, too—I'll open it and let it dry.

(*She goes out with the things through the second door on the right.* PASTOR MANDERS *takes off his travelling-bag and lays it and his hat on a chair. Meanwhile* REGINA *comes in again.*)

MANDERS. Ah! it's a comfort to get safe under cover. Everything going on well here?

REGINA. Yes, thank you, sir.

MANDERS. You have your hands full, I suppose, in preparation for to-morrow?

REGINA. Yes, there's plenty to do, of course.

MANDERS. And Mrs. Alving is at home, I trust?

REGINA. Oh dear, yes. She's just upstairs looking after the young master's chocolate.

MANDERS. Yes, by-the-bye—I heard down at the pier that Oswald had arrived.

REGINA. Yes, he came the day before yesterday. We didn't expect him before to-day.

MANDERS. Quite strong and well, I hope?

REGINA. Yes, thank you, quite; but dreadfully tired with the journey. He has made one rush all the way from Paris. I believe he came the whole way in one train. He's sleeping a little now, I think; so perhaps we'd better talk a little quietly.

MANDERS. Hush!—as quietly as you please.

REGINA (*arranging an arm-chair beside the table*). Now, do sit down, Pastor Manders, and make yourself comfortable. (*He sits down; she puts a footstool under his feet.*) There! are you comfortable now, sir?

MANDERS. Thanks, thanks, I'm most comfortable. (*Looks at her.*) Do you know, Miss Engstrand, I positively believe you've grown since I last saw you.

REGINA. Do you think so, sir? Mrs. Alving says my figure has developed too.

MANDERS. Developed? Well, perhaps a little; just enough. (*Short pause.*)

REGINA. Shall I tell Mrs. Alving you are here?

MANDERS. Thanks, thanks, there's no hurry, my dear child. By-the-bye, Regina, my good girl, just tell me: how is your father getting on out here?

REGINA. Oh, thank you, he's getting on well enough.

MANDERS. He called upon me last time he was in town.

REGINA. Did he, indeed? He's always so glad of a chance of talking to you, sir.

MANDERS. And you often look in upon him at his work, I daresay?

REGINA. I? Oh, of course, when I have time, I——

MANDERS. Your father is not a man of strong character, Miss Engstrand. He stands terribly in need of a guiding hand.

REGINA. Oh, yes; I daresay he does.

MANDERS. He needs to have some one near him whom he cares for, and whose judgment he respects. He frankly admitted that when he last came to see me.

REGINA. Yes, he mentioned something of the sort to me. But I don't know whether Mrs. Alving can spare me; especially now that we've got the new Orphanage to attend to. And then I should be so sorry to leave Mrs. Alving; she has always been so kind to me.

MANDERS. But a daughter's duty, my good girl——. Of course we must first get your mistress's consent.

REGINA. But I don't know whether it would be quite proper for me, at my age, to keep house for a single man.

MANDERS. What! My dear Miss Engstrand! When the man is your own father!

REGINA. Yes, that may be; but all the same——. Now if it were in a thoroughly respectable house, and with a real gentleman——

MANDERS. But, my dear Regina——

REGINA. ——one I could love and respect, and be a daughter to——

MANDERS. Yes, but my dear, good child——

REGINA. Then I should be glad to go to town. It's very lonely out here; you know yourself, sir, what it is to be alone in the world. And I can assure you I'm both quick and willing. Don't you know of any such place for me, sir?

MANDERS. I? No, certainly not.

REGINA. But, dear, dear sir, do remember me if——

MANDERS (*rising*). Yes, yes, certainly, Miss Engstrand.

REGINA. For if I——

MANDERS. Will you be so good as to fetch your mistress?

REGINA. I will, at once, sir. (*She goes out to the left.*)

MANDERS (*paces the room two or three times, stands a moment in the background with his hands behind his back, and looks out over the garden. Then he returns to the table, takes up a book, and looks at the title-page; starts, and looks at several*). Hm—indeed!

(MRS. ALVING *enters by the door on the left; she is followed by* REGINA, *who immediately goes out by the first door on the right.*)

MRS. ALVING (*holds out her hand*). Welcome, my dear Pastor.

MANDERS. How do you do, Mrs. Alving? Here I am as I promised.

MRS. ALVING. Always punctual to the minute.

MANDERS. You may believe it wasn't so easy for me to get away. With all the Boards and Committees I belong to——

MRS. ALVING. That makes it all the kinder of you to come so early. Now we can get through our business before dinner. But where's your luggage?

MANDERS (*quickly*). I left it down at the inn. I shall sleep there to-night.

MRS. ALVING (*suppressing a smile*). Are you really not to be persuaded, even now, to pass the night under my roof?

MANDERS. No, no, Mrs. Alving; many thanks. I shall stay down there as usual. It's so convenient for starting again.

MRS. ALVING. Well, you must have your own

way. But I really should have thought we two old people——

MANDERS. Now you're making fun of me. Ah! you're naturally in great spirits to-day—what between to-morrow's festival and Oswald's return.

MRS. ALVING. Yes; you can think what a delight it is to me! It's more than two years since he was home last. And now he has promised to stay with me all winter.

MANDERS. Has he really? That's very nice and dutiful of him. For I can well believe that life in Rome and Paris has far more attractions.

MRS. ALVING. True. But here he has his mother, you see. My own darling boy, he hasn't forgotten his old mother!

MANDERS. It would be grievous indeed, if absence and absorption in art and that sort of thing were to blunt his natural feelings.

MRS. ALVING. Yes, you may well say so. But there's nothing of that sort to fear in him. I'm quite curious to see whether you'll know him again. He'll be down presently; he's upstairs just now, resting a little on the sofa. But do sit down, my dear Pastor.

MANDERS. Thank you. Are you quite at liberty——?

MRS. ALVING. Certainly. (*She sits by the table.*)

MANDERS. Very well. Then you shall see—— (*He goes to the chair where his travelling-bag lies, takes out a packet of papers, sits down on the opposite side of the table, and tries to find a clear space for the papers.*) Now, to begin with, here is——(*breaking off*)—Tell me, Mrs. Alving, how do these books come here?

MRS. ALVING. These books? They are books I am reading.

MANDERS. Do you read this sort of literature?

MRS. ALVING. Certainly I do.

MANDERS. Do you feel better or happier for reading of this kind?

MRS. ALVING. I feel, so to speak, more secure.

MANDERS. That's strange. How do you mean?

MRS. ALVING. Well, I seem to find explanation and confirmation of all sorts of things I myself have been thinking. For that's the wonderful part of it, Pastor Manders; there's really nothing new in these books, nothing but what most people think and believe. Only most people either don't formulate it to themselves, or else keep quiet about it.

MANDERS. Great heavens! Do you really believe that most people——?

MRS. ALVING. I do, indeed.

MANDERS. But surely not in this country? Not here, among us?

MRS. ALVING. Yes, certainly, among us too.

MANDERS. Well, I really must say——!

MRS. ALVING. For the rest, what do you object to in these books?

MANDERS. Object to in them? You surely don't suppose that I have nothing to do but study such productions as these?

MRS. ALVING. That is to say, you know nothing of what you are condemning.

MANDERS. I have read enough *about* these writings to disapprove of them.

MRS. ALVING. Yes; but your own opinion——

MANDERS. My dear Mrs. Alving, there are many occasions in life when one must rely upon others. Things are so ordered in this world; and it's well that they are. How could society get on otherwise?

MRS. ALVING. Well, I daresay you're right there.

MANDERS. Besides, I of course don't deny that there may be much that is interesting in such books. Nor can I blame you for wishing to keep up with the intellectual movements that are said to be going on in the great world, where you have let your son pass so much of his life. But——

MRS. ALVING. But?

MANDERS (*lowering his voice*). But one shouldn't talk about it, Mrs. Alving. One is certainly not bound to account to everybody for what one reads and thinks within one's own four walls.

MRS. ALVING. Of course not; I quite think so.

MANDERS. Only think, now, how you are bound to consider the interests of this Orphanage which you decided on founding at a time when you thought very differently on spiritual matters—so far as I can judge.

MRS. ALVING. Oh yes; I quite admit that. But it was about the Orphanage——

MANDERS. It was about the Orphanage we were to speak; yes. All I say is: prudence, my dear lady! And now we'll get to business. (*Opens the packet, and takes out a number of papers.*) Do you see these?

MRS. ALVING. The documents?

MANDERS. All—and in perfect order. I can tell you it was hard work to get them in time. I had to put on strong pressure. The authorities are almost painfully scrupulous when you want them to come to the point. But here they are at last. (*Looks through the bundle.*) See! here is the formal deed of gift of the parcel of ground know as Solvik in the Manor of Rosenvold, with all the newly-constructed buildings, schoolrooms, master's house, and chapel. And here is the legal fiat for the endowment and for the Regulations of the Institution. Will you look at them? (*Reads.*) "Regulations for the Children's Home to be known as 'Captain Alving's Foundation.'"

MRS. ALVING (*looks long at the paper*). So there it is.

MANDERS. I have chosen the designation "Captain" rather than "Chamberlain." "Captain" looks less pretentious.

MRS. ALVING. Oh, yes; just as you think best.

MANDERS. And here you have the Bank Account of the capital lying at interest to cover the current expenses of the Orphanage.

MRS. ALVING. Thank you; but please keep it—it will be more convenient.

MANDERS. With pleasure. I think we will leave the money in the Bank for the present. The interest is certainly not what we could wish—four per cent. and six months' notice of withdrawal. If a good mortgage could be found later on—of course it must be a first mortgage and an undoubted security—then we could consider the matter.

MRS. ALVING. Certainly, my dear Pastor Manders. You are the best judge in these things.

MANDERS. I will keep my eyes open at any rate

But now there's one thing more which I have several times been intending to ask you.

MRS. ALVING. And what's that?

MANDERS. Shall the Orphanage buildings be insured or not?

MRS. ALVING. Of course they must be insured.

MANDERS. Well, stop a minute, Mrs. Alving. Let us look into the matter a little more closely.

MRS. ALVING. I have everything insured; buildings and movables and stock and crops.

MANDERS. Of course you have—on your own estate. And so have I—of course. But here, you see, it's quite another matter. The Orphanage is to be consecrated, as it were, to a higher purpose.

MRS. ALVING. Yes, but that's no reason——

MANDERS. For my own part, I should not see the smallest impropriety in guarding against all contingencies——

MRS. ALVING. No, I should think not.

MANDERS. But what is the general feeling in the neighbourhood? You, of course, know better than I.

MRS. ALVING. Hm—the general feeling——

MANDERS. Is there any considerable number of people—really responsible people—who might be scandalised?

MRS. ALVING. What do you mean by "really responsible people?"

MANDERS. Well, I mean people in such independent and influential positions that one cannot help allowing some weight to their opinions.

MRS. ALVING. There are several people of that sort here, who would very likely be shocked if——

MANDERS. There, you see! In town we have many such people. Think of all my colleague's adherents! People would be only too ready to interpret our action as a sign that neither you nor I had the right faith in a Higher Providence.

MRS. ALVING. But for your own part, my dear Pastor, you can at least tell yourself that——

MANDERS. Yes, I know—I know; my conscience would be quite easy, that is true enough. But nevertheless we should not escape grave misinterpretation; and that might very likely react unfavourably upon the Orphanage.

MRS. ALVING. Well, in that case, then——

MANDERS. Nor can I lose sight of the difficult—I may even say painful—position *I* might perhaps get into. In the leading circles of the town people are much taken up about this Orphanage. It is, of course, founded partly for the benefit of the town, as well; and it is to be hoped it will, to a considerable extent, result in lightening our Poor Rates. Now, as I have been your adviser, and have had the business matters in my hands, I cannot but fear that I may have to bear the brunt of fanaticism.

MRS. ALVING. Oh, you mustn't run the risk of that.

MANDERS. To say nothing of the attacks that would assuredly be made upon me in certain papers and periodicals, which——

MRS. ALVING. Enough, my dear Pastor Manders. That consideration is quite decisive.

MANDERS. Then you do not wish the Orphanage insured?

MRS. ALVING. No. We'll let it alone.

MANDERS (*leaning back in his chair*). But if a disaster were to happen?—one can never tell. Would you be able to make good the damage?

MRS. ALVING. No; I tell you plainly I should do nothing of the kind.

MANDERS. Then I must tell you, Mrs. Alving, we are taking no small responsibility upon ourselves.

MRS. ALVING. Do you think we can do otherwise?

MANDERS. No, that's just the thing; we really cannot do otherwise. We must not expose ourselves to misinterpretation; and we have no right whatever to give offence to our neighbours.

MRS. ALVING. You, as a clergyman, certainly should not.

MANDERS. I really think, too, we may trust that such an institution has fortune on its side; in fact, that it stands under a Special Providence.

MRS. ALVING. Let us hope so, Pastor Manders.

MANDERS. Then we'll let the matter alone.

MRS. ALVING. Yes, certainly.

MANDERS. Very well. Just as you think best. (*Makes a note.*) Then—no insurance.

MRS. ALVING. It's rather curious that you should just happen to mention the matter to-day.

MANDERS. I have often thought of asking you about it——

MRS. ALVING. ——for we very nearly had a fire down there yesterday.

MANDERS. You don't say so!

MRS. ALVING. Oh, it was of no importance. A

heap of shavings had caught fire in the carpenter's workshop.

MANDERS. Where Engstrand works?

MRS. ALVING. Yes. They say he's often very careless with matches.

MANDERS. He has so many things in his head, that man—so many temptations. Thank God, he's now striving to lead a decent life, I hear.

MRS. ALVING. Indeed! Who says so?

MANDERS. He himself assures me of it. And he's certainly a capital workman.

MRS. ALVING. Oh, yes; so long as he's sober.

MANDERS. Yes, that's a sad weakness. But he's often driven to it by his bad leg, he says. Last time he was in town I was really touched by him. He came and thanked me so warmly for having got him work here, so that he might be near Regina.

MRS. ALVING. He doesn't see much of *her*.

MANDERS. Oh, yes; he has a talk with her every day. He told me so himself.

MRS. ALVING. Well, it may be so.

MANDERS. He feels so acutely that he needs some one to hold him back when temptation comes. That's what I can't help liking about Jacob Engstrand; he comes to you helplessly, accusing himself and confessing his own weakness. The last time he was talking to me—Believe me, Mrs. Alving, supposing it were a real necessity for him to have Regina home again——

MRS. ALVING (*rising hastily*). Regina!

MANDERS. ——you must not set yourself against it.

MRS. ALVING. Indeed I shall set myself against

it! And besides—Regina is to have a position in the Orphanage.

MANDERS. But, after all, remember he's her father——

MRS. ALVING. Oh! I know best what sort of a father he has been to her. No! she shall never go to him with my goodwill.

MANDERS (*rising*). My dear lady, don't take the matter so warmly. You misjudge Engstrand sadly. You seem to be quite terrified——

MRS. ALVING (*more quietly*). It makes no difference. I have taken Regina into my house, and there she shall stay. (*Listens.*) Hush, my dear Mr. Manders; don't say any more about it. (*Her face lights up with gladness.*) Listen! there's Oswald coming downstairs. Now we'll think of no one but him.

(OSWALD ALVING, *in a light overcoat, hat in hand and smoking a large meerschaum, enters through the door on the left; he stops in the doorway.*)

OSWALD. Oh! I beg your pardon; I thought you were in the study. (*Comes forward.*) Good-morning, Pastor Manders?

MANDERS (*staring*). Ah——! How strange——!

MRS. ALVING. Well now, what do you think of him, Mr. Manders?

MANDERS. I—I—can it really be——?

OSWALD. Yes, it's really the Prodigal Son, sir.

MANDERS (*protesting*). My dear young friend——!

OSWALD. Well, then, the Reclaimed Son.

MRS. ALVING. Oswald remembers how much you were opposed to his becoming a painter.

MANDERS. To our human eyes many a step seems dubious which afterwards proves——(*wrings his hand*). Anyhow, welcome, welcome home. Why, my dear Oswald—I suppose I may call you by your Christian name?

OSWALD. What else should you call me?

MANDERS. Very good. What I wanted to say was this, my dear Oswald—you mustn't believe that I utterly condemn the artist's calling. I have no doubt there are many who can keep their inner self unharmed in that profession, as in any other.

OSWALD. Let us hope so.

MRS. ALVING (*beaming with delight*). I know one who has kept both his inner and outer self unharmed. Just look at him, Mr. Manders.

OSWALD (*moves restlessly about the room*). Yes, yes, my dear mother; let's say no more about it.

MANDERS. Why, certainly—that's undeniable. And you have begun to make a name for yourself already. The newspapers have often spoken of you, most favourably. By-the-bye, just lately they haven't mentioned you so often, I fancy.

OSWALD (*up in the conservatory*). I haven't been able to paint so much lately.

MRS. ALVING. Even a painter needs a little rest now and then.

MANDERS. I can quite believe it. And meanwhile he can be gathering his forces for some great work.

OSWALD. Yes.—Mother, will dinner soon be ready?

MRS. ALVING. In less than half-an-hour. He has a capital appetite, thank God.

MANDERS. And a taste for tobacco, too.

OSWALD. I found my father's pipe in my room, and so——

MANDERS. Aha! then that accounts for it.

MRS. ALVING. For what?

MANDERS. When Oswald stood there, in the doorway, with the pipe in his mouth, I could have sworn I saw his father, large as life.

OSWALD. No, really?

MRS. ALVING. Oh! how can you say so? Oswald takes after me.

MANDERS. Yes, but there's an expression about the corners of the mouth—something about the lips that reminds one exactly of Alving; at any rate, now that he's smoking.

MRS. ALVING. Not in the least. Oswald has rather a clerical curve about his mouth, I think.

MANDERS. Yes, yes; some of my colleagues have much the same expression.

MRS. ALVING. But put your pipe away, my dear boy; I won't have smoking in here.

OSWALD (*does so*). By all means. I only wanted to try it; for I once smoked it when I was a child.

MRS. ALVING. You?

OSWALD. Yes. I was quite small at the time. I recollect I came up to father's room one evening when he was in great spirits.

MRS. ALVING. Oh, you can't recollect anything of these times.

OSWALD. Yes, I recollect distinctly. He took me up on his knees, and gave me the pipe. "Smoke, boy," he said; "smoke away, boy." And I smoked as hard as I could, until I felt I was growing quite pale, and the perspiration stood in great drops on my forehead. Then he burst out laughing heartily——

MANDERS. That was most extraordinary.

MRS. ALVING. My dear friend, it's only something Oswald has dreamt.

OSWALD. No, mother, I assure you I didn't dream it. For—don't you remember *this?*—you came and carried me out into the nursery. Then I was sick, and I saw that you were crying.—Did father often play such pranks?

MANDERS. In his youth he overflowed with the joy of life——*

OSWALD. And yet he managed to do so much in the world; so much that was good and useful; and he died so young, too.

MANDERS. Yes, you have inherited the name of an active and worthy man, my dear Oswald Alving. No doubt it will be an incentive to you——

OSWALD. It ought to, indeed.

MANDERS. It was good of you to come home for the ceremony in his honour.

OSWALD. I could do no less for my father.

MRS. ALVING. And I am to keep him so long! That's the best of all.

MANDERS. You're going to pass the winter at home, I hear.

OSWALD. My stay is indefinite, sir. But, oh! how delightful it is to be at home again!

* "Var en særdeles livsglad mand"—literally, "was a man who took the greatest pleasure in life," *la joie de vivre*—an expression which frequently recurs in this play.

MRS. ALVING (*beaming*). Yes, isn't it?

MANDERS (*looking sympathetically at him*). You went out into the world early, my dear Oswald.

OSWALD. I did. I sometimes wonder whether it wasn't *too* early.

MRS. ALVING. Oh, not at all. A healthy lad is all the better for it; especially when he's an only child. He oughtn't to hang on at home with his mother and father and get spoilt.

MANDERS. It's a very difficult question, Mrs. Alving. A child's proper place is, and must be, the home of his fathers.

OSWALD. There I quite agree with you, Pastor Manders.

MANDERS. Only look at your own son—there's no reason why we shouldn't say it in his presence—what has the consequence been for him? He's six or seven and twenty, and has never had the opportunity of learning what home life really is.

OSWALD. I beg your pardon, Pastor; there you're quite mistaken.

MANDERS. Indeed? I thought you had lived almost exclusively in artistic circles.

OSWALD. So I have.

MANDERS. And chiefly among the younger artists.

OSWALD. Yes, certainly.

MANDERS. But I thought few of these young fellows could afford to set up house and support a family.

OSWALD. There are many who can't afford to marry, sir.

MANDERS. Yes, that's just what I say.

OSWALD. But they can have a home for all that. And several of them have, as a matter of fact; and very pleasant, comfortable homes they are, too.

(MRS. ALVING *follows with breathless interest; nods, but says nothing.*)

MANDERS. But I am not talking of bachelors' quarters. By a "home" I understand the home of a family, where a man lives with his wife and children.

OSWALD. Yes; or with his children and his children's mother.

MANDERS (*starts; clasps his hands*). But, good heavens——!

OSWALD. Well?

MANDERS. Lives with—his children's mother!

OSWALD. Yes. Would you have him turn his children's mother out of doors?

MANDERS. Then it's illicit relations you are talking of! Irregular marriages, as people call them!

OSWALD. I have never noticed anything particularly irregular about the life these people lead.

MANDERS. But how is it possible that a—a young man or young woman with any decent principles can endure to live in that way?—in the eyes of all the world!

OSWALD. What are they to do? A poor young artist—a poor girl—it costs a lot to get married. What are they to do?

MANDERS. What are they to do? Let me tell you, Mr. Alving, what they ought to do. They ought to exercise self-restraint from the first; that's what they ought to do.

OSWALD. Such talk won't go far with warm-blooded young people, over head and ears in love.

MRS. ALVING. No, it wouldn't go far.

MANDERS (*continuing*). How can the authorities tolerate such things? Allow them to go on in the light of day? (*To* MRS. ALVING.) Had I not cause to be deeply concerned about your son? In circles where open immorality prevails, and has even a sort of prestige——!

OSWALD. Let me tell you, sir, that I have been a constant Sunday-guest in one or two such irregular homes——

MANDERS. On Sunday of all days!

OSWALD. Isn't that the day to enjoy oneself? Well, never have I heard an offensive word, and still less have I witnessed anything that could be called immoral. No; do you know when and where I have come across immorality in artistic circles?

MANDERS. No, thank heaven, I don't!

OSWALD. Well, then, allow me to inform you. I have met with it when one or other of our pattern husbands and fathers has come to Paris to have a look round on his own account, and has done the artists the honour of visiting their humble haunts. *They* knew what was what. These gentlemen could tell us all about places and things we had never dreamt of.

MANDERS. What! Do you mean to say that respectable men from home here would——?

OSWALD. Have you never heard these respectable men, when they got home again, talking about the way in which immorality was running rampant abroad?

MANDERS. Yes, of course.

MRS. ALVING. I have too.

OSWALD. Well, you may take their word for it. They know what they're talking about! (*Presses his hands to his head.*) Oh! that that great, free, glorious life out there should be defiled in such a way!

MRS. ALVING. You mustn't get excited, Oswald. You will do yourself harm.

OSWALD. Yes; you're quite right, mother. It's not good for me. You see, I'm wretchedly worn out. I'll go for a little turn before dinner. Excuse me, Pastor; I know you can't take my point of view; but I couldn't help speaking out.

(*He goes out through the second door to the right.*)

MRS. ALVING. My poor boy!

MANDERS. You may well say so. Then that's what he has come to!

(MRS. ALVING *looks at him silently.*)

MANDERS (*walking up and down*). He called himself the Prodigal Son—alas! alas!

(MRS. ALVING *continues looking at him.*)

MANDERS. And what do you say to all this?

MRS. ALVING. I say that Oswald was right in every word.

MANDERS (*stands still*). Right! Right! In such principles?

MRS. ALVING. Here, in my loneliness, I have come to the same way of thinking, Pastor Manders. But I've never dared to say anything. Well! now my boy shall speak for me.

MANDERS. You are much to be pitied, Mrs. Alving. But now I must speak seriously to you.

And now it is no longer your business manager and adviser, your own and your late husband's early friend, who stands before you. It is the priest—the priest who stood before you in the moment of your life when you had gone most astray.

MRS. ALVING. And what has the priest to say to me?

MANDERS. I will first stir up your memory a little. The time is well chosen. To-morrow will be the tenth anniversary of your husband's death. To-morrow the memorial in his honour will be unveiled. To-morrow I shall have to speak to the whole assembled multitude. But to-day I will speak to you alone.

MRS. ALVING. Very well, Pastor Manders. Speak.

MANDERS. Do you remember that after less than a year of married life you stood on the verge of an abyss? That you forsook your house and home? That you fled from your husband? Yes, Mrs. Alving—fled, fled, and refused to return to him, however much he begged and prayed you?

MRS. ALVING. Have you forgotten how infinitely miserable I was in that first year?

MANDERS. It is only the spirit of rebellion that craves for happiness in this life. What right have we human beings to happiness? No, we have to do our duty! And your duty was to hold firmly to the man you had once chosen and to whom you were bound by a holy tie.

MRS. ALVING. You know very well what sort of life Alving was leading — what excesses he was guilty of.

MANDERS. I know very well what rumours there were about him, and I am the last to approve the life he led in his young days, if report did not wrong him. But a wife is not to be her husband's judge. It was your duty to bear with humility the cross which a Higher Power had, for your own good, laid upon you. But instead of that you rebelliously throw away the cross, desert the backslider whom you should have supported, go and risk your good name and reputation, and—nearly succeed in ruining other people's reputation into the bargain.

MRS. ALVING. Other people's? One other person's, you mean.

MANDERS. It was incredibly reckless of you to seek refuge with me.

MRS. ALVING. With our clergyman? With our intimate friend?

MANDERS. Just on that account. Yes, you may thank God that I possessed the necessary firmness; that I dissuaded you from your wild designs; and that it was vouchsafed me to lead you back to the path of duty, and home to your lawful husband.

MRS. ALVING. Yes, Pastor Manders, it was certainly your work.

MANDERS. I was but a poor instrument in a Higher Hand. And what a blessing has it not been to you, all the days of your life, that I got you to resume the yoke of duty and obedience! Did not everything happen as I foretold? Did not Alving turn his back on his errors, as a man should? Did he not live with you from that time, lovingly and blamelessly, all his days? Did he not become a benefactor to the whole district? And did he not raise you up to him, so that you little by little became his assistant in all his undertakings? And a capital assistant, too—Oh! I know, Mrs. Alving, that praise is due to you. But now I come to the next great error in your life.

MRS. ALVING. What do you mean?

MANDERS. Just as you once disowned a wife's duty, so you have since disowned a mother's.

MRS. ALVING. Ah!

MANDERS. You have been all your life under the dominion of a pestilent spirit of self-will. All your efforts have been bent towards emancipation and lawlessness. You have never known how to endure any bond. Everything that has weighed upon you in life you have cast away without care or conscience, like a burden you could throw off at will. It did not please you to be a wife any longer, and you left your husband. You found it troublesome to be a mother, and you sent your child forth among strangers.

MRS. ALVING. Yes. That is true. I did so.

MANDERS. And thus you have become a stranger to him.

MRS. ALVING. No! no! I am not.

MANDERS. Yes, you are; you must be. And how have you got him back again? Bethink yourself well, Mrs. Alving. You have sinned greatly against your husband;—that you recognise by raising yonder memorial to him. Recognise now, also, how you have sinned against your son. There may be time to lead him back from the paths of error. Turn back yourself, and save what may yet be saved in him.

For (*with uplifted fore-finger*) verily, Mrs. Alving, you are a guilt-laden mother!—This I have thought it my duty to say to you. (*Silence.*)

MRS. ALVING (*slowly and with self-control*). You have now spoken out, Pastor Manders; and to-morrow you are to speak publicly in memory of my husband. I shall not speak to-morrow. But now I will speak frankly to you, as you have spoken to me.

MANDERS. To be sure; you will plead excuses for your conduct——

MRS. ALVING. No. I will only narrate.

MANDERS. Well?

MRS. ALVING. All that you have just said about me and my husband and our life after you had brought me back to the path of duty—as you called it—about all that you know nothing from personal observation. From that moment you, who had been our intimate friend, never set foot in our house again.

MANDERS. You and your husband left the town immediately after.

MRS. ALVING. Yes; and in my husband's lifetime you never came to see us. It was business that forced you to visit me when you undertook the affairs of the Orphanage.

MANDERS (*softly and uncertainly*). Helen—if that is meant as a reproach, I would beg you to bear in mind——

MRS. ALVING. ——the regard you owed to your position, yes; and that I was a runaway wife. One can never be too careful with such unprincipled creatures.

MANDERS. My dear—Mrs. Alving, you know that is an absurd exaggeration——

MRS. ALVING. Well well, suppose it is. My point is that your judgment as to my married life is founded upon nothing but current gossip.

MANDERS. Well, I admit that. What then?

MRS. ALVING. Well, then, Mr. Manders—I will tell you the truth. I have sworn to myself that one day you should know it—you alone!

MANDERS. What is the truth, then?

MRS. ALVING. The truth is that my husband died just as dissolute as he had lived all his days.

MANDERS (*feeling after a chair*). What do you say?

MRS. ALVING. After nineteen years of marriage, as dissolute—in his desires at any rate—as he was before you married us.

MANDERS. And those—those wild oats, those irregularities, those excesses, if you like, you call "a dissolute life"?

MRS. ALVING. Our doctor used the expression.

MANDERS. I don't understand you.

MRS. ALVING. You need not.

MANDERS. It almost makes me dizzy. Your whole married life, the seeming union of all these years, was nothing more than a hidden abyss!

MRS. ALVING. Nothing more. Now you know it.

MANDERS. This is—it will take me long to accustom myself to the thought. I can't grasp it! I can't realise it! But how was it possible to——? How could such a state of things be kept dark?

MRS. ALVING. That has been my ceaseless struggle, day after day. After Oswald's birth, I thought Alving seemed to be a little better. But it didn't last long. And then I had to struggle twice as hard, fighting for life or death, so that nobody should know what sort of a man my child's father was. And you know what power Alving had of winning people's hearts. Nobody seemed able to believe anything but good of him. He was one of those people whose life does not bite upon their reputation. But at last, Mr. Manders—for you must know the whole story—the most repulsive thing of all happened.

MANDERS. More repulsive than the rest?

MRS. ALVING. I had gone on bearing with him, although I knew very well the secrets of his life out of doors. But when he brought the scandal within our own walls——

MANDERS. Impossible! Here!

MRS. ALVING. Yes; here in our own home. It was there (*pointing towards the first door on the right*), in the dining-room, that I first got to know of it. I was busy with something in there, and the door was standing ajar. I heard our housemaid come up from the garden, with water for those flowers.

MANDERS. Well——?

MRS. ALVING. Soon after I heard Alving come too. I heard him say something softly to her. And then I heard—(*with a short laugh*)—oh! it still sounds in my ears, so hateful and yet so ludicrous—I heard my own servant-maid whisper, "Let me go, Mr. Alving! Let me be."

MANDERS. What unseemly levity on his part! But it cannot have been more than levity, Mrs. Alving; believe me, it cannot.

MRS. ALVING. I soon knew what to believe. Mr. Alving had his way with the girl; and that connection had consequences, Mr. Manders.

MANDERS (*as though petrified*). Such things in this house! in this house!

MRS. ALVING. I had borne a great deal in this house. To keep him at home in the evenings—and at night—I had to make myself his boon companion in his secret orgies up in his room. There I have had to sit alone with him, to clink glasses and drink with him, and to listen to his ribald, silly talk. I have had to fight with him to get him dragged to bed——

MANDERS (*moved*). And you were able to bear all that?

MRS. ALVING. I had to bear it for my little boy's sake. But when the last insult was added; when my own servant-maid—— Then I swore to myself: This shall come to an end. And so I took the reins into my own hand—the whole control over him and everything else. For now I had a weapon against him, you see; he dared not oppose me. It was then I sent Oswald from home. He was in his seventh year, and was beginning to observe and ask questions, as children do. That I could not bear. It seemed to me the child must be poisoned by merely breathing the air of this polluted home. That was why I sent him away. And now you can see, too, why he was never allowed to set foot inside his home so long as his father lived. No one knows what it has cost me.

MANDERS. You have indeed had a life of trial.

MRS. ALVING. I could never have borne it if I hadn't had my work. For I may truly say that I have worked! All those additions to the estate—all the improvements—all the useful appliances, that won Alving such general praise—do you suppose *he* had energy for anything of the sort?—he who lay all day on the sofa and read an old court guide! No; this I will tell you too: it was I who urged him on when he had his better intervals; it was I who had to drag the whole load when he relapsed into his evil ways, or sank into querulous wretchedness.

MANDERS. And to that man you raise a memorial?

MRS. ALVING. There you see the power of an evil conscience.

MANDERS. Evil——? What do you mean?

MRS. ALVING. It always seemed to me impossible but that the truth must come out and be believed. So the Asylum was to deaden all rumours and banish doubt.

MANDERS. In that you have certainly not missed your aim, Mrs. Alving.

MRS. ALVING. And besides, I had one other reason. I did not wish that Oswald, my own boy, should inherit anything whatever from his father.

MANDERS. Then it is Alving's fortune that——?

MRS. ALVING. Yes. The sums I have spent upon the Orphanage, year by year, make up the amount—I have reckoned it up precisely—the amount which made Lieutenant Alving a good match in his day.

MANDERS. I don't quite understand——

MRS. ALVING. It was my purchase-money. I do not choose that that money should pass into Oswald's hands. My son shall have everything from me—everything. (OSWALD ALVING *enters through the second door to the right; he has taken off his hat and over-coat in the hall.* MRS. ALVING *goes towards him.*) Are you back again already? my dear, dear boy!

OSWALD. Yes. What can a fellow do out of doors in this eternal rain? But I hear dinner's ready. That's capital!

REGINA (*with a parcel, from the dining-room*). A parcel has come for you, Mrs. Alving. (*Hands it to her.*)

MRS. ALVING (*with a glance at* MR. MANDERS). No doubt copies of the ode for to-morrow's ceremony.

MANDERS. Hm——

REGINA. And dinner is ready.

MRS. ALVING. Very well. We'll come directly. I'll just—— (*Begins to open the parcel.*)

REGINA (*to* OSWALD). Would Mr. Alving like red or white wine?

OSWALD. Both, if you please

REGINA. *Bien.* Very well, sir. (*She goes into the dining-room.*)

OSWALD. I may as well help to uncork it. (*He also goes into the dining-room, the door of which swings half open behind him.*)

MRS. ALVING (*who has opened the parcel*). Yes, as I thought. Here is the Ceremonial Ode, Pastor Manders.

MANDERS (*with folded hands*). With what

countenance I'm to deliver my discourse to-morrow ——!

MRS. ALVING. Oh! you'll get through it somehow.

MANDERS (*softly, so as not to be heard in the dining-room*). Yes; it would not do to provoke scandal.

MRS. ALVING (*under her breath, but firmly*). No. But then this long, hateful comedy will be ended. From the day after to-morrow it shall be for me as though he who is dead had never lived in this house. No one shall be here but my boy and his mother. (*From within the dining-room comes the noise of a chair overturned, and at the same moment is heard:*)

REGINA (*sharply, but whispering*). Oswald! take care! are you mad? Let me go!

MRS. ALVING (*starts in terror*). Ah!

(*She stares wildly towards the half-opened door.* OSWALD *is heard coughing and humming. A bottle is uncorked.*)

MANDERS (*excited*). What in the world is the matter? What is it, Mrs. Alving?

MRS. ALVING (*hoarsely*). Ghosts! The couple from the conservatory—risen again!

MANDERS. What! Is it possible! Regina——? Is she——?

MRS. ALVING. Yes. Come. Not another word!

(*She seizes* MR. MANDERS *by the arm, and walks unsteadily towards the dining-room.*)

Act Second.

(*The same room. The mist still lies heavy over the land-scape.* MANDERS *and* MRS. ALVING *enter from the dining-room.*)

MRS. ALVING (*still in the doorway*). *Velbekomme*,[1] Mr. Manders. (*Turns back towards the dining-room.*) Aren't you coming too, Oswald?

OSWALD (*from within*). No, thank you. I think I shall go out a little.

MRS. ALVING. Yes, do. The weather seems brighter now. (*She shuts the dining-room door, goes to the hall door, and calls:*) Regina!

REGINA (*outside*). Yes, Mrs. Alving.

MRS. ALVING. Go down to the laundry, and help with the garlands.

REGINA. I'll go directly, Mrs. Alving.

(MRS. ALVING *assures herself that* REGINA *goes; then shuts the door.*)

MANDERS. I suppose he can't overhear us in there?

MRS. ALVING. Not when the door is shut. Besides, he's just going out.

MANDERS. I'm still quite upset. I can't think how I could get down a morsel of dinner.

[1] A phrase equivalent to the German *Prosit die Mahlzeit*—"May good digestion wait on appetite"

MRS. ALVING (*controlling her nervousness, walks up and down*). No more can I. But what's to be done now?

MANDERS. Yes; what's to be done? Upon my honour, I don't know. I'm so utterly without experience in matters of this sort.

MRS. ALVING. I'm quite convinced that, so far, no mischief has been done.

MANDERS. No; heaven forbid! But it's an unseemly state of things, nevertheless.

MRS. ALVING. The whole thing is an idle fancy of Oswald's; you may be sure of that.

MANDERS. Well, as I say, I'm not accustomed to affairs of the kind. But I should certainly think——

MRS. ALVING. Out of the house she must go, and that immediately. That's as clear as daylight.

MANDERS. Yes, of course she must.

MRS. ALVING. But where to? It would not be right to——

MANDERS. Where to? Home to her father, of course.

MRS. ALVING. To whom did you say?

MANDERS. To her—— But then, Engstrand is not——? Good God, Mrs. Alving, it's impossible! You must be mistaken after all.

MRS. ALVING. Alas! I'm mistaken in nothing. Johanna confessed all to me, and Alving could not deny it. So there was nothing to be done but to get the matter hushed up.

MANDERS. No, you could do nothing else.

MRS. ALVING. The girl left our service at once, and got a good sum of money to hold her tongue for the time. The rest she managed for herself when she got into the town. She renewed her old acquaintance with Engstrand, no doubt gave him to understand how much money she had received, and told him some tale about a foreigner who put in here with a yacht that summer. So she and Engstrand got married in hot haste. Why, you married them yourself.

MANDERS. But then how to account for——? I recollect distinctly Engstrand coming to give notice of the marriage. He was broken down with contrition, and reproached himself so bitterly for the misbehaviour he and his sweetheart had been guilty of.

MRS. ALVING. Yes; of course he had to take the blame upon himself.

MANDERS. But such a piece of duplicity on his part! And towards me too! I never could have believed it of Jacob Engstrand. I shan't fail to give him a serious talking to; he may be sure of that. And then the immorality of such a connection! For money! How much did the girl receive?

MRS. ALVING. Three hundred dollars.

MANDERS. There! think of that! for a miserable three hundred dollars to go and marry a fallen woman!

MRS. ALVING. Then what have you to say of me? I went and married a fallen man.

MANDERS. But—good heavens!—what are you talking about? A fallen man?

MRS. ALVING. Do you think Alving was any purer when I went with him to the altar than Johanna was when Engstrand married her?

MANDERS. Well, but there's a world of difference between the two cases——

MRS. ALVING. Not so much difference after all, except in the price—a wretched three hundred dollars and a whole fortune.

MANDERS. How can you compare the two cases? You had taken counsel with your own heart and with your friends.

MRS. ALVING (*without looking at him*). I thought you understood where what you call my heart had strayed to at the time.

MANDERS (*distantly*). Had I understood anything of the kind, I should not have continued a daily guest in your husband's house.

MRS. ALVING. Well, the fact remains that with myself I took no counsel whatever.

MANDERS. Well then, with your nearest relatives —as your duty bade you—with your mother and both your aunts.

MRS. ALVING. Yes, that's true. Those three cast up the account for me. Oh! it's marvellous how clearly they made out that it would be downright madness to refuse such an offer. If mother could only see me now, and know what all that grandeur has come to!

MANDERS. Nobody can be held responsible for the result. This, at least, remains clear: your marriage was in accordance with law and order.

MRS. ALVING (*at the window*). Oh! that perpetual law and order! I often think that's what does all the mischief here in the world.

MANDERS. Mrs. Alving, that is a sinful way of talking.

MRS. ALVING. Well, I can't help it; I can endure all this constraint and cowardice no longer. It's too much for me. I must work my way out to freedom.

MANDERS. What do you mean by that?

MRS. ALVING (*drumming on the window-sill*). I ought never to have concealed the facts of Alving's life. But at that time I was afraid to do anything else—afraid on my own account. I was such a coward.

MANDERS. A coward?

MRS. ALVING. If people had come to know anything, they would have said—"Poor man! with a runaway wife, no wonder he kicks over the traces."

MANDERS. Such remarks might have been made with a certain show of right.

MRS. ALVING (*looking steadily at him*). If I were what I ought to be, I should go to Oswald and say, "Listen, my boy; your father was self-indulgent and vicious——"

MANDERS. Merciful heavens——!

MRS. ALVING. ——and then I should tell him all I have told you—every word of it.

MANDERS. The idea is shocking, Mrs. Alving.

MRS. ALVING. Yes; I know that. I know that very well. I'm shocked at it myself. (*Goes away from the window.*) I'm such a coward.

MANDERS. You call it "cowardice" to do your plain duty? Have you forgotten that a son should love and honour his father and mother?

MRS. ALVING. Don't let us talk in such general terms. Let us ask: should Oswald love and honour Chamberlain Alving?

MANDERS. Is there no voice in your mother's heart that forbids you to destroy your son's ideals?

MRS. ALVING. But what about the truth?

MANDERS. But what about the ideals?

MRS. ALVING. Oh! Ideals! Ideals! If only I weren't such a coward!

MANDERS. Do not despise ideals, Mrs. Alving; they will avenge themselves cruelly. Take Oswald's case; he, unfortunately, seems to have few enough ideals as it is; but I can see that his father stands before him as an ideal.

MRS. ALVING. You're right there.

MANDERS. And this habit of mind you have yourself implanted and fostered by your letters.

MRS. ALVING. Yes; in my superstitious awe for Duty and Decency I lied to my boy, year after year. Oh! what a coward, what a coward I've been!

MANDERS. You have established a happy illusion in your son's heart, Mrs. Alving, and assuredly you ought not to undervalue it.

MRS. ALVING. Hm; who knows whether it's so happy after all——? But, at any rate, I won't have any goings-on with Regina. He shan't go and ruin the poor girl.

MANDERS. No; good God! that would be dreadful!

MRS. ALVING. If I knew he was in earnest, and that it would be for his happiness——

MANDERS. What? What then?

MRS. ALVING. But it couldn't be; for I'm sorry to say Regina is not a girl to make him happy.

MANDERS. Well, what then? What do you mean?

MRS. ALVING. If I weren't such a pitiful coward I would say to him, "Marry her, or make what arrangement you please, only let us have nothing underhand about it."

MANDERS. Good heavens, would you let them *marry!* Anything so dreadful——! so unheard of——!

MRS. ALVING. Do you really mean "unheard of"? Frankly, Pastor Manders, do you suppose that throughout the country there aren't plenty of married couples as closely akin as they?

MANDERS. I don't in the least understand you.

MRS. ALVING. Oh yes, indeed you do.

MANDERS. Ah, you are thinking of the possibility that—— Yes, alas! family life is certainly not always so pure as it ought to be. But in such a case as you point to, one can never know—at least with any certainty. Here, on the other hand—that you, a mother, can think of letting your son——!

MRS. ALVING. But I can't—I wouldn't for anything in the world; that's precisely what I am saying.

MANDERS. No, because you are a "coward," as you put it. But if you were not a "coward," then——? Good God! a connection so shocking.

MRS. ALVING. So far as that goes, they say we're all sprung from connections of that sort. And who is it that arranged the world so, Pastor Manders?

MANDERS. Questions of that kind I must decline to discuss with you, Mrs. Alving; you are far from being in the right frame of mind for them. But that you dare to call your scruples "cowardly"——!

MRS. ALVING. Let me tell you what I mean. I

am timid and half-hearted because I cannot get rid of the Ghosts that haunt me.

MANDERS. What do you say haunts you?

MRS. ALVING. Ghosts! When I heard Regina and Oswald in there, I seemed to see Ghosts before me. I almost think we're all of us Ghosts, Pastor Manders. It's not only what we have inherited from our father and mother that "walks" in us. It's all sorts of dead ideas, and lifeless old beliefs, and so forth. They have no vitality, but they cling to us all the same, and we can't get rid of them. Whenever I take up a newspaper, I seem to see Ghosts gliding between the lines. There must be Ghosts all the country over, as thick as the sand of the sea. And then we are, one and all, so pitifully afraid of the light.

MANDERS. Ah! here we have the fruits of your reading! And pretty fruits they are, upon my word! Oh! those horrible, revolutionary, free-thinking books!

MRS. ALVING. You are mistaken, my dear Pastor. It was you yourself who set me thinking; and I thank you for it with all my heart.

MANDERS. I?

MRS. ALVING. Yes—when you forced me under the yoke you called Duty and Obligation; when you praised as right and proper what my whole soul rebelled against as something loathsome. It was then that I began to look into the seams of your doctrine. I wanted only to pick at a single knot; but when I had got that undone, the whole thing ravelled out. And then I understood that it was all machine-sewn.

MANDERS (*softly, with emotion*). And was that the upshot of my life's hardest battle?

MRS. ALVING. Call it rather your most pitiful defeat.

MANDERS. It was my greatest victory, Helen—the victory over myself.

MRS. ALVING. It was a crime against us both.

MANDERS. When you went astray, and came to me crying, "Here I am; take me!" I commanded you, saying, "Woman, go home to your lawful husband." Was that a crime?

MRS. ALVING. Yes, I think so.

MANDERS. We two do not understand each other.

MRS. ALVING. Not now, at any rate.

MANDERS. Never—never in my most secret thoughts have I regarded you otherwise than as another's wife.

MRS. ALVING. Oh!—indeed?

MANDERS. Helen——!

MRS. ALVING. People so easily forget their past selves.

MANDERS. I do not. I am what I always was.

MRS. ALVING (*changing the subject*). Well well well; don't let us talk of old times any longer. You are now over head and ears in Commissions and Boards of Direction, and I am fighting my battle with Ghosts both within me and without.

MANDERS. Those without I shall help you to lay. After all the shocking things I've heard from you to-day, I cannot in conscience permit an unprotected girl to remain in your house.

MRS. ALVING. Don't you think the best plan

would be to get her provided for?—I mean, by a good marriage.

MANDERS. No doubt. I think it would be desirable for her in every respect. Regina is now at the age when—— Of course I don't know much about these things, but——

MRS. ALVING. Regina matured very early.

MANDERS. Yes, did she not? I have an impression that she was remarkably well developed, physically, when I prepared her for confirmation. But in the meantime, she must go home, under her father's eye.—Ah! but Engstrand is not—— That he—that *he*—could so hide the truth from me!

(*A knock at the door into the hall.*)

MRS. ALVING. Who can that be? Come in!

ENGSTRAND (*in his Sunday clothes, in the doorway*). I beg your pardon humbly, but——

MANDERS. Ah! Hm——

MRS. ALVING. Is that you, Engstrand?

ENGSTRAND. ——there was none of the servants about, so I took the great liberty of just knocking.

MRS. ALVING. Oh! very well. Come in. Do you want to speak to me?

ENGSTRAND (*comes in*). No, I'm greatly obliged to you; it was with his Reverence I wanted to have a word or two.

MANDERS (*walking up and down the room*). Hm—indeed! You want to speak to me, do you?

ENGSTRAND. Yes, I should like so much to——

MANDERS (*stops in front of him*). Well; may I ask what you want?

ENGSTRAND. Well, it was just this, your Reverence; we've been paid off down yonder—my grateful thanks to you, ma'am,—and now everything's finished, I've been thinking it would be but right and proper if we, that have been working so honestly together all this time—well, I was thinking we ought to end up with a little prayer-meeting tonight.

MANDERS. A prayer-meeting? Down at the Orphanage?

ENGSTRAND. Oh, if your Reverence doesn't think it proper——

MANDERS. Oh yes! I do; but—hm——

ENGSTRAND. I've been in the habit of offering up a little prayer in the evenings, myself.

MRS. ALVING. Have you?

ENGSTRAND. Yes, every now and then—just a little exercise, you might call it. But I'm a poor, common man, and have little enough gift, God help me! and so I thought, as the Reverend Mr. Manders happened to be here, I'd——

MANDERS. Well, you see, Engstrand, I must first ask you a question. Are you in the right frame of mind for such a meeting? Do you feel your conscience clear and at ease?

ENGSTRAND. Oh! God help us, your Reverence! we'd better not talk about conscience.

MANDERS. Yes, that's just what we must talk about. What have you to answer?

ENGSTRAND. Why—one's conscience—it can be bad enough now and then.

MANDERS. Ah, you admit that. Then will you make a clean breast of it, and tell the truth about Regina?

MRS. ALVING (*quickly*). Mr. Manders!

MANDERS (*reassuringly*). Just let me——

ENGSTRAND. About Regina! Lord! how you frighten me! (*Looks at* MRS. ALVING.) There's nothing wrong about Regina, is there?

MANDERS. We'll hope not. But I mean, what is the truth about you and Regina? You pass for her father, eh!

ENGSTRAND (*uncertain*). Well—hm—your Reverence knows all about me and poor Johanna.

MANDERS. Come, no more prevarication! Your wife told Mrs. Alving the whole story before quitting her service.

ENGSTRAND. Well, then, may——! Now, did she really?

MANDERS. So you're found out, Engstrand.

ENGSTRAND. And she swore and took her Bible oath——

MANDERS. Did she take her Bible oath?

ENGSTRAND. No; she only swore; but she did it so earnestly.

MANDERS. And you have hidden the truth from me all these years? Hidden it from me! from me, who have trusted you without reserve, in everything.

ENGSTRAND. Well, I can't deny it.

MANDERS. Have I deserved this of you, Engstrand? Haven't I always been ready to help you in word and deed, so far as it stood in my power? Answer me. Have I not?

ENGSTRAND. It would have been a poor look-out for me many a time but for the Reverend Mr. Manders.

MANDERS. And you reward me thus! You cause me to enter falsehoods in the Church Register, and you withhold from me, year after year, the explanations you owed alike to me and to truth. Your conduct has been wholly inexcusable, Engstrand; and from this time forward all is over between us.

ENGSTRAND (*with a sigh*). Yes! I suppose it must be.

MANDERS. How can you possibly justify yourself?

ENGSTRAND. How could I think she'd gone and made bad worse by talking about it? Will your Reverence just fancy yourself in the same trouble as poor Johanna——

MANDERS. I!

ENGSTRAND. Lord bless you! I don't mean just exactly the same. But I mean, if your Reverence had anything to be ashamed of in the eyes of the world, as the saying is—— We men oughtn't to judge a poor woman too hardly, your Reverence.

MANDERS. I am not doing so. It's you I am reproaching.

ENGSTRAND. Might I make so bold as to ask your Reverence a bit of a question?

MANDERS. Yes, ask away.

ENGSTRAND. Isn't it right and proper for a man to raise up the fallen?

MANDERS. Most certainly it is.

ENGSTRAND. And isn't a man bound to keep his sacred word?

MANDERS. Why, of course he is; but——

ENGSTRAND. When Johanna had got into trouble

through that Englishman—or it might have been an American or a Russian, as they call them—well, you see, she came down into the town. Poor thing! she'd sent me about my business once or twice before: for she couldn't bear the sight of anything but what was handsome; and I'd got this damaged leg. Your Reverence recollects how I ventured up into a dancing-saloon, where seafaring people carried on with drink and devilry, as the saying goes. And then, when I was for giving them a bit of an admonition to lead a new life——

MRS. ALVING (*at the window*). Hm——

MANDERS. I know all about that, Engstrand; the ruffians threw you downstairs. You've told me of the affair already.

ENGSTRAND. I'm not puffed up about it, your Reverence. But what I wanted to say was, that then she came and confessed all to me, with weeping and gnashing of teeth. I can tell your Reverence I was sore at heart to hear it.

MANDERS. Were you indeed, Engstrand? Well, go on.

ENGSTRAND. So I said to her, "The American, he's sailing about on the boundless sea. And as for you, Johanna," said I, "you've committed a grievous sin and you're a fallen creature. But Jacob Engstrand," said I, "he's got two good legs to stand upon, *he* has——" You know, your Reverence, I was speaking figurative-like.

MANDERS. I understand quite well. Go on.

ENGSTRAND. Well, that was how I raised her up and made an honest woman of her, so that folks shouldn't get to know how she'd gone astray with foreigners.

MANDERS. All that was very good of you. Only I can't approve of your stooping to take money——

ENGSTRAND. Money? I? Not a farthing!

MANDERS (*inquiringly to* MRS. ALVING). But——

ENGSTRAND. Oh, wait a minute!—now I recollect. Johanna had a trifle of money. But I would have nothing to do with it. "No," said I, "that's mammon; that's the wages of sin. This dirty gold—or notes, or whatever it was—we'll just fling that back to the American," said I. But he was gone and away, over the stormy sea, your Reverence.

MANDERS. Was he really, my good fellow?

ENGSTRAND. Ay, sir. So Johanna and I, we agreed that the money should go to the child's education; and so it did, and I can account for every blessed farthing of it.

MANDERS. Why, this alters the case considerably.

ENGSTRAND. That's just how it stands, your Reverence. And I make so bold as to say I've been an honest father to Regina, so far as my poor strength went; for I'm but a poor creature, worse luck!

MANDERS. Well, well, my good fellow——

ENGSTRAND. But I may make bold to say that I've brought up the child, and lived kindly with poor Johanna, and ruled over my own house, as the Scripture has it. But I could never think of going up to your Reverence and puffing myself up and boasting because I too had done some good in the world. No, sir; when anything of that sort happens to Jacob Engstrand, he holds his tongue about it. It doesn't happen so very often, I daresay. And when I do come to see your Reverence, I find a mortal deal to say about what's wicked and weak. For I do say—as I was saying just now—one's conscience isn't always as clean as it might be.

MANDERS. Give me your hand, Jacob Engstrand.

ENGSTRAND. Oh, Lord! your Reverence——

MANDERS. Come, no nonsense (*wrings his hand*). There we are!

ENGSTRAND. And if I might humbly beg your Reverence's pardon——

MANDERS. You? On the contrary, it's I who ought to beg your pardon——

ENGSTRAND. Lord, no, sir!

MANDERS. Yes, certainly. And I do it with all my heart. Forgive me for misunderstanding you. And I wish I could give you some proof of my hearty regret, and of my good-will towards you——

ENGSTRAND. Would your Reverence?

MANDERS. With the greatest pleasure.

ENGSTRAND. Well then, there's the very opportunity now. With the money I've saved here, I was thinking I might set up a Sailors' Home down in the town.

MRS. ALVING. *You?*

ENGSTRAND. Yes; it too might be a sort of Orphanage, in a manner of speaking. There are many temptations for seafaring folk ashore. But in this Home of mine, a man might feel as under a father's eye, I was thinking.

MANDERS. What do you say to this, Mrs. Alving?

ENGSTRAND. It isn't much I've got to start with,

the Lord help me! But if I could only find a helping hand, why——

MANDERS. Yes, yes; we'll look into the matter. I entirely approve of your plan. But now, go before me and make everything ready, and get the candles lighted, so as to give the place an air of festivity. And then we'll pass an edifying hour together, my good fellow; for now I quite believe you're in the right frame of mind.

ENGSTRAND. Yes, I trust I am. And so I'll say good-bye, ma'am, and thank you kindly; and take good care of Regina for me—(*wipes a tear from his eye*)—poor Johanna's child; hm, it's an odd thing, now; but it's just as if she'd grown into the very apple of my eye. It is indeed.

(*He bows and goes out through the hall.*)

MANDERS. Well, what do you say of that man now, Mrs. Alving? That threw a totally different light on matters, didn't it?

MRS. ALVING. Yes, it certainly did.

MANDERS. It only shows how excessively careful one must be in judging one's fellow-creatures. But it's a great joy to ascertain that one has been mistaken. Don't you think so?

MRS. ALVING. I think you are, and will always be, a great baby, Manders.

MANDERS. I?

MRS. ALVING (*laying her two hands upon his shoulders*). And I say that I've half a mind to put my arms round your neck, and kiss you.

MANDERS (*stepping hastily back*). No, no! God bless me! What an idea!

MRS. ALVING (*with a smile*). Oh! you needn't be afraid of me.

MANDERS (*by the table*). You have sometimes such an exaggerated way of expressing yourself. Now, I'll just collect all the documents, and put them in my bag. (*He does so.*) There, now. And now, good-bye for the present. Keep your eyes open when Oswald comes back. I shall look in again later.

(*He takes his hat and goes out through the hall door.*)

MRS. ALVING (*sighs, looks for a moment out of the window, sets the room in order a little, and is about to go into the dining-room, but stops at the door with a half-suppressed cry*). Oswald, are you still at table?

OSWALD (*in the dining-room*). I'm only finishing my cigar.

MRS. ALVING. I thought you'd gone for a little walk.

OSWALD. In such weather as this? (*A glass clinks.* MRS. ALVING *leaves the door open, and sits down with her knitting on the sofa by the window.*) Wasn't that Pastor Manders that went out just now?

MRS. ALVING. Yes; he went down to the Orphanage.

OSWALD. Hm. (*The glass and decanter clink again.*)

MRS. ALVING (*with a troubled glance*). Dear Oswald, you should take care of that liqueur. It's strong.

OSWALD. It keeps out the damp.

MRS. ALVING. Wouldn't you rather come in to me?

OSWALD. I mayn't smoke in there.

MRS. ALVING. You know quite well you may smoke cigars.

OSWALD. Oh! all right then; I'll come in. Just a tiny drop more first! There! (*He comes into the room with his cigar, and shuts the door after him. A short silence.*) Where's Manders gone to?

MRS. ALVING. I've just told you; he went down to the Orphanage.

OSWALD. Oh, ah; so you did.

MRS. ALVING. You shouldn't sit so long at table after dinner, Oswald.

OSWALD (*holding his cigar behind him*). But I find it so pleasant, mother. (*Strokes and pets her.*) Just think what it is for me to come home and sit at mother's own table. in mother's room, and eat mother's delicious dinners.

MRS. ALVING. My dear, dear boy!

OSWALD (*somewhat impatiently walks about and smokes*). And what else can I do with myself here? I can't set to work at anything.

MRS. ALVING. Why can't you?

OSWALD. In such weather as this? Without a single ray of sunlight the whole day? (*Walks up the room.*) Oh! not to be able to work!

MRS. ALVING. Perhaps it was not quite wise of you to come home?

OSWALD. Oh, yes, mother; I had to.

MRS. ALVING. Why? I would ten times rather forego the joy of having you here than——

OSWALD (*stops beside the table*). Now just tell me, mother: does it really make you so very happy to have me home again?

MRS. ALVING. *Does* it make me happy!

OSWALD (*crumpling up a newspaper*). I should have thought it must be pretty much the same to you whether I was in existence or not.

MRS. ALVING. Have you the heart to say that to your mother, Oswald?

OSWALD. But you've got on very well without me all this time.

MRS. ALVING. Yes; I've got on without you. That's true.

(*A silence. Twilight gradually falls.* OSWALD *walks to and fro across the room. He has laid his cigar down.*)

OSWALD (*stops beside* MRS. ALVING). Mother, may I sit on the sofa beside you?

MRS. ALVING (*makes room for him*). Yes do, my dear boy.

OSWALD (*sits down*). Now I'm going to tell you something, mother.

MRS. ALVING (*anxiously*). Well?

OSWALD (*looks fixedly before him*). For I can't go on hiding it any longer.

MRS. ALVING. Hiding what? What is it?

OSWALD (*as before*). I could never bring myself to write to you about it; and since I've come home——

MRS. ALVING (*seizes him by the arm*). Oswald, what *is* the matter?

OSWALD (*as before*). Both yesterday and to-day

I've tried to put the thoughts away from me—to get free from them; but it won't do.

MRS. ALVING (*rising*). Now you must speak out, Oswald.

OSWALD (*draws her down to the sofa again*). Sit still; and then I'll try to tell you. I complained of fatigue after my journey——

MRS. ALVING. Well, what then?

OSWALD. But it isn't that that's the matter with me; it isn't any ordinary fatigue——

MRS. ALVING (*tries to jump up*). You're not ill, Oswald?

OSWALD (*draws her down again*). Do sit still, mother. Only take it quietly. I'm not downright ill, either; not what's commonly called "ill." (*Clasps his hands above his head.*) Mother, my mind is broken down—ruined—I shall never be able to work again. (*With his hands before his face, he buries his head in her lap, and breaks into bitter sobbing.*)

MRS. ALVING (*white and trembling*). Oswald! Look at me! No, no; it isn't true.

OSWALD (*looks up with despair in his eyes*). Never to be able to work again! Never! never! It will be like living death! Mother, can you imagine anything so horrible?

MRS. ALVING. My poor boy! How has this horrible thing come over you?

OSWALD (*sits upright*). That's just what I can't possibly grasp or understand. I've never led a dissipated life—never, in any respect. You mustn't believe that of me, mother. I've never done that.

MRS. ALVING. I'm sure you haven't, Oswald.

OSWALD. And yet this has come over me just the same—this awful misfortune!

MRS. ALVING. Oh, but it will pass away, my dear, blessed boy. It's nothing but over-work. Trust me, I am right.

OSWALD (*sadly*). I thought so too at first; but it isn't so.

MRS. ALVING. Tell me the whole story from beginning to end.

OSWALD. Well, I will.

MRS. ALVING. When did you first notice it?

OSWALD. It was directly after I had been home last time, and had got back to Paris again. I began to feel the most violent pains in my head—chiefly in the back of my head, I thought. It was as though a tight iron ring was being screwed round my neck and upwards.

MRS. ALVING. Well, and then?

OSWALD. At first I thought it was nothing but the ordinary headache I had been so plagued with when I was growing up——

MRS. ALVING. Yes, yes——

OSWALD. But it wasn't that. I soon found that out. I couldn't work. I wanted to begin upon a big new picture, but my powers seemed to fail me; all my strength was crippled; I couldn't form any definite images; everything swam before me—whirling round and round. Oh! it was an awful state! At last I sent for a doctor, and from him I learned the truth.

MRS. ALVING. How do you mean?

OSWALD. He was one of the first doctors in Paris.

I told him my symptoms, and then he set to work asking me a heap of questions which I thought had nothing to do with the matter. I couldn't imagine what the man was after——

MRS. ALVING. Well?

OSWALD. At last he said: "You have been worm-eaten from your birth." He used that very word—*vermoulu.*

MRS. ALVING (*breathlessly*). What did he mean by that?

OSWALD. I didn't understand either, and begged him to explain himself more clearly. And then the old cynic said—(*clenching his fist*) Oh——!

MRS. ALVING. What did he say?

OSWALD. He said, "The sins of the fathers are visited upon the children."

MRS. ALVING (*rising slowly*). The sins of the fathers——!

OSWALD. I very nearly struck him in the face——

MRS. ALVING (*walks away across the floor*). The sins of the fathers——

OSWALD (*smiles sadly*). Yes; what do you think of that? Of course I assured him that such a thing was out of the question. But do you think he gave in? No, he stuck to it; and it was only when I produced your letters and translated the passages relating to father——

MRS. ALVING. But then?

OSWALD. Then of course he was bound to admit that he was on the wrong track; and so I got to know the truth—the incomprehensible truth! I ought to have held aloof from my bright and happy life among my comrades. It had been too much for my strength. So I had brought it upon myself!

MRS. ALVING. Oswald! Oh no, don't believe it!

OSWALD. No other explanation was possible, he said. That's the awful part of it. Incurably ruined for life—by my own heedlessness! All that I meant to have done in the world—I never dare think of again—I'm not *able* to think of it. Oh! if I could but live over again, and undo all I've done! (*He buries his face in the sofa.* MRS. ALVING *wrings her hands and walks, in silent struggle, backwards and forwards.* OSWALD, *after a while, looks up and remains resting upon his elbow.*) If it had only been something inherited, something one wasn't responsible for! But this! To have thrown away so shamefully, thoughtlessly, recklessly, one's own happiness, one's own health, everything in the world—one's future, one's very life!

MRS. ALVING. No, no, my dear, darling boy! It's impossible. (*Bends over him.*) Things are not so desperate as you think.

OSWALD. Oh! you don't know—— (*Springs up.*) And then, mother, to cause you all this sorrow! Many a time I've almost wished and hoped that at bottom you didn't care so very much about me.

MRS. ALVING. I, Oswald? My only boy! You are all I have in the world! The only thing I care about!

OSWALD (*seizes both her hands and kisses them*). Yes, mother dear, I see it well enough. When I'm at home, I see it, of course; and that's the hardest part for me. But now you know the whole story, and now we won't talk any more about it to-day. I daren't think of it for long together. (*Goes up the room.*) Get me something to drink, mother.

MRS. ALVING. Drink? What do you want to drink now?

OSWALD. Oh! anything you like. You have some cold punch in the house.

MRS. ALVING. Yes, but my dear Oswald——

OSWALD. Don't refuse me, mother. Do be nice, now! I must have something to wash down all these gnawing thoughts. (*Goes into the conservatory.*) And then——it's so dark here! (MRS. ALVING *pulls a bell-rope on the right.*) And this ceaseless rain! It may go on week after week for months together. Never to get a glimpse of the sun! I can't recollect ever having seen the sun shine all the times I've been at home.

MRS. ALVING. Oswald, you're thinking of going away from me.

OSWALD. Hm—(*drawing a deep breath*)—I'm not thinking of anything. I can't think of anything. (*In a low voice.*) I let thinking alone.

REGINA (*from the dining-room.*) Did you ring, ma'am?

MRS. ALVING. Yes; let us have the lamp in.

REGINA. I will, directly. It's ready lighted. (*Goes out.*)

MRS. ALVING (*goes across to* OSWALD). Oswald, be frank with me.

OSWALD. Well, so I am, mother. (*Goes to the table.*) I think I've told you enough.

(REGINA *brings the lamp and sets it upon the table.*)

MRS. ALVING. Regina, you might fetch us a half bottle of champagne.

REGINA. Very well, ma'am. (*Goes out.*)

OSWALD (*puts his arm round* MRS. ALVING'S *neck*). That's just what I wanted. I knew mother wouldn't let her boy be thirsty.

MRS. ALVING. My own, poor, darling Oswald, how could I deny you anything now?

OSWALD (*eagerly*). Is that true, mother? Do you mean it?

MRS. ALVING. How? What?

OSWALD. That you couldn't deny me anything.

MRS. ALVING. My dear Oswald——

OSWALD. Hush!

REGINA (*brings a tray with a half-bottle of champagne and two glasses, which she sets on the table*). Shall I open it?

OSWALD. No, thanks. I'll do it myself.

(REGINA *goes out again.*)

MRS. ALVING (*sits down by the table*). What was it you meant, I mustn't deny you?

OSWALD (*busy opening the bottle*). First let's have a glass—or two.

(*The cork pops; he pours wine into one glass, and is about to pour it into the other.*)

MRS. ALVING (*holding her hand over it*). Thanks; not for me.

OSWALD. Oh! won't you? Then I will!

(*He empties the glass, fills, and empties it again; then he sits down by the table.*)

MRS. ALVING (*in expectation*). Well?

OSWALD (*without looking at her*). Tell me—I thought you and Pastor Manders seemed so odd—so quiet—at dinner to-day.

MRS. ALVING. Did you notice it?

OSWALD. Yes. Hm—— (*After a short silence.*) Tell me: what do you think of Regina?

MRS. ALVING. What I think?

OSWALD. Yes; isn't she splendid?

MRS. ALVING. My dear Oswald, you don't know her as I do——

OSWALD. Well?

MRS. ALVING. Regina, unfortunately, was allowed to stay at home too long. I ought to have taken her earlier into my house.

OSWALD. Yes, but isn't she splendid to look at, mother?

(*He fills his glass.*)

MRS. ALVING. Regina has many serious faults.

OSWALD. Oh, what does it matter?

(*He drinks again.*)

MRS. ALVING. But I'm fond of her, nevertheless, and I'm responsible for her. I wouldn't for all the world have any harm happen to her.

OSWALD (*springs up*). Mother! Regina is my only salvation.

MRS. ALVING (*rising*). What do you mean by that?

OSWALD. I can't go on bearing all this anguish of mind alone.

MRS. ALVING. Haven't you got your mother to share it with you?

OSWALD. Yes; that's what I thought; and so I came home to you. But that won't do. I see it won't do. I can't endure my life here.

MRS. ALVING. Oswald!

OSWALD. I must live differently, mother. That's why I must leave you. I won't have you looking on at it.

MRS. ALVING. My unhappy boy! But, Oswald, while you're so ill as this——

OSWALD. If it were only the illness, I should stay with you, mother, you may be sure; for you are the best friend I have in the world.

MRS. ALVING. Yes, indeed I am, Oswald; am I not?

OSWALD (*wanders restlessly about*). But it's all the torment, the remorse; and besides that, the great, killing dread. Oh! that awful dread!

MRS. ALVING (*walking after him*). Dread? What dread? What do you mean?

OSWALD. Oh, you mustn't ask me any more! I don't know. I can't describe it. (MRS. ALVING *goes over to the right and pulls the bell.*) What is it you want?

MRS. ALVING. I want my boy to be happy—that's what I want. He shan't go on racking his brains. (*To* REGINA, *who comes in at the door:*) More champagne—a whole bottle. (REGINA *goes.*)

OSWALD. Mother!

MRS. ALVING. Do you think we don't know how to live here at home?

OSWALD. Isn't she splendid to look at? How beautifully she's built! And so thoroughly healthy!

MRS. ALVING (*sits by the table*). Sit down, Oswald; let us talk quietly together.

OSWALD (*sits*). I daresay you don't know, mother, that I owe Regina some reparation.

MRS. ALVING. You?

OSWALD. For a bit of thoughtlessness, or whatever you like to call it—very innocent, anyhow. When I was home last time——

MRS. ALVING. Well?

OSWALD. She used often to ask me about Paris, and I used to tell her one thing and another. Then I recollect I happened to say to her one day, "Wouldn't you like to go there yourself?"

MRS. ALVING. Well?

OSWALD. I saw her face flush, and then she said, "Yes, I should like it of all things." "Ah, well," I replied, "it might perhaps be managed"—or something like that.

MRS. ALVING. And then?

OSWALD. Of course I'd forgotten the whole thing; but the day before yesterday I happened to ask her whether she was glad I was to stay at home so long——

MRS. ALVING. Yes?

OSWALD. And then she looked so strangely at me and asked, "But what's to become of my trip to Paris?"

MRS. ALVING. Her trip!

OSWALD. And so I got out of her that she had taken the thing seriously; that she had been thinking of me the whole time, and had set to work to learn French——

MRS. ALVING. So that was why she did it!

OSWALD. Mother! when I saw that fresh, lovely, splendid girl standing there before me—till then I had hardly noticed her—but when she stood there as though with open arms ready to receive me——

MRS. ALVING. Oswald!

OSWALD. ——then it flashed upon me that my salvation lay in her; for I saw that she was full of the joy of life.[1]

MRS. ALVING (*starts*). The joy of life? Can there be salvation in that?

REGINA (*from the dining-room, with a bottle of champagne*). I'm sorry to have been so long, but I had to go to the cellar. (*Puts the bottle on the table.*)

OSWALD. And now fetch another glass.

REGINA (*looks at him in surprise*). There is Mrs. Alving's glass, Mr. Alving.

OSWALD. Yes, but fetch one for yourself, Regina (REGINA *starts and gives a lightning-like side glance at* MRS. ALVING.) Why do you wait?

REGINA (*softly and hesitatingly*). Is it Mrs. Alving's wish?

MRS. ALVING. Fetch the glass, Regina.

(REGINA *goes out into the dining-room.*)

OSWALD (*follows her with his eyes*). Have you noticed how she walks?—so firmly and lightly!

MRS. ALVING. It can never be, Oswald!

OSWALD. It's a settled thing. Can't you see that? It's no use saying anything against it. (REGINA *enters with an empty glass, which she keeps in her hand.*) Sit down, Regina.

[1] Livsglæde—"la joie de vivre."

(REGINA *looks inquiringly at* MRS. ALVING.)

MRS. ALVING. Sit down. (REGINA *sits on a chair by the dining-room door, still holding the empty glass in her hand.*) Oswald, what were you saying about the joy of life?

OSWALD. Ah! the joy of life, mother—that's a thing you don't know much about in these parts. I've never felt it here.

MRS. ALVING. Not when you're with me?

OSWALD. Not when I'm at home. But you don't understand that.

MRS. ALVING. Yes, yes; I think I almost understand it—now.

OSWALD. And then, too, the joy of work! At bottom, it's the same thing. But that, too, you know nothing about.

MRS. ALVING. Perhaps you're right, Oswald; tell me more about it.

OSWALD. Well, I only mean that here people are brought up to believe that work is a curse and a punishment for sin, and that life is something miserable, something we want to be done with, the sooner the better.

MRS. ALVING. "A vale of tears," yes; and we take care to make it one.

OSWALD. But in the great world people won't hear of such things. There, nobody really believes such doctrines any longer. There, you feel it bliss and ecstasy merely to draw the breath of life. Mother, have you noticed that everything I've painted has turned upon the joy of life?—always, always upon the joy of life?—light and sunshine and glorious air and faces radiant with happiness. That's why I'm afraid of remaining at home with you.

MRS. ALVING. Afraid? What are you afraid of here, with me?

OSWALD. I'm afraid lest all my instincts should be warped into ugliness.

MRS. ALVING (*looks steadily at him*). Do you think that would be the way of it?

OSWALD. I know it. You may live the same life here as there, and yet it won't be the same life.

MRS. ALVING (*who has been listening eagerly, rises, her eyes big with thought, and says:*) Now I see the connection.

OSWALD. What is it you see?

MRS. ALVING. I see it now for the first time. And now I can speak.

OSWALD (*rising*). Mother, I don't understand you.

REGINA (*who has also risen*). Perhaps I ought to go?

MRS. ALVING. No. Stay here. Now I can speak. Now, my boy, you shall know the whole truth. And then you can choose. Oswald! Regina!

OSWALD. Hush! Here's Manders——

MANDERS (*comes in by the hall door*). There! We've had a most edifying time down there.

OSWALD. So have we.

MANDERS. We must stand by Engstrand and his Sailors' Home. Regina must go to him and help him——

REGINA. No thank you, sir.

MANDERS (*noticing her for the first time*). What? You here? and with a glass in your hand!

REGINA (*hastily putting the glass down*). *Pardon!*

OSWALD. Regina is going with me, Mr. Manders.

MANDERS. Going with you!

OSWALD. Yes; as my wife—if she wishes it.

MANDERS. But, good God——!

REGINA. I can't help it, sir.

OSWALD. Or she'll stay here, if I stay.

REGINA (*involuntarily*). Here!

MANDERS. I am thunderstruck at your conduct, Mrs. Alving.

MRS. ALVING. They will do neither one thing nor the other; for now I can speak out plainly.

MANDERS. You surely won't do that. No, no, no!

MRS. ALVING. Yes, I can speak and I will. And no ideal shall suffer after all.

OSWALD. Mother! What on earth are you hiding from me?

REGINA (*listening*). Oh, ma'am! listen! Don't you hear shouts outside.

(*She goes into the conservatory and looks out.*)

OSWALD (*at the window on the left*). What's going on? Where does that light come from?

REGINA (*cries out*). The Orphanage is on fire!

MRS. ALVING (*rushing to the window*). On fire?

MANDERS. On fire! Impossible! I've just come from there.

OSWALD. Where's my hat? Oh, never mind it—Father's Orphanage!

(*He rushes out through the garden door.*)

MRS. ALVING. My shawl, Regina! It's blazing!

MANDERS. Terrible! Mrs. Alving, it's a judgment upon this abode of sin.

MRS. ALVING. Yes, of course. Come, Regina.

(*She and* REGINA *hasten out through the hall.*)

MANDERS (*clasps his hands together*). And uninsured, too!

(*He goes out the same way.*)

Act Third.

(*The room as before. All the doors stand open. The lamp is still burning on the table. It is dark out of doors; there is only a faint glow from the conflagration in the background to the left.*)

(MRS. ALVING, *with a shawl over her head, stands in the conservatory and looks out.* REGINA, *also with a shawl on, stands a little behind her.*)

MRS. ALVING. All burnt!—burnt to the ground!

REGINA. The basement is still burning.

MRS. ALVING. How is it Oswald doesn't come home? There's nothing to be saved.

REGINA. Would you like me to take down his hat to him?

MRS. ALVING. Hasn't he even got his hat on?

REGINA (*pointing to the hall*). No; there it hangs.

MRS. ALVING. Let it be. He must come up now. I'll go and look for him myself.

(*She goes out through the garden door.*)

MANDERS (*comes in from the hall*). Isn't Mrs. Alving here?

REGINA. She's just gone down the garden.

MANDERS. This is the most terrible night I ever went through.

REGINA. Yes; isn't it a dreadful misfortune, sir?

MANDERS. Oh, don't talk about it! I can hardly bear to think of it.

REGINA. How *can* it have happened?

MANDERS. Don't ask me, Regina! How should *I* know? Do *you*, too——? Isn't it enough that your father——?

REGINA. What about him?

MANDERS. Oh! he has driven me clean out of my mind——

ENGSTRAND (*comes through the hall*). Your Reverence!

MANDERS (*turns round in terror*). Are you after me here, too?

ENGSTRAND. Yes, strike me dead, but I must—— Oh, Lord! what am I saying? It's an awfully ugly business, your Reverence.

MANDERS (*walks to and fro.*) Alas! alas!

REGINA. What's the matter?

ENGSTRAND. Why, it all came of that prayer-meeting, you see. (*Softly.*) The bird's limed, my girl. (*Aloud.*) And to think that it's my fault that it's his Reverence's fault!

MANDERS. But I assure you, Engstrand——

ENGSTRAND. There wasn't another soul except your Reverence that ever touched the candles down there.

MANDERS (*stops*). Ah! so you declare. But I certainly can't recollect that I ever had a candle in my hand.

ENGSTRAND. And I saw as clear as daylight how your Reverence took the candle and snuffed it with your fingers, and threw away the snuff among the shavings.

MANDERS. And you stood and looked on?

ENGSTRAND. Yes; I saw it as plain as a pike-staff.

MANDERS. It's quite beyond my comprehension. Besides, it's never been my habit to snuff candles with my fingers.

ENGSTRAND. And very risky it looked, that it did! But is there so much harm done after all, your Reverence?

MANDERS (*walks restlessly to and fro*). Oh, don't ask me!

ENGSTRAND (*walks with him*). And your Reverence hadn't insured it, neither?

MANDERS (*continuing to walk up and down*). No, no, no; you've heard that already.

ENGSTRAND (*following him*). Not insured! And then to go right down and set light to the whole thing. Lord! Lord! what a misfortune!

MANDERS (*wipes the sweat from his forehead*). Ay, you may well say that, Engstrand.

ENGSTRAND. And to think that such a thing should happen to a benevolent Institution, that was to have been a blessing both to town and country, as the saying is! The newspapers won't handle your Reverence very gently, I expect.

MANDERS. No; that's just what I'm thinking of. That's almost the worst of it. All the malignant attacks and accusations——! Oh! it's terrible only to imagine it.

MRS. ALVING (*comes in from the garden*). He can't be got away from the fire.

MANDERS. Ah! there you are, Mrs. Alving!

MRS. ALVING. So you've escaped your Inaugural Address, Pastor Manders.

MANDERS. Oh! I should so gladly——

MRS. ALVING (*in an undertone*). It's all for the best. That Orphanage would have done no good to anybody.

MANDERS. Do you think not?

MRS. ALVING. Do you think it would?

MANDERS. It's a terrible misfortune, all the same.

MRS. ALVING. Let us speak plainly of it, as a piece of business. Are you waiting for Mr. Manders, Engstrand?

ENGSTRAND (*at the hall door*). Ay, ma'am; indeed I am.

MRS. ALVING. Then sit down meanwhile.

ENGSTRAND. Thank you, ma'am; I'd rather stand.

MRS. ALVING (*to* MANDERS). I suppose you're going by the steamer?

MANDERS. Yes; it starts in an hour.

MRS. ALVING. Be so good as to take all the papers with you. I won't hear another word about this affair. I have other things to think about.

MANDERS. Mrs. Alving——

MRS. ALVING. Later on I shall send you a Power of Attorney to settle everything as you please.

MANDERS. That I shall very readily undertake. The original destination of the endowment must now be completely changed, alas!

MRS. ALVING. Of course it must.

MANDERS. I think, first of all, I shall arrange that the Solvik property shall pass to the parish. The land is by no means without value. It can always be turned to account for some purpose or other. And the interest of the money in the Bank I could, perhaps, best apply for the benefit of some undertaking that has proved itself a blessing to the town.

MRS. ALVING. Do just as you please. The whole matter is now completely indifferent to me.

ENGSTRAND. Give a thought to my Sailors' Home, your Reverence.

MANDERS. Yes, that's not a bad suggestion. That must be considered.

ENGSTRAND. Oh, devil take considering—I beg your pardon!

MANDERS (*with a sigh*). And I'm sorry to say I don't know how long I shall be able to retain control of these things—whether public opinion may not compel me to retire. It entirely depends upon the result of the official inquiry into the fire——

MRS. ALVING. What are you talking about?

MANDERS. And the result can by no means be foretold.

ENGSTRAND (*comes close to him*). Ay, but it can though. For here stands Jacob Engstrand.

MANDERS. Well well, but——?

ENGSTRAND (*more softly*). And Jacob Engstrand isn't the man to desert a noble benefactor in the hour of need, as the saying is.

MANDERS. Yes, but my good fellow—how——?

ENGSTRAND. Jacob Engstrand may be likened to a guardian angel, he may, your Reverence.

MANDERS. No, no; I can't accept that.

ENGSTRAND. Oh! you will though, all the same.

I know a man that's taken others' sins upon himself before now, I do.

MANDERS. Jacob! (*Wrings his hand.*) You are a rare character. Well, you shall be helped with your Sailors' Home. That you may rely upon. (ENGSTRAND *tries to thank him, but cannot for emotion.* MR. MANDERS *hangs his travelling-bag over his shoulder.*) And now let's be off. We two go together.

ENGSTRAND (*at the dining-room door, softly to* REGINA). You come along too, girl. You shall live as snug as the yolk in an egg.

REGINA (*tosses her head*). *Merci!*

(*She goes out into the hall and fetches* MANDERS'S *overcoat.*)

MANDERS. Good-bye, Mrs. Alving! and may the spirit of Law and Order descend upon this house, and that quickly.

MRS. ALVING. Good-bye, Manders.

(*She goes up towards the conservatory, as she sees* OSWALD *coming in through the garden door.*)

ENGSTRAND (*while he and* REGINA *help* MANDERS *to get his coat on*). Good-bye, my child. And if any trouble should come to you, you know where Jacob Engstrand is to be found. (*Softly.*) Little Harbour Street, hm——! (*To* MRS. ALVING *and* OSWALD.) And the refuge for wandering mariners shall be called "Captain Alving's Home," that it shall! And if I'm spared to carry on that house in my own way, I venture to promise that it shall be worthy of his memory.

MANDERS (*in the doorway*). Hm—hm!—Now come, my dear Engstrand. Good-bye! Good-bye!

(*He and* ENGSTRAND *go out through the hall.*)

OSWALD (*goes towards the table*). What house was he talking about?

MRS. ALVING. Oh, a kind of Home that he and Manders want to set up.

OSWALD. It will burn down like the other.

MRS. ALVING. What makes you think so?

OSWALD. Everything will burn. All that recalls father's memory is doomed. Here am I, too, burning down.

(REGINA *starts and looks at him.*)

MRS. ALVING. Oswald! you oughtn't to have remained so long down there, my poor boy!

OSWALD (*sits down by the table*). I almost think you're right.

MRS. ALVING. Let me dry your face, Oswald; you're quite wet.

(*She dries his face with her pocket-handkerchief.*)

OSWALD (*stares indifferently in front of him*). Thanks, mother.

MRS. ALVING. Aren't you tired, Oswald? Would you like to sleep?

OSWALD (*nervously*). No, no—I can't sleep. I never sleep. I only pretend to. (*Sadly.*) That will come soon enough.

MRS. ALVING (*looking sorrowfully at him*). Yes, you really are ill, my blessed boy.

REGINA (*eagerly*). Is Mr. Alving ill?

OSWALD (*impatiently*). Oh, do shut all the doors! This killing dread——

MRS. ALVING. Shut the doors, Regina.

(REGINA *shuts them and remains standing by the hall door.* MRS. ALVING *takes her shawl off.* REGINA *does the same.* MRS. ALVING *draws a chair across to* OSWALD'S, *and sits by him.*)

MRS. ALVING. There now! I'm going to sit beside you——

OSWALD. Ah! do. And Regina shall stay here, too. Regina shall be with me always. You'll come to the rescue, Regina, won't you?

REGINA. I don't understand——

MRS. ALVING. To the rescue?

OSWALD. Yes—in the hour of need.

MRS. ALVING. Oswald, have you not your mother to come to the rescue?

OSWALD. You? (*Smiles.*) No, mother; *that* rescue you will never bring me. (*Laughs sadly.*) You! ha ha! (*Looks earnestly at her.*) Though, after all, it lies nearest to you. (*Impetuously.*) Why don't you say "thou"[1] to me, Regina? Why don't you call me "Oswald"?

REGINA (*softly*). I don't think Mrs. Alving would like it.

MRS. ALVING. You shall soon have leave to do it. And sit over here beside us, won't you?

(REGINA *sits down quietly and hesitatingly at the other side of the table.*)

MRS. ALVING. And now, my poor suffering boy, I'm going to take the burden off your mind——

OSWALD. You, mother?

[1] "Sige du" = Fr. *tutoyer*.

MRS. ALVING. ——All the gnawing remorse and self-reproach you speak of.

OSWALD. And you think you can do that?

MRS. ALVING. Yes, now I can, Oswald. You spoke of the joy of life; and at that word a new light burst for me over my life and all it has contained.

OSWALD (*shakes his head*). I don't understand you.

MRS. ALVING. You ought to have known your father when he was a young lieutenant. He was brimming over with the joy of life!

OSWALD. Yes, I know he was.

MRS. ALVING. It was like a breezy day only to look at him. And what exuberant strength and vitality there was in him!

OSWALD. Well——?

MRS. ALVING. Well then, child of joy as he was—for he *was* like a child at that time—he had to live here at home in a half-grown town, which had no joys to offer him—only dissipations. He had no object in life—only an official position. He had no work into which he could throw himself heart and soul; he had only business. He had not a single comrade that knew what the joy of life meant—only loungers and boon-companions——

OSWALD. Mother!

MRS. ALVING. So the inevitable happened.

OSWALD. The inevitable?

MRS. ALVING. You said yourself, this evening, what would happen to you if you stayed at home.

OSWALD. Do you mean to say that father——?

MRS. ALVING. Your poor father found no outlet

for the overpowering joy of life that was in him. And I brought no brightness into his home.

OSWALD. Not even you?

MRS. ALVING. They had taught me a lot about duties and so on, which I had taken to be true. Everything was marked out into duties—into my duties, and his duties, and—I'm afraid I made home intolerable for your poor father, Oswald.

OSWALD. Why did you never write me anything about all this?

MRS. ALVING. I have never before seen it in such a light that I could speak of it to you, his son.

OSWALD. In what light did you see it then?

MRS. ALVING (*slowly*). I saw only this one thing, that your father was a broken-down man before you were born.

OSWALD (*softly*). Ah!

(*He rises and walks away to the window.*)

MRS. ALVING. And then, day after day, I dwelt on the one thought that by rights Regina should be at home in this house—just like my own boy.

OSWALD (*turning round quickly*). Regina!

REGINA (*springs up and asks, with bated breath*). I?

MRS. ALVING. Yes, now you know it, both of you.

OSWALD. Regina!

REGINA (*to herself*). So mother was that kind of woman, after all.

MRS. ALVING. Your mother had many good qualities, Regina.

REGINA. Yes, but she was one of that sort, all the same. Oh! I've often suspected it; but—— And now, if you please, ma'am, may I be allowed to go away at once?

MRS. ALVING. Do you really wish it, Regina?

REGINA. Yes, indeed I do.

MRS. ALVING. Of course you can do as you like; but——

OSWALD (*goes towards* REGINA). Go away now? Isn't this your home?

REGINA. *Merci*, Mr. Alving!—or now, I suppose, I may say Oswald. But I can tell you this wasn't what I expected.

MRS. ALVING. Regina, I have not been frank with you——

REGINA. No, that you haven't, indeed. If I'd known that Oswald was ill, why—— And now, too, that it can never come to anything serious between us—— I really can't stop out here in the country and wear myself out nursing sick people.

OSWALD. Not even one who is so near to you?

REGINA. No, that I can't. A poor girl must make the best of her young days, or she'll be left out in the cold before she knows where she is. And I, too, have the joy of life in me, Mrs. Alving.

MRS. ALVING. Yes, I see you have. But don't throw yourself away, Regina.

REGINA. Oh! what must be, must be. If Oswald takes after his father, I take after my mother, I dare-say. May I ask, ma'am, if Mr. Manders knows all this about me?

MRS. ALVING. Mr. Manders knows all about it.

REGINA (*puts on her shawl hastily*). Well then, I'd better make haste and get away by this steamer.

Pastor Manders is so nice to deal with; and I certainly think I've as much right to a little of that money as he has—that brute of a carpenter.

MRS. ALVING. You're heartily welcome to it, Regina.

REGINA (*looks hard at her*). I think you might have brought me up as a gentleman's daughter, ma'am; it would have suited me better. (*Tosses her head.*) But it's done now—it doesn't matter! (*With a bitter side glance at the corked bottle.*) All the same, I may come to drink champagne with gentlefolks yet.

MRS. ALVING. And if you ever need a home, Regina, come to me.

REGINA. No, thank you, ma'am. Mr. Manders will look after me, I know. And if the worst comes to the worst, I know of one house where I've every right to a place.

MRS. ALVING. Where is that?

REGINA. "Captain Alving's Home."

MRS. ALVING. Regina—now I see it—you're going to your ruin.

REGINA. Oh, stuff! Good-bye.

(*She nods and goes out through the hall.*)

OSWALD (*stands at the window and looks out*). Is she gone?

MRS. ALVING. Yes.

OSWALD (*murmuring aside to himself*). I think it's a great mistake, all this.

MRS. ALVING (*goes behind him and lays her hands on his shoulders*). Oswald, my dear boy; has it shaken you very much?

OSWALD (*turns his face towards her*). All that about father, do you mean?

MRS. ALVING. Yes, about your unhappy father. I'm so afraid it may have been too much for you.

OSWALD. Why should you fancy that? Of course it came upon me as a great surprise; but, after all, it can't matter much to me.

MRS. ALVING (*draws her hands away*). Can't matter! That your father was so infinitely miserable!

OSWALD. Of course I can pity him as I would anybody else; but——

MRS. ALVING. Nothing more? Your own father!

OSWALD (*impatiently*). Oh, there! "father," "father"! I never knew anything of father. I don't remember anything about him except that he once made me sick.

MRS. ALVING. That's a terrible way to speak! Should a son not love his father, all the same?

OSWALD. When a son has nothing to thank his father for? has never known him? Do you really cling to that old superstition?—you who are so enlightened in other ways?

MRS. ALVING. Is it only a superstition——?

OSWALD. Yes; can't you see it, mother? It's one of those notions that are current in the world, and so——

MRS. ALVING (*deeply moved*). Ghosts!

OSWALD (*crossing the room*). Yes; you may well call them Ghosts.

MRS. ALVING (*wildly*). Oswald!—then you don't love me, either!

OSWALD. You I know, at any rate.

MRS. ALVING. Yes, you know me; but is that all?

OSWALD. And of course I know how fond you are of me, and I can't but be grateful to you. And you can be so very useful to me, now that I'm ill.

MRS. ALVING. Yes, can't I, Oswald? Oh! I could almost bless the illness that has driven you home to me. For I can see very plainly you are not mine; I have to win you.

OSWALD (*impatiently*). Yes yes yes; all these are just so many phrases. You must recollect I'm a sick man, mother. I can't be much taken up with other people; I have enough to do thinking about myself.

MRS. ALVING (*in a low voice*). I shall be patient and easily satisfied.

OSWALD. And cheerful too, mother.

MRS. ALVING. Yes, my dear boy, you're quite right. (*Goes towards him.*) Have I relieved you of all remorse and self-reproach now?

OSWALD. Yes, you have. But who's to relieve me of the dread?

MRS. ALVING. The dread?

OSWALD (*walks across the room*). Regina could have been got to do it.

MRS. ALVING. I don't understand you. What is all this about dread—and Regina?

OSWALD. Is it very late, mother?

MRS. ALVING. It's early morning. (*She looks out through the conservatory.*) The day is dawning over the hills; and the weather is fine, Oswald. In a little while you shall see the sun.

OSWALD. I'm glad of that. Oh! I may still have much to rejoice in and live for——

MRS. ALVING. Yes, much—much, indeed!

OSWALD. Even if I can't work——

MRS. ALVING. Oh! you'll soon be able to work again, my dear boy, now that you haven't got all those gnawing and depressing thoughts to brood over any longer.

OSWALD. Yes, I'm glad you were able to rid me of all those fancies; and when I've got one thing more arranged—— (*Sits on the sofa.*) Now we'll have a little talk, mother.

MRS. ALVING. Yes, let us.

(*She pushes an arm-chair towards the sofa, and sits down close to him.*)

OSWALD. And meantime the sun will be rising. And then you'll know all. And then I shan't have that dread any longer.

MRS. ALVING. What am I to know?

OSWALD (*not listening to her*). Mother, didn't you say, a little while ago, that there was nothing in the world you wouldn't do for me, if I asked you.

MRS. ALVING. Yes, to be sure I said it.

OSWALD. And you'll stick to it, mother?

MRS. ALVING. You may rely on that, my dear and only boy! I have nothing in the world to live for but you alone.

OSWALD. All right, then; now you shall hear. Mother, you have a strong, steadfast mind, I know. Now you're to sit quite still when you hear it.

MRS. ALVING. What dreadful thing can it be——?

OSWALD. You're not to scream out. Do you hear? Do you promise me that? We'll sit and talk about it quite quietly. Promise me, mother?

MRS. ALVING. Yes, yes; I promise. Only speak.

OSWALD. Well, you must know that all this fatigue, and my inability to think of work—all that is not the illness itself——

MRS. ALVING. Then what is the illness itself?

OSWALD. The disease I have as my birthright (*he points to his forehead and adds very softly*)—is seated here.

MRS. ALVING (*almost voiceless*). Oswald! No, no!

OSWALD. Don't scream. I can't bear it. Yes, it's seated here—waiting. And it may break out any day—at any moment.

MRS. ALVING. Oh! what horror!

OSWALD. Now, do be quiet. That's how it stands with me——

MRS. ALVING (*jumps up*). It's not true, Oswald It's impossible. It can't be so.

OSWALD. I have had one attack down there already. It was soon over. But when I got to know what had been the matter with me, then the dread came upon me raging and tearing; and so I set off home to you as fast as I could.

MRS. ALVING. Then this is the dread——!

OSWALD. Yes, for it's so indescribably loathsome, you know. Oh! if it had only been an ordinary mortal disease——! For I'm not so afraid of death —though I should like to live as long as I can.

MRS. ALVING. Yes, yes, Oswald, you must!

OSWALD. But this is so unutterably loathsome! To become a little baby again! To have to be fed! To have to—— Oh, it's not to be spoken of!

MRS. ALVING. The child has his mother to nurse him.

OSWALD (*jumps up*). No, never; that's just what I won't have. I can't endure to think that perhaps I should lie in that state for many years—get old and grey. And in the meantime you might die and leave me. (*Sits in* MRS. ALVING'S *chair.*) For the doctor said it wouldn't necessarily prove fatal at once. He called it a sort of softening of the brain—or something of the kind. (*Smiles sadly.*) I think that expression sounds so nice. It always sets me thinking of cherry-coloured velvet—something soft and delicate to stroke.

MRS. ALVING (*screams*). Oswald!

OSWALD (*springs up and paces the room*). And now you have taken Regina from me. If I'd only had her! She would have come to the rescue, I know.

MRS. ALVING (*goes to him*). What do you mean by that, my darling boy? Is there any help in the world that I wouldn't give you?

OSWALD. When I got over my attack in Paris, the doctor told me that when it came again—and it will come again—there would be no more hope.

MRS. ALVING. He was heartless enough to——

OSWALD. I demanded it of him. I told him I had preparations to make. (*He smiles cunningly.*) And so I had. (*He takes a little box from his inner breast pocket and opens it.*) Mother, do you see this?

MRS. ALVING. What is that?

OSWALD. Morphia.

MRS. ALVING (*looks horrified at him*). Oswald—my boy!

OSWALD. I've scraped together twelve pilules——

MRS. ALVING (*snatches at it*). Give me the box, Oswald.

OSWALD. Not yet, mother.

(*He hides the box again in his pocket.*)

MRS. ALVING. I shall never survive this!

OSWALD. It must be survived. Now if I'd had Regina here, I should have told her how things stood with me, and begged her to come to the rescue at the last. She would have done it. I'm certain she would.

MRS. ALVING. Never!

OSWALD. When the horror had come upon me, and she saw me lying there helpless, like a little new-born baby, impotent, lost, hopeless, past all saving——

MRS. ALVING. Never in all the world would Regina have done this.

OSWALD. Regina would have done it. Regina was so splendidly light-hearted. And she would soon have wearied of nursing an invalid like me——

MRS. ALVING. Then heaven be praised that Regina is not here.

OSWALD. Well then, it's you that must come to the rescue, mother.

MRS. ALVING (*screams aloud*). I!

OSWALD. Who is nearer to it than you?

MRS. ALVING. I! your mother!

OSWALD. For that very reason.

MRS. ALVING. I, who gave you life!

OSWALD. I never asked you for life. And what sort of a life have you given me? I won't have it. You shall take it back again.

MRS. ALVING. Help! Help!

(*She runs out into the hall.*)

OSWALD (*going after her*). Don't leave me. Where are you going?

MRS. ALVING (*in the hall*). To fetch the doctor, Oswald. Let me go.

OSWALD (*also outside*). You shall not go. And no one shall come in. (*The locking of a door is heard.*)

MRS. ALVING (*comes in again*). Oswald—Oswald!—my child!

OSWALD (*follows her*). Have you a mother's heart for me, and yet can see me suffer from this unutterable dread?

MRS. ALVING (*after a moment's silence, commands herself, and says:*) Here's my hand upon it.

OSWALD. Will you——?

MRS. ALVING. If it's ever necessary. But it will never be necessary. No, no; it's impossible.

OSWALD. Well, let us hope so, and let us live together as long as we can. Thank you, mother.

(*He seats himself in the arm-chair which* MRS. ALVING *has moved to the sofa. Day is breaking. The lamp is still burning on the table.*)

MRS. ALVING (*drawing near cautiously*). Do you feel calm now?

OSWALD. Yes.

MRS. ALVING (*bending over him*). It has been a dreadful fancy of yours, Oswald—nothing but a fancy. All this excitement has been too much for you. But now you shall have a long rest; at home with your mother, my own blessed boy. Everything you point to you shall have, just as when you were a little child. There now. That crisis is over now. You see how easily it passed. Oh! I was sure it would—— And do you see, Oswald, what a lovely day we're going to have? Brilliant sunshine! Now you'll really be able to see your home.

(*She goes to the table and puts the lamp out. Sunrise. The glacier and the snow-peaks in the background glow in the morning light.*)

OSWALD (*sits in the arm-chair with his back towards the landscape, without moving. Suddenly he says:*) Mother, give me the sun.

MRS. ALVING (*by the table, starts and looks at him*). What do you say?

OSWALD (*repeats, in a dull, toneless voice:*) The sun. The sun.

MRS. ALVING (*goes to him*). Oswald, what's the matter with you? (OSWALD *seems to shrink together in the chair; all his muscles relax; his face is expressionless, his eyes have a glassy stare.* MRS. ALVING *is quivering with terror.*) What is this? (*Shrieks.*) Oswald, what's the matter with you? (*Falls on her knees beside him and shakes him.*) Oswald, Oswald! look at me! Don't you know me?

OSWALD (*tonelessly as before*). The sun. The sun.

MRS. ALVING (*springs up in despair, entwines her hands in her hair and shrieks*). I can't bear it (*whispers, as though petrified*); I can't bear it! Never! (*Suddenly.*) Where has he got them? (*Fumbles hastily in his breast.*) Here! (*Shrinks back a few steps and screams.*) No; no; no! Yes!—No; no!

(*She stands a few steps from him with her hands twisted in her hair, and stares at him in speechless terror.*)

OSWALD (*sits motionless as before and says:*) The sun. The sun

AN ENEMY OF THE PEOPLE.

(1882.)

Characters.

DOCTOR THOMAS STOCKMANN, *medical officer of the Baths.*
MRS. STOCKMANN, *his wife.*
PETRA, *their daughter, a teacher.*
EILIF, } *their sons, boys of thirteen.*
MORTEN, }
PETER STOCKMANN, *the doctor's elder brother, Burgomaster*[1] *and chief of police, chairman of the Baths Committee, etc.*
MORTEN KIIL, *master tanner, Mrs. Stockmann's foster-father.*
HOVSTAD, *editor of the "People's Messenger."*
BILLING, *on the staff.*
HORSTER, *a ship's captain.*
ASLAKSEN, *a printer.*

Townsfolk present at the meeting; all sorts and conditions of men, some women, and a flock of school-boys.

SCENE: *A town on the South Coast of Norway.*

1 "Burgomaster" is the most convenient substitute for "Byfogd," but "Town Clerk" would perhaps be a nearer approach to a literal rendering of the term. It is impossible to find exact counterparts in English for the different grades of the Norwegian bureaucracy.

AN ENEMY OF THE PEOPLE.

PLAY IN FIVE ACTS.

Act First.

(*Evening.* DR. STOCKMANN'S *sitting-room; simply but neatly fitted and furnished. In the wall to the right are two doors, the first leading to the Doctor's study, the second to an anteroom. In the opposite wall, facing the anteroom door, a door leading to the other rooms. Near the middle of this wall stands the stove; further towards the foreground a sofa, with a mirror above it, and in front of it an oval table with a cover. On the table a lighted lamp, with a shade. In the back wall an open door leading to the dining-room, in which is seen a supper-table, with a lamp on it.*)

(BILLING *is seated at the table, a napkin under his chin.* MRS. STOCKMANN *stands by the table and hands him a plate with a large slice of roast beef. The other seats round the table are empty; the table is in disorder, as after a meal.*)

MRS. STOCKMANN. Well, if you're an hour late, Mr. Billing, you must put up with a cold supper.

BILLING (*eating*). It's excellent, delicious!

MRS. STOCKMANN. You know how Stockmann insists on regular meal-hours——

BILLING. Oh, I don't mind at all. I almost think it tastes better when I can sit down like this and have it all to myself, undisturbed.

MRS. STOCKMANN. Well, if you're satisfied—— (*Listening in the direction of the anteroom.*) Surely that's Hovstad coming too.

BILLING. Very likely.

(BURGOMASTER STOCKMANN *enters, wearing an overcoat and an official gold-laced cap, and carrying a stick.*)

BURGOMASTER. Good evening, sister-in-law.

MRS. STOCKMANN (*coming into the sitting-room*). Oh, good evening; is it you? It's very nice of you to look in.

BURGOMASTER. I was just passing, and so—— (*Looks towards the dining-room.*) Ah! I see you have company.

MRS. STOCKMANN (*rather embarrassed*). Oh, no! Not at all; it's the merest chance. (*Hurriedly.*) Won't you come and have something?

BURGOMASTER. I? No, thanks. Good gracious! hot meat in the evening! that wouldn't suit *my* digestion.

MRS. STOCKMANN. Oh! for once in a way——

BURGOMASTER. No, no. Much obliged to you. I stick to tea and bread and butter. It's more wholesome in the long run—and rather more economical, too.

MRS. STOCKMANN (*smiling*). You mustn't think Thomas and I are mere spendthrifts, either.

BURGOMASTER. You're not, sister-in-law; far be it from me to say that. (*Pointing to the Doctor's study.*) Is he not at home?

MRS. STOCKMANN. No, he's gone for a little turn after supper—with the boys.

BURGOMASTER. I wonder if that's good for him? (*Listening.*) There he is.

MRS. STOCKMANN. No, that's not he. (*A knock.*) Come in! (HOVSTAD *enters from the anteroom.*) Ah! it's Mr. Hovstad——

HOVSTAD. You must excuse me; I was detained at the printer's. Good evening, Burgomaster.

BURGOMASTER (*bowing rather stiffly*). Mr. Hovstad! Come on business, I presume?

HOVSTAD. Partly. About something for the paper.

BURGOMASTER. So I supposed. I hear my brother's an extremely prolific contributor to the *People's Messenger.*

HOVSTAD. Yes, he's good enough to give the *Messenger* the benefit when he wants to relieve his mind on any special subject.

MRS. STOCKMANN (*to* HOVSTAD). But won't you——? (*Points to the dining-room.*)

BURGOMASTER. God forbid I should blame him for writing for the class of readers he finds most in sympathy with him. And, personally, I've no reason to bear your paper any ill-will, Mr. Hovstad.

HOVSTAD. No, I should think not.

BURGOMASTER. On the whole, there's a great deal of mutual toleration in our town;—an excellent public spirit. And that's because we have a great common interest to hold us together—an interest in which all right-minded citizens are equally concerned.

HOVSTAD. Yes—the Baths.

BURGOMASTER. Just so. We have our magnificent new Baths. You'll see! The whole life of the town will centre around the Baths, Mr. Hovstad, beyond a doubt!

MRS. STOCKMANN. That's just what Thomas says.

BURGOMASTER. How marvellously the place has developed, even within the last few years. Money has come into circulation, and brought life and movement with it. Houses and ground-rents rise in value every day.

HOVSTAD. And the difficulty of getting work is decreasing.

BURGOMASTER. That's true. There's a gratifying diminution in the burden imposed on the well-to-do classes by the poor-rates; and they will be still further lightened if only we have a really good summer this year—plenty of visitors—lots of invalids, to give the Baths a reputation.

HOVSTAD. I hear there's every prospect of that.

BURGOMASTER. Things look most promising. Inquiries about apartments and so forth are flowing in every day.

HOVSTAD. Then the Doctor's paper will come in very opportunely.

BURGOMASTER. Has he been writing again?

HOVSTAD. It's a thing he wrote in the winter; eulogising the Baths, and enlarging on the excellent sanitary conditions of the town. But at the time I held it over.

BURGOMASTER. Ha! I suppose there was some little hitch.

HOVSTAD. Not at all. But I thought it better to keep it till the spring, when people are beginning to look about them, and think of their summer quarters.

BURGOMASTER. You're right, quite right, Mr. Hovstad.

MRS. STOCKMANN. Yes, Thomas is really indefatigable where the Baths are concerned.

BURGOMASTER. Well, you know, he's one of the staff.

HOVSTAD. And of course he was really their creator.

BURGOMASTER. Was he? I hear now and then that certain persons are of that opinion. But I should have thought that I too had a modest share in that undertaking.

MRS. STOCKMANN. Yes, that's what Thomas is always saying.

HOVSTAD. Who wants to deny it, Burgomaster? You set the thing going, and put it on a practical footing; everybody knows that. I only meant that the original idea was the doctor's.

BURGOMASTER. Yes, my brother has certainly had ideas enough in his time—worse luck! But when it comes to realising them, Mr. Hovstad, we want men of another stamp. I should have expected that in this house at least——

MRS. STOCKMANN. Why, my dear brother-in-law——

HOVSTAD. Burgomaster, how can you——?

MRS. STOCKMANN. Do go in and take something, Mr. Hovstad; my husband is sure to be in directly.

HOVSTAD. Thanks; just a mouthful, perhaps.

(*He goes into the dining-room.*)

BURGOMASTER (*speaking in a low voice*). It's

extraordinary how people who spring directly from the peasant-class never can get rid of a want of tact.

MRS. STOCKMANN. But why should you care? Can't you and Thomas share the honour, like brothers?

BURGOMASTER. Yes, one would suppose so; but it seems a share of the honour isn't enough for some persons.

MRS. STOCKMANN. What nonsense! You and Thomas always get on so well together. (*Listening.*) There, I think I hear him.

(*Goes and opens the door of the anteroom.*)

DR. STOCKMANN (*laughing and talking loudly without*). Here's another visitor for you, Katrine. Isn't it jolly, eh? Come in, Captain Horster. Hang your coat on that peg. What! you don't wear an overcoat? Fancy, Katrine, I caught him in the street, and I could hardly get him to come along. (CAPTAIN HORSTER *enters and bows to* MRS. STOCKMANN. *The* DOCTOR *is by the door.*) In with you, boys. They're famished again! Come on, Captain; you must have some of our roast beef——

(*He forces* HORSTER *into the dining-room.* EILIF *and* MORTEN *join them.*)

MRS. STOCKMANN. But, Thomas, don't you see——

DR. STOCKMANN (*turning round in the doorway*). Oh! is that you, Peter? (*Goes up to him and holds out his hand.*) Now this is really jolly.

BURGOMASTER. Unfortunately, I must be off directly——

DR. STOCKMANN. Nonsense! We'll have some

toddy in a minute. You're not forgetting the toddy, Katrine?

MRS. STOCKMANN. Of course not; the water's boiling.

(*She goes into the dining-room.*)

BURGOMASTER. Toddy too——!

DR. STOCKMANN. Yes; sit down, and let's enjoy ourselves.

BURGOMASTER. Thanks; I never join in drinking-parties.

DR. STOCKMANN. But this isn't a party.

BURGOMASTER. It seems to me—— (*Looks towards the dining-room.*) It's wonderful how they can get through all that food.

DR. STOCKMANN (*rubbing his hands*). Yes, doesn't it do one good to see young people eat? Always hungry! That's as it should be! They must eat. They need strength! It's they that have got to keep the ferment of the future astir, Peter.

BURGOMASTER. May I ask what there is to be "kept astir," as you call it?

DR. STOCKMANN. You'll have to ask the young people that—when the time comes. *We* shan't see it, of course. Two old fogies like you and me——

BURGOMASTER. Come, come—surely that's a very extraordinary expression to use——

DR. STOCKMANN. Oh, you mustn't mind my nonsense, Peter. I'm in glorious spirits, you see. I feel so unspeakably happy in the midst of all this growing, germinating life. After all, what a glorious time we live in! It seems as though a whole new world were springing up around us.

BURGOMASTER. Do you really think so?

DR. STOCKMANN. Of course you can't see it as clearly as I do. You've passed your life in the midst of it all; and that deadens the impression. But I, who had to vegetate all those years in that little hole in the north, hardly ever seeing a soul that could speak a stimulating word to me—all this affects me as if I had suddenly dropped into the heart of some great metropolis——

BURGOMASTER. Hm; metropolis——

DR. STOCKMANN. Oh! I know well enough that things are on a small scale here compared with many other places. But there's vitality and promise—an infinity of things to work and strive for; and that's the main point. (*Calling.*) Katrine, haven't there been any letters?

MRS. STOCKMANN (*in the dining-room*). No, none at all.

DR. STOCKMANN. And then a good income, Peter! That's a thing one learns to appreciate when one has lived on starvation wages——

BURGOMASTER. Good heavens——!

DR. STOCKMANN. Oh yes! I can tell you we had often hard times of it up there. And now we can live like princes! To-day, for example, we had roast beef for dinner, and we've had some of it for supper too. Won't you have some! Come along—just look at it, anyhow.

BURGOMASTER. No no; certainly not——

DR. STOCKMANN. Well then, look here. Do you see we've bought a table-cover?

BURGOMASTER. Yes, so I observed.

DR. STOCKMANN. And a lamp-shade too. Do you see? Katrine has been saving up for them. They make the room look comfortable, don't they? Come over here. No no no, not there! So—yes—do you see what a rich light it throws down?—I really think it looks very nice. Eh?

BURGOMASTER. Yes, when one can afford such luxuries——

DR. STOCKMANN. Oh yes, I can afford it now. Katrine says I make almost as much as we spend.

BURGOMASTER. Yes—almost!

DR. STOCKMANN. Besides, a man of science must live in some style. Why, I believe a mere sheriff[1] spends much more a year than I do.

BURGOMASTER. Yes, I daresay! A member of the superior magistracy!

DR. STOCKMANN. Well then, even a common merchant! A man of that sort will get through many times as much——

BURGOMASTER. That's natural, in your relative positions——

DR. STOCKMANN. And, after all, I really don't spend anything unnecessarily, Peter. But I can't deny myself the delight of having people about me. I must have them. After being so long isolated, I find it a necessity of life to have bright, cheerful, freedom-loving, hard-working young men around me—and that's what they are, all of them, sitting there eating so heartily. I wish you knew more of Hovstad——

BURGOMASTER. Ah, Hovstad! He was telling

[1] *Amtmand*, the chief official of an *Amt* or county; consequently a high dignitary in the bureaucratic hierarchy.

me that he's going to publish another article of yours.

DR. STOCKMANN. An article of mine?

BURGOMASTER. Yes, about the Baths. An article you wrote last winter——

DR. STOCKMANN. Oh, that one! But I don't want that to appear just now.

BURGOMASTER. Why not? It seems to me this is the very time for it.

DR. STOCKMANN. Very likely—under ordinary circumstances—— (*Crosses the room.*)

BURGOMASTER (*looking after him*). And what's unusual in the circumstances now?

DR. STOCKMANN (*standing still*). Peter, I really can't tell you yet—not this evening, at all events. There may prove to be a great deal that's unusual in the circumstances. On the other hand, there may be nothing at all. Very likely it's only my fancy.

BURGOMASTER. Upon my word, you're very enigmatical. Is there anything in the wind? Anything I'm to be kept in the dark about? I should think, as Chairman of the Bath Committee——

DR. STOCKMANN. And I should think that I—— There! don't let's get our backs up, Peter.

BURGOMASTER. God forbid! I'm not in the habit of "getting my back up," as you express it. But I must absolutely insist that everything shall be carried on in a business-like manner, and through the proper authorities. I can't be a party to crooked or underhand ways.

DR. STOCKMANN. Have *I* ever been given to crooked or underhand ways?

BURGOMASTER. Anyhow, you have an ingrained propensity to going your own way. And that, in a well-ordered community, is almost as inadmissible. The individual must submit to society, or, more precisely, to the authorities whose business it is to watch over the welfare of society.

DR. STOCKMANN. Maybe. But what the devil has that to do with me?

BURGOMASTER. Why that's the very thing, my dear Thomas, that it seems you won't learn. But take care; you'll have to pay for it sooner or later. Now I've warned you. Good-bye.

DR. STOCKMANN. Are you quite mad? You're on a totally wrong track——

BURGOMASTER. I'm not usually on the wrong track. Besides, I must beg you not to—— (*Bowing towards dining-room.*) Good-bye, sister-in-law; good-bye, gentlemen.

(*He goes.*)

MRS. STOCKMANN (*entering the sitting-room*). Is he gone?

DR. STOCKMANN. Yes, and in a fine temper, too.

MRS. STOCKMANN. Why, my dear Thomas, what have you been saying to him now?

DR. STOCKMANN. Nothing at all. He can't expect me to account to him for everything—before the time comes.

MRS. STOCKMANN. What are you to account to him for?

DR. STOCKMANN. Hm! Never mind about that, Katrine. It's very odd that there are no letters.

(HOVSTAD, BILLING, *and* HORSTER *have risen from table and come forward into the sitting-room.* EILIF *and* MORTEN *presently follow.*)

BILLING (*stretching himself*). Ah! Strike me dead if one doesn't feel a new man after such a meal.

HOVSTAD. The Burgomaster didn't seem in the best of tempers this evening.

DR. STOCKMANN. That's his stomach. He has a very poor digestion.

HOVSTAD. It's the staff of the *Messenger* he finds it hardest to stomach.

MRS. STOCKMANN. I thought you got on with him well enough.

HOVSTAD. Oh, yes! But it's only a sort of armistice between us.

BILLING. That's it. That word sums up the situation.

DR. STOCKMANN. We must remember that Peter's a bachelor, poor devil! He has no home to be happy in; only business, business. And then all that cursed weak tea he goes and pours down his throat! Now then, put chairs round the table, boys! Katrine, shan't we have the toddy now?

MRS. STOCKMANN (*going towards the dining-room*). I'm just getting it.

DR. STOCKMANN. And you, Captain Horster, sit down by me on the sofa. So rare a guest as you—— Be seated, gentlemen.

(*The men sit round the table;* MRS. STOCKMANN *brings in a tray with kettle, glasses, decanters, etc.*)

MRS. STOCKMANN. There you are! Here's arrak, and this is rum, and this cognac. Now, help yourselves.

DR. STOCKMANN (*taking a glass*). So we will! (*While the toddy is being mixed.*) And now out with the cigars. Eilif, I'm sure you know where the box is. And you, Morten, may fetch my pipe. (*The boys go into the room, right.*) I have a suspicion that Eilif cribs a cigar now and then, but I pretend not to notice it. (*Calls.*) And my smoking-cap, Morten. Katrine, can't you tell him where I left it? Ah! he's got it. (*The boys bring in the things.*) Now, friends, help yourselves. You know I stick to my pipe;—this one has been on many a stormy journey with me, up there in the north. (*They clink glasses.*) Your health! Ah, I can tell you it's better fun to sit cosily here, safe from wind and weather.

MRS. STOCKMANN (*who sits knitting*). Do you sail soon, Captain Horster?

HORSTER. I hope to be ready for a start by next week.

MRS. STOCKMANN. And you're going to America?

HORSTER. Yes, that's the intention.

BILLING. But then you'll miss the election of the new Town Council.

HORSTER. Is there to be an election again?

BILLING. Didn't you know?

HORSTER. No, I don't bother about these things.

BILLING. But I suppose you take an interest in public affairs?

HORSTER. No, I don't understand anything about them.

BILLING. Still one ought to make use of one's vote.

HORSTER. Even those who don't understand anything about it?

BILLING. Understand? Now, what do you mean by that? Society's like a ship: every man must put his hand to the helm.

HORSTER. That may be all right on shore; but at sea it wouldn't do at all.

HOVSTAD. It's remarkable how little sailors care about public affairs, as a rule.

BILLING. Most extraordinary.

DR. STOCKMANN. Sailors are like birds of passage: they're at home both in the south and in the north. So the rest of us have to be all the more energetic, Mr. Hovstad. Will there be anything of public interest in the *People's Messenger* to-morrow?

HOVSTAD. Nothing of local interest. But the day after to-morrow I'm thinking of printing your article——

DR. STOCKMANN. Oh confound it, I say! You'll have to hold that over.

HOVSTAD. Really? We happen to have plenty of space, and I should say this was the very time for it——

DR. STOCKMANN. Yes yes, you may be right, but you'll have to hold it over all the same. I'll explain to you by-and-by——

(PETRA, *wearing a hat and cloak, and with a number of exercise books under her arm, comes in from the anteroom.*)

PETRA. Good evening!

DR. STOCKMANN. Good evening, Petra! Is that you?

(*General greetings.* PETRA *puts her cloak, hat, and books on a chair by the door.*)

PETRA. Here you all are, enjoying yourselves, while I've been out slaving!

DR. STOCKMANN. Well then, you come and enjoy yourself too.

BILLING. May I mix you a little——?

PETRA (*coming towards the table*). Thanks, I'll help myself—you always make it too strong. But, by the way, father, I've a letter for you.

(*Goes to the chair where her things are lying.*)

DR. STOCKMANN. A letter! From whom?

PETRA (*searching in the pocket of her cloak*). I got it from the postman just as I was going out——

DR. STOCKMANN (*rising and going towards her*). And you only bring it me now?

PETRA. I really hadn't time to run up again. Here it is.

DR. STOCKMANN (*seizing the letter*). Let me see, let me see, child. (*Reads the address.*) Yes; that's it——

MRS. STOCKMANN. Is it the one you've been expecting so, Thomas?

DR. STOCKMANN. Yes, it is. I must go at once—— Where shall I find a light, Katrine? Is there no lamp in my study again?

MRS. STOCKMANN. Yes—the lamp's lit. It's on the writing-table.

DR. STOCKMANN. Good. Excuse me one moment——

(*He goes into the room on the right.*)

PETRA. What can it be, mother?

MRS. STOCKMANN. I don't know. For the last few days he's been continually on the look-out for the postman.

BILLING. Probably a country patient——

PETRA. Poor father! He'll soon have far too much to do. (*Mixes her toddy.*) Ah! this'll be good.

HOVSTAD. Have you been teaching in the night school as well to-day?

PETRA (*sipping her glass*). Two hours.

BILLING. And four hours in the morning at the institute——

PETRA (*sitting down by the table*). Five hours.

MRS. STOCKMANN. And I see you've some exercises to correct this evening.

PETRA. Yes, a heap of them.

HORSTER. It seems to me you've plenty to do, too.

PETRA. Yes; but I like it. One feels so delightfully tired after it.

BILLING. Do you like that?

PETRA. Yes, for then one sleeps so well.

MORTEN. I say, Petra, you must be a great sinner.

PETRA. A sinner!

MORTEN. Yes, if you work so hard. Mr. Rörlund[1] says work is a punishment for our sins.

EILIF (*contemptuously*). Bosh! What a silly you are to believe such stuff as that!

MRS. STOCKMANN. Come come, Eilif.

BILLING (*laughing*). Capital, capital!

[1] See *The Pillars of Society*.

HOVSTAD. Wouldn't you like to work so hard, Morten?

MORTEN. No, I shouldn't.

HOVSTAD. What do you intend to be, then?

MORTEN. I should like to be a Viking.

EILIF. But then you'd have to be a heathen.

MORTEN. Well, so I would.

BILLING. There I agree with you, Morten. I say just the same.

MRS. STOCKMANN (*making a sign to him*). No, no, Mr. Billing, you don't.

BILLING. Strike me dead but I do, though. I *am* a heathen, and I'm proud of it. You'll see we shall all be heathens soon.

MORTEN. And shall we be able to do anything we like then?

BILLING. Well, you see, Morten——

MRS. STOCKMANN. Now run away, boys; I'm sure you've some lessons to prepare for to-morrow.

EILIF. You might let me stay just a little longer——

MRS. STOCKMANN. No, you must go too. Be off, both of you.

(*The boys say good-night and go into the room on the left.*)

HOVSTAD. Do you really think it can hurt the boys to hear these things?

MRS. STOCKMANN. Well, I don't know; but I don't like it.

PETRA. Well mother, I think you're quite wrong there.

MRS. STOCKMANN. Maybe! But I don't like it—here, at home.

PETRA. There's no end of hypocrisy both at home and at school. At home you must hold your tongue, and at school you have to stand up and lie to the children.

HORSTER. To lie?

PETRA. Yes; do you think we don't have to teach many and many a thing we don't believe ourselves?

BILLING. Yes, we know that well enough.

PETRA. If only I could afford it, I'd start a school myself, and things should be very different there.

BILLING. Oh, afford it——!

HORSTER. If you're really thinking of doing that, Miss Stockmann, I shall be delighted to let you have a room at my place. My father's old house is nearly empty; there's a large dining-room on the ground floor——

PETRA (*laughing*). Oh, thank you very much—but nothing will come of it.

HOVSTAD. Oh no! I fancy Miss Petra will rather go in for journalism. By the way, have you had time to look into the English novel you promised to translate for us——?

PETRA. Not yet. But you shall have it in good time.

(DR. STOCKMANN *enters from his room, with the letter open in his hand.*)

DR. STOCKMANN (*flourishing the letter*). Here's news, I can tell you, that'll wake up the town!

BILLING. News?

MRS. STOCKMANN. What news?

DR. STOCKMANN. A great discovery, Katrine.

HOVSTAD. What?

MRS. STOCKMANN. Made by you?

DR. STOCKMANN. Yes—by me! (*Walks up and down.*) *Now* let them go on accusing me of fads and crack-brained notions. But they'll not dare to Ha-ha! I know they won't.

PETRA. Father, do tell us what it is.

DR. STOCKMANN. Well well, give me time, and you shall hear all about it. If only Peter were here now! This just shows how we men can go about forming judgments like the blindest moles——

HOVSTAD. What do you mean, doctor?

DR. STOCKMANN (*standing beside the table*). Isn't it generally supposed that our town is healthy?

HOVSTAD. Of course.

DR. STOCKMANN. Indeed a quite exceptionally healthy place,—a place to be confidently recommended, both to invalids and people in health——

MRS. STOCKMANN. My dear Thomas——

DR. STOCKMANN. And certainly we haven't failed to recommend and belaud it. I've written again and again, both in the *Messenger* and in pamphlets——

HOVSTAD. Well, what then?

DR. STOCKMANN. These Baths, that we've called the pulse of the town, its spinal nerve, and—and the devil knows what else——

BILLING. "The town's palpitating heart," I was once moved to call them in a convivial moment——

DR. STOCKMANN. Yes, I daresay. But do you know what they really are, these mighty, magnificent, belauded Baths, that have cost so much money—do you know what they are?

HOVSTAD. No, what are they?

MRS. STOCKMANN. Do tell us.

DR. STOCKMANN. Simply a pestiferous hole.

PETRA. The Baths, father?

MRS. STOCKMANN (*at the same time*). Our Baths!

HOVSTAD (*also at the same time*). But, Doctor——!

BILLING. Oh, it's incredible!

DR. STOCKMANN. I tell you the whole place is a poisonous whited-sepulchre; noxious in the highest degree! All that filth up there in the Mill Dale, with its horrible stench, taints the water in the feed-pipes of the Baths; and the same confounded poisonous refuse oozes out by the beach——

HOVSTAD. Where the sea-baths are?

DR. STOCKMANN. Exactly.

HOVSTAD. But how are you so sure of all this, Doctor?

DR. STOCKMANN. I've investigated the whole thing as conscientiously as possible. I've long had my doubts about it. Last year we had some extraordinary cases of illness among the patients—both typhoid and gastric attacks——

MRS. STOCKMANN. Yes, I remember.

DR. STOCKMANN. At the time we thought the visitors had brought the infection with them; but afterwards—last winter—I began to question that. So I set about testing the water as well as I could.

MRS. STOCKMANN. It was that you were working so hard at!

DR. STOCKMANN. Yes, you may well say I've

worked, Katrine. But here, you know, I hadn't the necessary scientific appliances; so I sent samples both of our drinking-water and of our sea-water to the University for exact analysis by a chemist.

HOVSTAD. And you've received his report?

DR. STOCKMANN (*showing letter*). Here it is. And it proves beyond dispute the presence of putrifying organic matter in the water—millions of infusoria. It's absolutely noxious to health, whether used internally or externally.

MRS. STOCKMANN. What a blessing you found it out in time!

DR. STOCKMANN. Yes, you may well say that.

HOVSTAD. And what do you intend to do now, Doctor?

DR. STOCKMANN. Why, to set things right, of course.

HOVSTAD. Do you think that can be done?

DR. STOCKMANN. It must be done. Else the whole Baths are useless, ruined. But there's no fear. I'm quite clear as to what is required.

MRS. STOCKMANN. But, my dear Thomas, why should you have made such a secret of all this?

DR. STOCKMANN. Would you have had me rush all over the town and chatter about it before I was quite certain? No, thanks! I'm not so mad as that.

PETRA. But to us at home——

DR. STOCKMANN. I couldn't say a word to a living soul. But to-morrow you may look in at the Badger's——

MRS. STOCKMANN. Oh, Thomas!

DR. STOCKMANN. Well well, at your grandfather's. The old fellow *will* be astonished! He thinks I'm not quite right in my head—yes, and plenty of others think the same, I've noticed. But now these good people shall see—yes, they shall see now! (*Walks up and down rubbing his hands.*) What a stir there'll be in the town, Katrine! Just think of it! All the water-pipes will have to be relaid.

HOVSTAD (*rising*). All the water-pipes?

DR. STOCKMANN. Why, of course. The intake is too low down; it must be moved much higher up.

PETRA. So you were right, after all.

DR. STOCKMANN. Yes, do you remember, Petra? I wrote against it when they were beginning the works. But then no one would listen to me. Now, you may be sure, I'll give them my full broadside—for of course I've prepared a statement for the Directors; it's been lying there ready a whole week; I've only been waiting for this report. (*Points to letter.*) But now they shall have it at once. (*Goes into his room and returns with a packet of papers.*) See! Four closely-written sheets. And I'll enclose the report. A newspaper, Katrine! Get me something to wrap them up in. There—that's it. Give it to—to—— (*Stamps.*) What the devil's her name? Give it to the girl, I mean, and tell her to take it at once to the Burgomaster.

(MRS. STOCKMANN *goes out with packet through the dining-room.*)

PETRA. What do you think Uncle Peter will say, father?

DR. STOCKMANN. What should he say? He's

bound to be pleased at the discovery of so important a fact.

HOVSTAD. I suppose you'll let me put a short notice of your discovery in the *Messenger.*

DR. STOCKMANN. Yes, I shall be very glad if you will.

HOVSTAD. It's highly desirable that the public should know about it as soon as possible.

DR. STOCKMANN. Yes, certainly.

MRS. STOCKMANN (*returning*). She's gone with it.

BILLING. Strike me dead if you won't be the first man in the town, Doctor.

DR. STOCKMANN (*walks up and down in high glee*). Oh, nonsense! After all, I've done no more than my duty. I've been a lucky treasure-hunter, that's all. But all the same——

BILLING. Hovstad, don't you think the town ought to do homage to Dr. Stockmann in a torch-light procession?

HOVSTAD. I shall certainly propose it.

BILLING. And I'll talk it over with Aslaksen.

DR. STOCKMANN. No, dear friends; let all such claptrap alone. I won't hear of anything of the sort. And if the Directors want to raise my salary, I won't accept it. I tell you, Katrine, I will not accept it.

MRS. STOCKMANN. Quite right, Thomas.

PETRA (*raising her glass*). Your health, father.

HOVSTAD *and* BILLING. Your health, your health, Doctor!

HORSTER (*touching glasses with the* DOCTOR). I wish you nothing but joy of your discovery.

DR. STOCKMANN. Thanks, thanks, my dear

friends. I can't tell you how happy I am——! Oh, what a blessing it is to feel that you've deserved well of your native town and your fellow-citizens. Hurrah, Katrine!

(*He puts both his arms round her neck, and whirls her round with him.* MRS. STOCKMANN *screams and struggles. A burst of laughter, applause, and cheers for the* DOCTOR. *The boys thrust their heads in at the door.*)

Act Second.

(*The* DOCTOR'S *sitting-room. The dining-room door is closed. Morning.*)

MRS. STOCKMANN (*enters from the dining-room with a sealed letter in her hand, goes to the first door on the right, and peeps in*). Are you there, Thomas?

DR. STOCKMANN (*within*). Yes, I've just come in. (*Enters.*) What is it?

MRS. STOCKMANN. A letter from your brother.

(*Hands him the letter.*)

DR. STOCKMANN. Ah! let's see. (*Opens the envelope and reads.*) "The MS. sent me is returned herewith——" (*Reads on, muttering.*) Hm——!

MRS. STOCKMANN. Well, what does he say?

DR. STOCKMANN (*putting the paper in his pocket*). Nothing; only that he'll come up himself about mid-day.

MRS. STOCKMANN. Then be sure you remember to stop at home.

DR. STOCKMANN. Oh, I can easily manage that; I've finished my morning's work.

MRS. STOCKMANN. I'm very curious to know how he takes it.

DR. STOCKMANN. You'll see he won't be over pleased that it's I, and not he himself, that have made the discovery.

MRS. STOCKMANN. Ah, that's just what I'm afraid of.

DR. STOCKMANN. Of course at bottom he'll be glad. But still—Peter is damnably unwilling that any one but himself should do anything for the good of the town.

MRS. STOCKMANN. Do you know, Thomas, I think you might stretch a point, and share the honour with him. Couldn't you make out that it was he that put you on the track——?

DR. STOCKMANN. By all means, for aught I care. If only I can get things put straight, I——

(*Old* MORTEN KIIL *peeps in through the anteroom door, looks round inquiringly, and asks slyly.*)

MORTEN KIIL. Is it—is it true?

MRS. STOCKMANN (*going towards him*). Father, is that you?

DR. STOCKMANN. Hallo, father-in-law! good morning, good morning.

MRS. STOCKMANN. But do come in.

MORTEN KIIL. Yes, if it's true; if not, I'm off again.

DR. STOCKMANN. If what is true?

MORTEN KIIL. This business about the water-works. Now, *is* it true?

DR. STOCKMANN. Why, of course it is. But how did you come to hear of it.

MORTEN KIIL (*coming in*). Petra looked in on her way to the school——

DR. STOCKMANN. Oh, did she?

MORTEN KIIL. Ay ay—and she told me—— I thought she was only making game of me; but that's not like Petra either.

DR. STOCKMANN. No, indeed; how could you think so?

MORTEN KIIL. Oh, you can never be sure of anybody. You may be made a fool of before you know where you are. So it is true, after all?

DR. STOCKMANN. Most certainly it is. Do sit down, father-in-law. (*Forces him down on the sofa.*) Now isn't it a real blessing for the town——?

MORTEN KIIL (*suppressing his laughter*). A blessing for the town?

DR. STOCKMANN. Yes, that I made the discovery in time——

MORTEN KIIL (*as before*). Yes yes yes; but I could never have believed you'd have played your very own brother such a trick.

DR. STOCKMANN. Such a trick!

MRS. STOCKMANN. Oh, my dear father——

MORTEN KIIL (*resting his hands and chin on the top of his stick and winking slyly at the* DOCTOR). What was it again? Wasn't it that some animals had got into the water-pipes?

DR. STOCKMANN. Yes; infusorial animals.

MORTEN KIIL. And any number of these animals had got in, Petra said; an enormous lot.

DR. STOCKMANN. Certainly; hundreds of thousands of them.

MORTEN KIIL. But no one can see them—isn't that so?

DR. STOCKMANN. Quite right; no one can see them.

MORTEN KIIL (*with a quiet, chuckling laugh*). I'll be damned if that isn't the best thing I've heard of you yet.

DR. STOCKMANN. What do you mean?

MORTEN KIIL. But you'll never in this world make the Burgomaster take in anything of the sort.

DR. STOCKMANN. Well, that we'll see.

MORTEN KIIL. Do you really think he'll be so crazy?

DR. STOCKMANN. I hope the whole town will be so crazy.

MORTEN KIIL. The whole town! Well, I don't say but it may. But it serves them right; it'll teach them a lesson. They wanted to be so much cleverer than we old fellows. They hounded me out of the Town Council. Yes; I tell you they hounded me out like a dog, that they did. But now it's their turn. Just you keep up the game with them, Stockmann.

DR. STOCKMANN. Yes, but, father-in-law——

MORTEN KIIL. Keep it up, I say. (*Rising.*) If you can make the Burgomaster and his friends swallow all that, I'll give a hundred crowns straight away to the poor.

DR. STOCKMANN. That's good of you.

MORTEN KIIL. Of course I've little enough to throw away; but if you manage that, I'll certainly give the poor fifty crowns at Christmas.

(HOVSTAD *enters from anteroom.*)

HOVSTAD. Good morning! (*Pausing.*) Oh! I beg your pardon——

DR. STOCKMANN. Not at all. Come in, come in.

MORTEN KIIL (*chuckling again*). He! Is he in it too?

HOVSTAD. What do you mean?

DR. STOCKMANN. Yes, of course he's in it.

MORTEN KIIL. I might have known it! It's to go into the papers. Ah! you're the one, Stockmann! Think of what I've been saying. Now I'm off.

DR. STOCKMANN. Oh no! Stop a little, father-in-law.

MORTEN KIIL. No, I'm off now. Play them all the tricks you can. Deuce take me but you shan't lose by it.

(*He goes*, MRS. STOCKMANN *accompanying him.*)

DR. STOCKMANN (*laughing*). What do you think——? The old fellow doesn't believe a word of all this about the water-works.

HOVSTAD. Was that what he——?

DR. STOCKMANN. Yes; that was what we were talking about. And perhaps you've come on the same business?

HOVSTAD. Yes. Have you a moment to spare, Doctor?

DR. STOCKMANN. As many as you like, my dear fellow.

HOVSTAD. Have you heard anything from the Burgomaster?

DR. STOCKMANN. Not yet. He'll be here presently.

HOVSTAD. I've been thinking over the matter since last evening.

DR. STOCKMANN. Well——?

HOVSTAD. To you, as a doctor and a man of science, this business of the water-works is an isolated affair. I fancy it hasn't occurred to you that a good many other things are bound up with it?

DR. STOCKMANN. Yes?—how? Let's sit down, my dear fellow. No—there, on the sofa.

(HOVSTAD *sits on sofa; the* DOCTOR *in an easy-chair on the other side of the table.*)

DR. STOCKMANN. Well, so you think——?

HOVSTAD. You said yesterday that the water is polluted by impurities in the soil——

DR. STOCKMANN. Yes, undoubtedly; the mischief comes from that poisonous swamp up in the Mill Dale.

HOVSTAD. Excuse me, Doctor, but I think it comes from quite another swamp.

DR. STOCKMANN. What swamp may that be?

HOVSTAD. The swamp in which our whole municipal life is rotting.

DR. STOCKMANN. The devil, Mr. Hovstad! What notion is this you've got hold of?

HOVSTAD. All the affairs of the town have gradually drifted into the hands of a pack of bureaucrats.

DR. STOCKMANN. Come now, they're not all bureaucrats.

HOVSTAD. No; but those who aren't are the friends and adherents of those who are. We're entirely governed by a ring of wealthy men, men of old family and position in the town.

DR. STOCKMANN. Yes, but they're also men of ability and insight.

HOVSTAD. Did they show ability and insight when they laid the water-pipes where they are?

DR. STOCKMANN. No; that was a piece of stupidity, of course. But that'll be set right now.

HOVSTAD. Do you think it'll go so smoothly?

DR. STOCKMANN. Well, smoothly or not, it'll have to be done.

HOVSTAD. Yes, if the press exerts its influence.

DR. STOCKMANN. Not at all necessary, my dear fellow; I'm sure my brother——

HOVSTAD. Excuse me, Doctor, but I must tell you that I think of taking the matter up.

DR. STOCKMANN. In the paper?

HOVSTAD. Yes. When I took over the *People's Messenger*, I was determined to break up this ring of obstinate old blockheads who hold everything in their hands.

DR. STOCKMANN. But you told me yourself what came of it. You nearly ruined the paper.

HOVSTAD. Yes, we had to draw in our horns then, that's true enough. The whole Bath scheme might have fallen through if these men had been sent about their business. But now the Baths are an accomplished fact, and we can get on without these august personages.

DR. STOCKMANN. Get on without them, yes; but still we owe them much.

HOVSTAD. The debt shall be amply acknowledged. But a journalist of my democratic tendencies can't let such an opportunity slip through his fingers. We must explode the tradition of official infallibility. That rubbish must be got rid of, like every other superstition.

DR. STOCKMANN. I'm with you with all my heart, Mr. Hovstad. If it's a superstition, away with it.

HOVSTAD. I should be sorry to attack the Burgomaster, as he's your brother. But I know you think with me—the truth before all other considerations.

DR. STOCKMANN. Why, of course. (*Vehemently.*) But then—! but then——!

HOVSTAD. You mustn't think ill of me. I'm neither more self-interested nor more ambitious than other men.

DR. STOCKMANN. Why, my dear fellow, who says you are?

HOVSTAD. I come of humble folk, as you know, and I've had occasion to see what the lower classes really require. And that is to have a share in the direction of public affairs, Doctor. That's what develops ability and knowledge and self-respect——

DR. STOCKMANN. I understand that perfectly.

HOVSTAD. Yes; and I think a journalist incurs a heavy responsibility when he neglects an opportunity of helping to emancipate the downtrodden masses. I know well enough that our oligarchy will denounce me as an agitator, and so forth; but what do I care? If only my conscience is clear, I——

DR. STOCKMANN. Just so, just so, my dear Mr. Hovstad. But still—deuce take it——! (*A knock at the door.*) Come in!

(ASLAKSEN, *the printer, appears at the door of the anteroom. He is humbly but neatly dressed in black, wearing a white necktie slightly crumpled, and carrying gloves and a silk hat.*)

ASLAKSEN (*bowing*). I beg pardon, Doctor, for making so bold——

DR. STOCKMANN (*rising*). Hallo! If it isn't Mr. Aslaksen!

ASLAKSEN. Yes, it's me, Doctor.

HOVSTAD (*rising*). Do you want me, Aslaksen?

ASLAKSEN. No, not at all. I didn't know you were here. No, it's the Doctor himself——

DR. STOCKMANN. Well, what can I do for you?

ASLAKSEN. Is it true what Mr. Billing says, that you're going to get us a better set of water-works?

DR. STOCKMANN. Yes, for the Baths.

ASLAKSEN. Of course, of course. Then I just looked in to say that I'll back up the movement with all my might.

HOVSTAD (*to the* DOCTOR). You see!

DR. STOCKMANN. I'm sure I thank you heartily; but——

ASLAKSEN. It'll do you no harm to have us middle-class men at your back. We now form what you may call a compact majority in the town—when we want to, that's to say. And it's always well to have the majority with you, Doctor.

DR. STOCKMANN. No doubt, no doubt; but I can't conceive that any special measures will be necessary. I should think in so clear and straight-forward a matter——

ASLAKSEN. Yes, but all the same, it can do no harm; I know the local authorities well. The powers that be are not over ready to adopt suggestions from outsiders. So I think it wouldn't be amiss if we made some sort of a demonstration.

HOVSTAD. I think so too.

DR. STOCKMANN. A demonstration, you say? But how do you mean to demonstrate?

ASLAKSEN. Of course with great moderation, Doctor. I'm always in favour of moderation; for moderation is a citizen's first virtue—at least that's my way of thinking.

DR. STOCKMANN. We all know that, Mr. Aslaksen.

ASLAKSEN. Yes, I think my moderation is generally recognised. And this affair of the water-works is very important for us small middle-class men. The Baths bid fair to become a little gold-mine for the town. We'll all have to live by the Baths, especially we householders. We want to support the Baths all we can; and as I'm Chairman of the Householders' Association——

DR. STOCKMANN. Well——?

ASLAKSEN. And as I'm an active worker for the Temperance[1] Society—of course you know, Doctor, that I'm a temperance man?

DR. STOCKMANN. To be sure, to be sure.

ASLAKSEN. Well, you'll understand that I come in contact with a great many people. And as I'm known to be a prudent and law-abiding citizen, as you yourself admitted, Doctor, I have a certain influence in the town, and hold some power in my hands—though I say it that shouldn't.

DR. STOCKMANN. I know that very well, Mr. Aslaksen.

ASLAKSEN. Well you see, it would be easy for me to get up an address, if it came to a pinch.

DR. STOCKMANN. An address?

ASLAKSEN. Yes, a kind of vote of thanks to you, from the citizens of the town, for your action in a

[1] The word "mådehold," in Norwegian, means both "moderation" and "temperance."

matter of such general concern. Of course it will have to be drawn up with befitting moderation, so as to give no offence to the authorities and persons of position. But so long as we're careful about that, no one can take it ill, I should think.

HOVSTAD. Well, even if they didn't particularly like it——

ASLAKSEN. No no no; no offence to the powers that be, Mr. Hovstad. No opposition to people that can take it out of us again so easily. I've had enough of that in my time; no good ever comes of it. But no one can object to the free but temperate expression of a citizen's opinion.

DR. STOCKMANN (*shaking his hand*). I can't tell you, my dear Mr. Aslaksen, how heartily it delights me to find so much support among my fellow-townsmen. I'm so happy—so happy! Come, you'll have a glass of sherry? Eh?

ASLAKSEN. No, thank you; I never take wine.

DR. STOCKMANN. Well, then, a glass of beer—what do you say to that?

ASLAKSEN. Thanks, not that either, Doctor. I never take anything so early in the day. And now I'll be off round the town, and talk to some of the householders, and prepare public opinion.

DR. STOCKMANN. It's extremely kind of you, Mr. Aslaksen; but I really can't get it into my head that all these preparations are necessary; it seems to me the affair's as simple as possible.

ASLAKSEN. The authorities always move slowly, Doctor—God forbid I should blame them for it——

HOVSTAD. We'll stir them up in the paper to-morrow, Aslaksen.

ASLAKSEN. No violence, Mr. Hovstad. Proceed with moderation, or you'll do nothing with them. Take my advice; I've picked up experience in the school of life. And now I'll say good-morning, Doctor. You know now that at least you have us small middle-class men behind you, solid as a wall. You have the compact majority on your side, Doctor!

DR. STOCKMANN. Many thanks, my dear Mr. Aslaksen. (*Holds out his hand.*) Good-bye, good-bye.

ASLAKSEN. Are you coming to the office, Mr. Hovstad?

HOVSTAD. I'll come on presently. I've something to settle first.

ASLAKSEN. All right.

(*Bows, and goes.* DR. STOCKMANN *accompanies him into the anteroom.*)

HOVSTAD (*as the* DOCTOR *re-enters*). Well, what do you say to that, Doctor? Don't you think it's high time we should strike a blow at all this weak-kneed trimming and cowardice?

DR. STOCKMANN. Are you speaking of Aslaksen?

HOVSTAD. Yes, I am. He's a decent enough fellow, but he's one of those who are sunk in the swamp. And most people here are just like him; they're for ever see-sawing from side to side; what with scruples and misgivings, they never dare advance a step.

DR. STOCKMANN. Yes, but Aslaksen seems to me thoroughly well-intentioned.

HOVSTAD. There's one thing I value more highly than good intentions; and that is an attitude of manly self-reliance.

DR. STOCKMANN. There I'm quite with you.

HOVSTAD. So I'm going to seize this opportunity, and see whether I can't for once put a little grit into their good intentions. The worship of authority must be rooted up in this town. This gross, inexcusable blunder of the water-works should be enough to open the eyes of every voter.

DR. STOCKMANN. Very well! If you think it's for the good of the community, so be it; but not till I've spoken to my brother.

HOVSTAD. Anyhow, I'll be writing my leader in the meantime. And if the Burgomaster won't take the matter up——

DR. STOCKMANN. But how can you conceive his refusing?

HOVSTAD. Oh, it's not inconceivable. And then——?

DR. STOCKMANN. Well then, I promise you——; look here—then you may print my paper—put it in just as it is.

HOVSTAD. May I? Is that a promise?

DR. STOCKMANN (*handing him the manuscript*). There it is; take it with you. You may as well read it in any case; you can return it to me afterwards.

HOVSTAD. Very good; I'll do so. And now, good-bye, Doctor.

DR. STOCKMANN. Good-bye, good-bye. You'll see it'll all go smoothly, Mr Hovstad—as smoothly as possible.

HOVSTAD. Hm! We shall see.

(*Bows and goes out through the anteroom.*)

DR. STOCKMANN (*going to the dining-room door and looking in*). Katrine! Hallo! you back, Petra?

PETRA (*entering*). Yes, I've just got back from school.

MRS. STOCKMANN (*entering*). Hasn't he been here yet?

DR. STOCKMANN. Peter? No; but I've been having a long talk with Hovstad. He's quite enthusiastic about my discovery. You see, it's of much wider import than I thought at first. So he's placed his paper at my disposal, if I should require it.

MRS. STOCKMANN. Do you think you will——?

DR. STOCKMANN. Not I! But all the same, one's proud to know that the enlightened, independent press is on one's side. And what do you think? I've had a visit from the Chairman of the Householders' Association too.

MRS. STOCKMANN. Really! What did he want?

DR. STOCKMANN. To assure me of his support. They'll stand by me at a pinch. Katrine, do you know what I have behind me?

MRS. STOCKMANN. Behind you? No. What have you behind you?

DR. STOCKMANN. The compact majority!

MRS. STOCKMANN. Oh! Is that good for you, Thomas?

DR. STOCKMANN. Yes, indeed; I should think it was good! (*Rubbing his hands as he walks up and down.*) Great God! what a delight it is to feel oneself in such brotherly concord with one's fellow-townsmen.

PETRA. And to do so much that's good and useful, father!

DR. STOCKMANN. And all for one's native town, too!

MRS. STOCKMANN. There's the bell.

DR. STOCKMANN. That must be he. (*Knock at the door.*) Come in!

(*Enter* BURGOMASTER STOCKMANN *from the anteroom.*)

BURGOMASTER. Good-morning.

DR. STOCKMANN. I'm glad to see you, Peter.

MRS. STOCKMANN. Good-morning, brother-in-law. How are you?

BURGOMASTER. Oh, thanks, so-so. (*To the* DOCTOR.) Yesterday evening, after office hours, I received from you a dissertation upon the water at the Baths.

DR. STOCKMANN. Yes. Have you read it?

BURGOMASTER. I have.

DR. STOCKMANN. And what do you think of the affair?

BURGOMASTER. Hm—— (*Glancing at the women.*)

MRS. STOCKMANN. Come, Petra.

(*She and* PETRA *go into the room, left.*)

BURGOMASTER (*after a pause*). Was it necessary to make all these investigations behind my back?

DR. STOCKMANN. Yes, till I was absolutely certain, I——

BURGOMASTER. So you're certain now?

DR. STOCKMANN. You found no uncertainty in my statement of the case, did you?

BURGOMASTER. Is it your intention to submit

this statement to the Board of Directors, as a sort of official document?

DR. STOCKMANN. Of course. Something must be done in the matter, and that promptly.

BURGOMASTER. As usual, you use very strong expressions in your statement. Amongst other things, you say that what we offer our visitors is a slow poison!

DR. STOCKMANN. Why, Peter, can you call it anything else? Only think—poisoned water both internally and externally! And that to poor invalids who come to us in all confidence, and pay us liberally to cure them!

BURGOMASTER. And then you announce as your conclusion that we must build a sewer to carry off all the alleged impurities from the Mill Dale, and relay all the water-pipes.

DR. STOCKMANN. Yes. Can you suggest any alternative?—I know of none.

BURGOMASTER. I made an excuse for looking in at the town engineer's this morning, and—in a half-jesting way—I mentioned these alterations as things we might possibly have to consider, at some future time.

DR. STOCKMANN. At some future time!

BURGOMASTER. Of course he smiled at what he thought my extravagance. Have you taken the trouble to think what your proposed alterations would cost? From what the engineer said, I gathered that the expenses would probably mount up to several hundred thousand crowns.

DR. STOCKMANN. So much as that?

BURGOMASTER. Yes. But that's not the worst. The work would take at least two years.

DR. STOCKMANN. Two years! Do you mean to say two whole years?

BURGOMASTER. At least. And what are we to do with the Baths in the meanwhile? Are we to close them? Of course we'd have to. Do you think any one would come here, if it got abroad that the water was pestilential?

DR. STOCKMANN. But, Peter, that's just what it is.

BURGOMASTER. And all this now, just now, when the Baths are doing so well! Neighbouring towns, too, are not without their claims to rank as health-resorts. Do you think they wouldn't at once set to work to divert the full stream of visitors to themselves? Undoubtedly they would; and we should be left stranded. We should probably have to give up the whole costly undertaking; and so you would have ruined your native town.

DR. STOCKMANN. I—ruined——!

BURGOMASTER. It's only through the Baths that the town has any future worth speaking of. You surely know that as well as I do.

DR. STOCKMANN. But what do you think should be done?

BURGOMASTER. I have not succeeded in convincing myself that the condition of the water at the Baths is as serious as your statement represents.

DR. STOCKMANN. I tell you it's if anything worse—or will be in the summer, when the hot weather sets in.

BURGOMASTER. I repeat that I believe you exaggerate greatly. A competent physician should know what measures to take in order to obviate injurious influences, and to counteract them in case they should make themselves unmistakably felt.

DR. STOCKMANN. Indeed——? And then——?

BURGOMASTER. The existing water-works are, after all, a fact, and must naturally be treated as such. But when the time comes, the Directors will probably not be indisposed to consider whether it may not be possible, without unreasonable pecuniary sacrifices, to introduce certain improvements.

DR. STOCKMANN. And do you imagine I could ever be a party to such dishonesty?

BURGOMASTER. Dishonesty?

DR. STOCKMANN. Yes, it would be dishonesty—a fraud, a lie, an absolute crime against the public, against society as a whole!

BURGOMASTER. I have not, as I before remarked, been able to convince myself that there is really any such imminent danger.

DR. STOCKMANN. You have—you must have! I'm sure my demonstration is absolutely clear and convincing. And you know that perfectly, Peter, only you won't admit it. It was you who insisted that both the Bath-buildings and the water-works should be placed where they now are; and it's *that*—it's that damned blunder that you won't confess. Pshaw! Do you think I don't see through you?

BURGOMASTER. And even if it were so? If I do watch over my reputation with a certain anxiety, I do it for the good of the town. Without moral authority

I cannot guide and direct affairs in the way I consider most conducive to the general welfare. Therefore—and on various other grounds—it is of great moment to me that your statement should not be submitted to the Board of Directors. It must be kept back, for the good of the community. Later on I will bring up the matter for discussion, and we'll do the best we can, quietly; but not a word, not a whisper, of this unfortunate business must come to the public ears.

DR. STOCKMANN. But it can't be prevented now, my dear Peter.

BURGOMASTER. It must and shall be prevented.

DR. STOCKMANN. It can't be, I tell you; far too many people know about it already.

BURGOMASTER. Know about it! Who? Surely not those fellows on the *People's Messenger*——?

DR. STOCKMANN. Oh yes; they know. The liberal, independent press will take good care you do your duty.

BURGOMASTER (*after a short pause*). You're an amazingly reckless man, Thomas. Haven't you reflected what the consequences of this may be to yourself?

DR. STOCKMANN. Consequences?—Consequences to me?

BURGOMASTER. Yes—to you and yours.

DR. STOCKMANN. What the devil do you mean?

BURGOMASTER. I believe I've always shown myself ready and willing to lend you a helping hand.

DR. STOCKMANN. Yes, you have, and I thank you for it.

BURGOMASTER. I ask for no thanks. I was in

some measure forced to act as I did—for my own sake. I always hoped I should be able to keep you within certain bounds, if I helped to improve your pecuniary position.

DR. STOCKMANN. What! So it was only for your own sake——!

BURGOMASTER. In a measure, I say. It is painful for a man in an official position, when his nearest relation goes and compromises himself time after time.

DR. STOCKMANN. And you think I do that?

BURGOMASTER. Yes, unfortunately, you do, without knowing it. Yours is a turbulent, pugnacious, rebellious spirit. And then you have an unhappy propensity for rushing into print upon every possible and impossible occasion. You no sooner hit upon an idea than you must needs write a newspaper article or a whole pamphlet about it.

DR. STOCKMANN. Isn't it a citizen's duty, when he has conceived a new idea, to communicate it to the public!

BURGOMASTER. Pshaw! The public doesn't need new ideas. The public gets on best with the good old recognised ideas it has already.

DR. STOCKMANN. You say that right out!

BURGOMASTER. Yes, I must speak frankly to you for once. Hitherto I've tried to avoid it, for I know how irritable you are; but now I'm bound to tell you the truth, Thomas. You've no conception how much you injure yourself by your rashness. You complain of the authorities, ay, of the Government itself—you cry them down and maintain you've been slighted, persecuted. But what else can you expect, with your impossible disposition.

DR. STOCKMANN. Oh, indeed! So I'm impossible, am I?

BURGOMASTER. Yes, Thomas, you're an impossible man to work with. I know that from experience. You have no consideration; you seem quite to forget that you have me to thank for your position as medical officer of the Baths——

DR. STOCKMANN. It was mine by right! Mine, and no one else's! I was the first to discover the town's capabilities as a watering-place; I saw them, and, at that time, I alone. For years I fought single-handed for this idea of mine; I wrote and wrote——

BURGOMASTER. No doubt; but then the right time hadn't come. Of course in that out-of-the-world corner you couldn't judge of that. As soon as the propitious moment came, I—and others—took the matter in hand——

DR. STOCKMANN. Yes, and you bungled the whole of my glorious plan. Oh, we see now what a set of wiseacres you were!

BURGOMASTER. All *I* can see is that you're again seeking an outlet for your pugnacity. You want to make an onslaught on your superiors—that's an old habit of yours. You can't endure any authority over you; you look askance at any one who has a higher post than your own; you regard him as a personal enemy—and then it's all one to you what kind of weapon you use against him. But now I've shown you how much is at stake for the town, and consequently for me too. And therefore

I warn you, Thomas, that I'm inexorable in the demand I am about to make of you!

DR. STOCKMANN. What demand?

BURGOMASTER. As you haven't had the sense to refrain from chattering to outsiders about this delicate business, which should have been kept an official secret, of course it can't now be hushed up. All sorts of rumours will get abroad, and evil-disposed persons will invent all sorts of additions to them. It will therefore be necessary for you publicly to contradict these rumours.

DR. STOCKMANN. I? How? I don't understand you.

BURGOMASTER. We expect that after further investigation you will come to the conclusion that the affair is not nearly so serious or pressing as you had at first imagined.

DR. STOCKMANN. Aha! So you expect that?

BURGOMASTER. Furthermore, we expect you to express your confidence that the Board of Directors will thoroughly and conscientiously carry out all measures for the removal of any possible drawback.

DR. STOCKMANN. Yes, but you'll never be able to do that, so long as you go on tinkering and patching. I tell you that, Peter; and it's my deepest, sincerest conviction——

BURGOMASTER. As an official, you have no right to have any individual conviction.

DR. STOCKMANN (*starting*). No right to any——?

BURGOMASTER. As an official, I say. In your private capacity, of course, it's another matter. But as a subordinate official of the Baths, you've no right to express any conviction at issue with that of your superiors.

DR. STOCKMANN. This is too much! I, a doctor, a man of science, have no right to——

BURGOMASTER. The matter in question is not a purely scientific one; it's a complex affair; it has both a technical and an economic side.

DR. STOCKMANN. Pshaw! What's that to me? What the devil do I care! I will be free to speak my mind upon any subject on earth!

BURGOMASTER. As you please—so long as it doesn't concern the Baths. With them we forbid you to meddle.

DR. STOCKMANN (*shouts*). You forbid——! you! —a set of——

BURGOMASTER. *I* forbid it—*I*, your chief; and you must obey my prohibition.

DR. STOCKMANN (*controlling himself*). Upon my word, Peter, if you weren't my brother——

PETRA (*tears open the door*). Father, you shan't submit to this!

MRS. STOCKMANN (*following her*). Petra, Petra!

BURGOMASTER. Ah! so we've been listening!

MRS. STOCKMANN. The partition's so thin, we couldn't help——

PETRA. I stood and listened on purpose.

BURGOMASTER. Well, on the whole, I'm not sorry——

DR. STOCKMANN (*coming nearer to him*). You spoke to me of forbidding and obeying——

BURGOMASTER. You forced me to adopt that tone.

DR. STOCKMANN. And I am to give myself the lie, in a public declaration?

BURGOMASTER. We consider it absolutely necessary that you should issue a statement in the terms indicated.

DR. STOCKMANN. And if I don't obey?

BURGOMASTER. Then we shall ourselves put forth a statement to reassure the public.

DR. STOCKMANN. Well and good; then I'll write against you. I shall stick to my point and prove that *I* am right, and you wrong. And what will you do then?

BURGOMASTER. Then I shall be unable to prevent your dismissal.

DR. STOCKMANN. What——!

PETRA. Father! Dismissal!

MRS. STOCKMANN. Dismissal!

BURGOMASTER. Your dismissal from the Baths. I shall be obliged to move that notice be given you at once, and that you have henceforth no connection whatever with the Baths.

DR. STOCKMANN. You would dare to do that!

BURGOMASTER. It is you who are playing the daring game.

PETRA. Uncle, this is scandalous conduct towards a man like father.

MRS. STOCKMANN. Do be quiet, Petra.

BURGOMASTER (*looking at* PETRA). Aha! We have opinions of our own already, eh? Of course! (*To* MRS. STOCKMANN.) Sister-in-law, you are apparently the most sensible person in the house. Use all your influence with your husband; try to make him realise what all this will involve both for his family——

DR. STOCKMANN. My family concerns myself alone.

BURGOMASTER. ——Both for his family, I say, and for the town he lives in.

DR. STOCKMANN. It's I that have the real good of the town at heart! I want to lay bare the evils that, sooner or later, must come to light. Ah! You shall yet see that I love my native town.

BURGOMASTER. You, who, in your blind obstinacy, want to cut off the town's chief source of prosperity!

DR. STOCKMANN. The source is poisoned, man! Are you mad? We live by trafficking in filth and corruption. The whole of our flourishing social life is rooted in a lie!

BURGOMASTER. Idle fancies—or worse. The man who makes such offensive insinuations against his native place must be an enemy of society.

DR. STOCKMANN (*going towards him*). You dare to——

MRS. STOCKMANN (*throwing herself between them*). Thomas!

PETRA (*seizing her father's arm*). Keep calm, father.

BURGOMASTER. I won't expose myself to violence. You're warned now. Reflect upon what is due to yourself and to your family. Good-bye.

(*He goes.*)

DR. STOCKMANN (*walking up and down*). And I must put up with such treatment! In my own house, Katrine! What do you say to that?

MRS. STOCKMANN. Indeed it's a shame and a disgrace, Thomas——

PETRA. Oh, I'd like to give it to uncle——!

DR. STOCKMANN. It's my own fault. I ought to have bristled up against them long ago—to have shown my teeth—and made them feel them! And he called me an enemy of society. Me! I won't bear it; by Heaven, I won't!

MRS. STOCKMANN. But, my dear Thomas, after all, your brother has the power——

DR. STOCKMANN. Yes, but I have the right!

MRS. STOCKMANN. Ah yes, right, right! What's the good of having the right when you haven't the might?

PETRA. Oh mother! how can you talk so?

DR. STOCKMANN. What! No good, in a free society, to have right on your side? I like that, Katrine! And besides, haven't I the free and independent press with me, and the compact majority at my back? That's might enough, I should think!

MRS. STOCKMANN. Why, good heavens, Thomas! you're surely not thinking of——?

DR. STOCKMANN. What am I not thinking of?

MRS. STOCKMANN. Of setting yourself up against your brother, I mean.

DR. STOCKMANN. What the devil would you have me do, if not stick to what's right and true?

PETRA. Yes, that's what I'd like to know?

MRS. STOCKMANN. But it'll be of no earthly use. If they won't they won't.

DR. STOCKMANN. Ho-ho, Katrine! just wait a while and you'll see I can fight my own battles.

MRS. STOCKMANN. Yes, you'll fight—till you get your dismissal; that's what'll happen.

DR. STOCKMANN. Well then, I shall at any rate have done my duty towards the public, towards society—I who am called an enemy of society!

MRS. STOCKMANN. But towards your family, Thomas? Towards us at home? Do you think this is doing your duty towards those who are dependent on you?

PETRA. Oh mother, don't always think first of us.

MRS. STOCKMANN. Yes, it's all very well for you to talk; you can stand alone if need be.—But think of the boys, Thomas; and think a little of yourself too, and of me——

DR. STOCKMANN. You're surely out of your senses, Katrine. Am I to be such a miserable coward as to knuckle under to this Peter and his damned crew? Should I ever have another happy hour in all my life?

MRS. STOCKMANN. I don't know; but God preserve us from the happiness we shall all of us have if you stick to your point. There you would be again, with nothing to live on, with no regular income. I think we had enough of that in the old days. Remember them, Thomas; think of what it all means.

DR. STOCKMANN (*struggling with himself and clenching his hands*). And these jacks-in-office can bring all this upon a free and honest man! Isn't it disgusting, Katrine?

MRS. STOCKMANN. Yes, no doubt they're treating

you shamefully. But God knows there's plenty of injustice one must just submit to in this world.— Here are the boys, Thomas. Look at them! What's to become of them? Oh no, no! you can never have the heart——

(EILIF *and* MORTEN, *with school-books, have meanwhile entered.*)

DR. STOCKMANN. The boys——! (*With a sudden access of firmness and decision.*) Never, though the whole earth should crumble, will I bow my neck beneath the yoke.

(*Goes towards his room.*)

MRS. STOCKMANN (*following him*). Thomas, what are you going to do?

DR. STOCKMANN (*at the door*). I must have the right to look my boys in the face when they've grown into free men.

(*Goes into his room.*)

MRS. STOCKMANN (*bursts into tears*). Ah! God help us all!

PETRA. Father's all right! He'll never give in!

(*The boys ask wonderingly what it all means;* PETRA *signs to them to be quiet.*)

Act Third.

(*The Editor's Room; office of the "People's Messenger." In the background, to the left, a door; to the right another door, with glass panes, through which can be seen the printing-room. A door in the right-hand wall. In the middle of the room a large table covered with papers, newspapers, and books. In front, on the left, a window, and by it a writing-desk with a high stool. A couple of arm-chairs beside the table; some other chairs along the walls. The room is dingy and cheerless, the furniture shabby, the arm-chairs dirty and torn. Within the printing-room are seen a few compositors at work; further within, a hand-press in operation.*)

(HOVSTAD *is seated at the desk, writing. Presently* BILLING *enters from the right, with the* DOCTOR'S *manuscript in his hand.*)

BILLING. Well, I must say——

HOVSTAD (*writing*). Have you read it through?

BILLING (*laying MS. on the desk*). Yes, I should think I had.

HOVSTAD. Don't you think the Doctor comes out strong——?

BILLING. Strong! Why, strike me dead if he isn't crushing! Every word falls like a—well, like a sledge-hammer.

HOVSTAD. Yes, but these fellows won't collapse at the first blow.

BILLING. True enough; but we'll keep on hammering away, blow after blow, till the whole bureaucracy comes crashing down. As I sat in there reading that article, I seemed to hear the revolution thundering afar.

HOVSTAD (*turning round*). Hush! Don't let Aslaksen hear that.

BILLING (*in a lower voice*). Aslaksen's a white-livered, cowardly fellow, without a spark of manhood in him. But this time surely you'll have your own way? You'll print the Doctor's paper?

HOVSTAD. Yes, if only the Burgomaster doesn't give in——

BILLING. That would be deuced annoying.

HOVSTAD. Well, whatever happens, fortunately we can turn the situation to account. If the Burgomaster won't agree to the Doctor's proposal, he'll have all the small middle-class against him—all the Householders' Association, and the rest of them. And if he does agree to it, he'll fall out with the whole crew of big shareholders in the Baths, who have hitherto been his main support——

BILLING. Yes, of course; for it's certain they'll have to fork out a lot of money——

HOVSTAD. You may take your oath of that. And then, don't you see, when the ring is broken up, we'll din it into the public day by day that the Burgomaster is incompetent in every respect, and that all positions of trust in the town, the whole municipal government in short, must be entrusted to men of liberal ideas.

BILLING. Strike me dead if that isn't the square

truth. I see it, I see it: we're on the eve of a revolution!

(*A knock at the door.*)

HOVSTAD. Hush—(*calls*). Come in!

(DR. STOCKMANN *enters from the back, left.*)

HOVSTAD (*going towards him*). Ah! here's the Doctor. Well?

DR. STOCKMANN. Print away, Mr. Hovstad!

HOVSTAD. So it's come to that?

BILLING. Hurrah!

DR. STOCKMANN. Print away, I tell you. To be sure it's come to that. Since they will have it so, they must! War is declared, Mr. Billing!

BILLING. War to the knife, say I! War to the death, Doctor!

DR. STOCKMANN. This article is only the beginning. I've got plans for four or five others in my head already. But where do you keep Aslaksen?

BILLING (*calling into the printing-room*). Aslaksen! just come here a moment.

HOVSTAD. Did you say four or five more articles? On the same subject?

DR. STOCKMANN. Not at all, my dear fellow. No; they'll deal with quite different matters. But they're all of a piece with the water-works and sewer question. One thing leads to another. It's like beginning to pick at an old house, don't you know?

BILLING. Strike me dead, but that's true! You feel you can't leave off till you've pulled the whole rubbish to pieces.

ASLAKSEN (*enters from the printing-room*). Pulled

to pieces! Surely the Doctor isn't thinking of pulling the Baths to pieces?

HOVSTAD. Not at all! Don't be alarmed.

DR. STOCKMANN. No, we were talking of something quite different. Well, what do you think of my article, Mr. Hovstad?

HOVSTAD. I think it's simply a masterpiece——

DR. STOCKMANN. Yes, isn't it? I'm glad you think so—so glad.

HOVSTAD. It's so clear and to the point. One doesn't in the least need to be a specialist to understand the gist of it. I'm sure every intelligent man will be on your side.

ASLAKSEN. And all the prudent ones too, I hope?

BILLING. Both the prudent and imprudent—in fact, almost the whole town.

ASLAKSEN. Then I suppose we may venture to print it.

DR. STOCKMANN. I should think so!

HOVSTAD. It shall go in to-morrow.

DR. STOCKMANN. Yes, plague take it, not a day must be lost. Look here, Mr. Aslaksen, this is what I wanted to ask you: won't you take personal charge of the article?

ASLAKSEN. Certainly I will.

DR. STOCKMANN. Be as careful as if it were gold. No printers' errors; every word is important. I'll look in again presently; perhaps you'll be able to let me see a proof. Ah! I can't tell you how I long to have the thing in print—to see it hurled forth——

BILLING. Yes, like a thunderbolt!

DR. STOCKMANN. ——and submitted to the

judgment of every intelligent citizen. Oh! you've no idea what I've had to put up with to-day. I've been threatened with all sorts of things. I was to be robbed of my clearest rights as a man——

BILLING. What! Your rights as a man——!

DR. STOCKMANN. ——I was to humble myself, and eat the dust; I was to set my personal interests above my deepest, holiest convictions——

BILLING. Strike me dead, but that's too outrageous!

HOVSTAD. Oh, what can you expect from that quarter?

DR. STOCKMANN. But they'll get the worst of it, I can promise them. I'll throw myself into the breach every day in the *Messenger*, bombard them with one explosive article after another——

ASLAKSEN. Yes, but look here——

BILLING. Hurrah! War! War!

DR. STOCKMANN. I'll smite them to the earth, I'll crush them, I'll level their entrenchments to the ground in the eyes of all right-thinking men! I'll do it!

ASLAKSEN. But above all things be temperate, Doctor; proceed with moderation——

BILLING. Not at all, not at all! don't spare the dynamite!

DR. STOCKMANN (*going on imperturbably*). For now it isn't merely a question of water-works and sewers, you see. No, society as a whole must be purged, disinfected——

BILLING. There sounded the word of salvation!

DR. STOCKMANN. All the old bunglers must be

got rid of, you understand. And that in every department! Such endless vistas have opened out before me to-day. I don't see everything quite clearly yet, but that'll soon come. It's young and vigorous standard-bearers we must look for, my friends; we must have new captains at all the outposts.

BILLING. Hear, hear!

DR. STOCKMANN. And if only we hold together, it'll go so smoothly, so smoothly! The whole revolution will be just like the launch of a ship. Don't you think so?

HOVSTAD. For my part, I believe we have now every prospect of placing our municipal affairs in the right hands.

ASLAKSEN. And if only we proceed with moderation, I really don't think there can be any danger.

DR. STOCKMANN. Who the devil cares whether there's danger or not? What I do, I do in the name of truth and for conscience sake.

HOVSTAD. You are a man to be backed up, Doctor.

ASLAKSEN. Yes, there's no doubt the Doctor's a true friend to the town; he's what I call a friend of society.

BILLING. Strike me dead if Dr. Stockmann isn't a Friend of the People, Aslaksen.

ASLAKSEN. I have no doubt the Householders' Association will soon adopt that expression.

DR. STOCKMANN (*shaking their hands, deeply moved*). Thanks, thanks, my dear, faithful friends; it does me good to hear you. My respected brother called me something very different. Never mind! I'll pay him back with interest! But I must be off now to see a poor devil of a patient. I'll look in again, though. Be sure you look after the article, Mr. Aslaksen; and for goodness' sake don't leave out any of my notes of exclamation! Rather put in a few more. Well, good-bye for the present, good-bye, good-bye.

(*Mutual salutations while they accompany him to the door. He goes out.*)

HOVSTAD. He'll be invaluable to us.

ASLAKSEN. Yes, so long as he confines himself to the Baths. But if he goes further, it won't be advisable to go with him.

HOVSTAD. Hm! Well, that depends——

BILLING. You're always so confoundedly timid, Aslaksen.

ASLAKSEN. Timid? Yes, when it's a question of attacking local authorities, I *am* timid, Mr. Billing; I have learnt caution in the school of experience, let me tell you. But go for the higher politics, attack the Government itself, and then see if I'm timid.

BILLING. No, you're not; but that's just where you're inconsistent.

ASLAKSEN. The fact is, I'm keenly alive to my responsibilities. If you attack the Government, you at least do society no harm, for the men attacked don't care a straw, you see; they stay where they are all the same. But *local* authorities *can* be turned out; and then we might get some incompetent set into power, to the irreparable injury both of householders and others.

HOVSTAD. But the education of citizens by self-government—what do you think of *that?*

ASLAKSEN. When a man has solid interests to protect, he can't think of everything, Mr. Hovstad.

HOVSTAD. Then I hope I may never have solid interests to protect.

BILLING. Hear, hear!

ASLAKSEN (*smiling*). Hm! (*Points to the desk.*) Governor Stensgård[1] sat in that editorial chair before you.

BILLING (*spitting*). Pooh! A turncoat like that!

HOVSTAD. I'm no weathercock—and never will be.

ASLAKSEN. A politician should never be too sure of anything on earth, Mr. Hovstad. And as for you, Mr. Billing, you ought to take in a reef or two, I should say; aren't you applying for the secretaryship to the Town Council?

BILLING. I——!

HOVSTAD. Is that so, Billing?

BILLING. Well, yes—but, deuce take it, you know, I'm only doing it to annoy those wiseacres.

ASLAKSEN. Well, that doesn't concern me. But if I'm to be accused of cowardice and inconsistency, I'd just like to point out this: My political record is open to every one. I've not changed at all, except that I'm perhaps more moderate. My heart still belongs to the people; but I don't deny that my reason

[1] This is the only case in which Ibsen introduces persons who have appeared in an earlier play. Aslaksen figures in *The League of Youth*, of which Stensgård is the central character. It should be noted that Stensgård has justified Lundestad's prophecy by attaining the high administrative dignity of "Stiftamtmand," here roughly translated "Governor."

inclines somewhat towards the authorities—the local ones, at any rate.

(*Goes into the printing-room.*)

BILLING. Don't you think we ought to get rid of him, Hovstad?

HOVSTAD. Do you know of any one else that'll back us up, financially?

BILLING. What a confounded nuisance it is to have no capital!

HOVSTAD (*sitting down by desk*). Yes, if we only had that——

BILLING. Suppose you applied to Dr. Stockmann?

HOVSTAD (*turning over his papers*). What would be the good? He hasn't a rap.

BILLING. No; but he has a good man behind him—old Morten Kiil—"The Badger," as they call him.

HOVSTAD (*writing*). Are you so sure he has money?

BILLING. Yes, strike me dead if he hasn't! And part of it must certainly go to Stockmann's family. He's bound to provide for them—anyhow, for the children.

HOVSTAD (*half turning*). Are you counting on *that?*

BILLING. Counting? How should I be counting on it?

HOVSTAD. Best not! And that secretaryship you shouldn't count on either; for I can assure you you won't get it.

BILLING. Do you think I don't know that? A refusal is the very thing I want. Such a rebuff fires your spirit of opposition, gives you a fresh supply of gall; and that's just what you need in a god-forsaken place like this, where there's so little to stimulate you.

HOVSTAD (*writing*). Yes, yes.

BILLING. Well—they'll soon hear of me! Now I'll go and write the appeal to the Householders' Association.

(*Goes into the room on the right.*)

HOVSTAD (*sits at his desk, gnawing his pen, and says slowly*). Hm!—so that's it—(*A knock at the door*). Come in. (PETRA *enters from the back, left.*)

HOVSTAD (*rising*). What! Is it you? Here?

PETRA. Yes; please excuse me——

HOVSTAD (*offering her an arm-chair*). Won't you sit down.

PETRA. No, thanks; I must go again directly.

HOVSTAD. I suppose it's something from your father——?

PETRA. No, I've come on my own account. (*Takes a book from the pocket of her cloak.*) Here's that English story.

HOVSTAD. Why have you brought it back?

PETRA. Because I won't translate it.

HOVSTAD. But you promised——

PETRA. Yes; but then I hadn't read it. I suppose you've not read it either?

HOVSTAD. No; you know I can't read English; but——

PETRA. Exactly; and that's why I wanted to tell you that you must find something else. (*Putting *book on table.*) This can't possibly go into the *Messenger.*

HOVSTAD. Why not?

PETRA. Because it flies in the face of all your convictions.

HOVSTAD. Well, for that matter——

PETRA. You don't understand me. It's all about a supernatural power that looks after the so-called good people in this world, and turns everything to their advantage at last; while all the bad people are punished.

HOVSTAD. Yes, but that's all right. It's the very thing the public like.

PETRA. And would you supply the public with such stuff? You don't believe a word of it yourself. You know well enough that things don't really happen like that.

HOVSTAD. Of course not; but an editor can't always do as he likes. He has often to yield to people's fancies in small matters. After all, politics is the chief thing in life—at any rate for a newspaper; and if I want the people to follow me along the path of emancipation and progress, I mustn't scare them away. If they find a moral story like this down in the cellar,[1] they're all the more willing to stand what's printed above it—they feel themselves safer.

PETRA. For shame! You're not such a hypocrite as to spread snares like that for your readers. You're not a spider.

HOVSTAD (*smiling*). Thanks for your good opinion. It's true that the idea is Billing's, not mine.

[1] The reference is to the continental feuilleton at the foot of the page.

PETRA. Billing's!

HOVSTAD. Yes, at least he was talking in that strain the other day. It was Billing that was so anxious to get the story into the paper; I don't even know the book.

PETRA. But how can Billing, with his advanced views——

HOVSTAD. Well, Billing is many-sided. He's applying for the secretaryship to the Town Council, I hear.

PETRA. I don't believe that, Hovstad. How could he descend to such a thing?

HOVSTAD. That you must ask *him*.

PETRA. I could never have thought it of Billing.

HOVSTAD (*looking more closely at her*). No? Is that such a revelation to you?

PETRA. Yes. And yet—perhaps not. Oh, I don't know.

HOVSTAD. We journalists aren't worth much, Miss Petra.

PETRA. Do you really say that?

HOVSTAD. I think so, now and then.

PETRA. Yes, in the little everyday squabbles—that I can understand. But now that you've taken up a great cause——

HOVSTAD. You mean this affair of your father's?

PETRA. Of course. I should think you must feel yourself worth more than the common herd now.

HOVSTAD. Yes, to-day I do feel something of the sort.

PETRA. Yes, surely you must. Oh, it's a glorious career you've chosen! To be the pioneer of unrecognised truths and new and courageous ways of thought!—to stand forth fearlessly in support of an injured man——

HOVSTAD. Especially when the injured man is—hm!—I hardly know how to put it——

PETRA. You mean when he is so upright and true?

HOVSTAD (*in a low voice*). I mean when he's your father——

PETRA (*suddenly taken aback*). *That?*

HOVSTAD. Yes, Petra—Miss Petra.

PETRA. So *that's* your main idea, is it? Not the cause itself? Not the truth? Not father's great, warm heart?

HOVSTAD. Oh, that too, of course.

PETRA. No thank you; you've said too much, Mr. Hovstad. Now I shall never trust you again in anything.

HOVSTAD. Can you be so hard on me because it's chiefly for your sake——?

PETRA. What I blame you for is that you haven't acted straightforwardly towards father. You've spoken to him as if you cared only for the truth and the good of the community. You've trifled with both father and me. You are not the man you pretended to be. And that I shall never forgive you—never!

HOVSTAD. You shouldn't say that so bitterly, Miss Petra—least of all now.

PETRA. Why not now?

HOVSTAD. Because your father can't do without my help.

PETRA (*looking scornfully at him*). So that's what you are! Oh, shame!

HOVSTAD. No, no. I spoke thoughtlessly. You mustn't believe that.

PETRA. I know what to believe. Good-bye.

(ASLAKSEN *enters from printing-room, hurriedly and mysteriously.*)

ASLAKSEN. Plague take it, Mr. Hovstad—(*seeing* PETRA). Ow, that's awkward——

PETRA. Well, there's the book. You must give it to some one else.

(*Going towards the main door.*)

HOVSTAD (*following her*). But, Miss Petra——

PETRA. Good-bye. (*She goes.*)

ASLAKSEN. I say, Mr. Hovstad!

HOVSTAD. Well well; what is it?

ASLAKSEN. The Burgomaster's out there, in the printing-office.

HOVSTAD. The Burgomaster?

ASLAKSEN. Yes. He wants to speak to you; he came in by the back way—he didn't want to be seen, you know.

HOVSTAD. What's the meaning of this? Stop, I'll go myself—— (*Goes towards the printing-room, opens the door, bows, and invites the* BURGOMASTER *to enter.*) Keep a look-out, Aslaksen, that no one——

ASLAKSEN. I understand.

(*Goes into the printing-room.*)

BURGOMASTER. You didn't expect to see me here, Mr. Hovstad.

HOVSTAD. No, I can't say I did.

BURGOMASTER (*looking about him*). You've got a very comfortable place here; quite charming.

HOVSTAD. Oh——

BURGOMASTER. And here have I come, without with your leave or by your leave, to take up your time——

HOVSTAD. You're very welcome, sir; I'm at your service. Let me take your cap and stick. (*He does so, and puts them on a chair.*) And won't you sit down?

BURGOMASTER (*sitting down by the table*). Thanks. (HOVSTAD *also sits by the table.*) I've been much—very much worried to-day, Mr. Hovstad.

HOVSTAD. Really? Well, I suppose with all your various duties, Burgomaster——

BURGOMASTER. It's the Doctor that's been worrying me to-day.

HOVSTAD. Indeed! The Doctor?

BURGOMASTER. He's been writing a sort of memorandum to the Directors about some supposed shortcomings in the Baths.

HOVSTAD. Has he really?

BURGOMASTER. Yes; hasn't he told you? I thought he said——

HOVSTAD. Oh yes, by-the-bye, he did say something——

ASLAKSEN (*from the printing-office*). Oh, I want the manuscrift——

HOVSTAD (*in a tone of vexation*). Hm; there it is on the desk.

ASLAKSEN (*finding it*). All right.

BURGOMASTER. Why, that's it——

ASLAKSEN. Yes, that's the Doctor's article, Burgomaster.

HOVSTAD. Oh! is *that* what you were speaking of?

BURGOMASTER. The very same. What do you think of it?

HOVSTAD. I'm not a specialist, and I've only glanced at it.

BURGOMASTER. And yet you're going to print it?

HOVSTAD. I can't very well refuse a signed communication——

ASLAKSEN. I have nothing to do with the editing of the paper, Burgomaster——

BURGOMASTER. Of course not.

ASLAKSEN. I merely print what's placed in my hands.

BURGOMASTER. Quite right, quite right.

ASLAKSEN. So I must——

(*Goes towards the printing-room.*)

BURGOMASTER. No, stop a moment, Mr. Aslaksen. With your permission, Mr. Hovstad——

HOVSTAD. By all means, Burgomaster.

BURGOMASTER. You're a discreet and thoughtful man, Mr. Aslaksen.

ASLAKSEN. I'm glad you think so, Burgomaster.

BURGOMASTER. And a man of very wide influence.

ASLAKSEN. Chiefly among the lower middle-class.

BURGOMASTER. The small tax-payers form the majority—here as everywhere.

ASLAKSEN. That's true enough.

BURGOMASTER. And I don't doubt that you know the general feeling among them. Am I right?

ASLAKSEN. Yes, I think I may say that I do, Burgomaster.

BURGOMASTER. Well—if there's such a praiseworthy spirit of self-sacrifice among the poorer citizens of the town, I——

ASLAKSEN. How so?

HOVSTAD. Self-sacrifice?

BURGOMASTER. It's an admirable instance of public spirit—a most admirable instance. I admit it's more than I should quite have expected. But, of course, you know public feeling better than I do.

ASLAKSEN. Yes but, Burgomaster——

BURGOMASTER. And assuredly it's no small sacrifice the town will have to make.

HOVSTAD. The town?

ASLAKSEN. But I don't understand—it's the Baths——

BURGOMASTER. At a rough provisional estimate, the alterations the Doctor thinks desirable will come to two or three hundred thousand crowns.

ASLAKSEN. That's a lot of money; but——

BURGOMASTER. Of course we shall be obliged to raise a municipal loan.

HOVSTAD (*rising*). You don't suppose that the town——?

ASLAKSEN. Would you come upon the rates? Upon the scanty savings of the lower middle-class?

BURGOMASTER. Why, my dear Mr. Aslaksen, where else are the funds to come from?

ASLAKSEN. That the shareholders in the Baths must look to.

BURGOMASTER. The shareholders are not in a position to go to further expense.

ASLAKSEN. Are you quite sure of that, Burgomaster?

BURGOMASTER. I have positive information. So if these extensive alterations are called for, the town itself will have to bear the cost.

ASLAKSEN. Oh, plague take it all!—I beg your pardon!—but this is quite another matter, Mr. Hovstad.

HOVSTAD. Yes, it certainly is.

BURGOMASTER. The worst of it is, that we shall be obliged to close the establishment for a couple of years.

HOVSTAD. To close it? Completely?

ASLAKSEN. For two years!

BURGOMASTER. Yes, the work will require that time at least.

ASLAKSEN. But, damn it all! we can't stand that, Burgomaster. What are we householders to live on in the meantime?

BURGOMASTER. It's extremely difficult to say, Mr Aslaksen. But what can you do? Do you think a single visitor will come here if we go about making them fancy that the water is poisoned, that the place is pestilential, that the whole town——

ASLAKSEN. And it's all nothing but fancy?

BURGOMASTER. With the best will in the world, I've failed to convince myself that it's anything else.

ASLAKSEN. But then it's quite inexcusable of Dr. Stockmann—beg pardon, Burgomaster, but——

BURGOMASTER. I'm sorry to say you're only

speaking the truth, Mr. Aslaksen. Unfortunately, my brother has always been noted for his rashness.

ASLAKSEN. And yet you were going to back him up, Mr. Hovstad!

HOVSTAD. But who could possibly have imagined that——!

BURGOMASTER. I have drawn up a short statement of the facts, as they appear from a sober-minded standpoint; and I've intimated that any drawbacks that may possibly exist can no doubt be remedied by measures compatible with the finances of the Baths.

HOVSTAD. Have you the article with you, Burgomaster?

BURGOMASTER (*searching in his pockets*). Yes; I brought it with me in case you——

ASLAKSEN (*quickly*). Plague take it, there he is!

BURGOMASTER. Who? My brother?

HOVSTAD. Where? where?

ASLAKSEN. He's coming through the printing-room.

BURGOMASTER. What a nuisance! I don't want to meet him here, and yet there are several things I want to talk to you about.

HOVSTAD (*pointing to the door on the right*). Go in there for a moment.

BURGOMASTER. But——?

HOVSTAD. You'll only find Billing there.

ASLAKSEN. Quick, quick, Burgomaster, he's just coming.

BURGOMASTER. Very well. Try to get rid of him quickly.

(*He goes out by the door on the right, which* ASLAKSEN *opens, and closes behind him.*)

HOVSTAD. Pretend to be busy, Aslaksen.

(*He sits down and writes.* ASLAKSEN *turns over a heap of newspapers on a chair, right.*)

DR. STOCKMANN (*entering from the printing-room*). Here I am, back again. (*Puts down his hat and stick.*)

HOVSTAD (*writing*). Already, Doctor? Make haste with what we were speaking of, Aslaksen. We've no time to lose to-day.

DR. STOCKMANN (*to* ASLAKSEN). No proof yet, I hear.

ASLAKSEN (*without turning round*). No; how could you expect it?

DR. STOCKMANN. Of course not; but you understand my impatience. I can have no rest or peace until I see the thing in print.

HOVSTAD. Hm; it'll take a good while yet. Don't you think so, Aslaksen?

ASLAKSEN. I'm almost afraid it will.

DR. STOCKMANN. All right, all right, my good friends; then I'll look in again. I'll look in twice if necessary. With so much at stake—the welfare of the whole town—upon my word, it's no time for idling. (*Is on the point of going, but stops and comes back.*) Oh, look here, there's one other thing I must speak to you about.

HOVSTAD. Excuse me; wouldn't some other time——?

DR. STOCKMANN. I can tell you in two words. You see it's this: when people read my statement in the paper to-morrow, and find I've spent the whole winter working quietly for the good of the town——

HOVSTAD. Yes but, Doctor——

DR. STOCKMANN. I know what you're going to say. You don't think it was a bit more than my duty—my simple duty as a citizen. Of course I know that, as well as you do. But you see, my fellow-citizens—good Lord! the poor souls think so much of me——

ASLAKSEN. Yes, the townspeople have thought very highly of you till to-day, Doctor.

DR. STOCKMANN. That's exactly why I'm afraid that,—what I wanted to say was this: when all this comes to them—especially to the poorer class—as a summons to take the affairs of the town into their own hands for the future——

HOVSTAD (*rising*). Hm, Doctor, I won't conceal from you——

DR. STOCKMANN. Aha! I thought there was something brewing! But I won't hear of it. If they're going to get up anything——

HOVSTAD. How so?

DR. STOCKMANN. Well, anything of any sort—a procession with banners, or a banquet, or a subscription for a testimonial, or whatever it may be—you must give me your solemn promise to put a stop to it. And you too, Mr. Aslaksen; do you hear?

HOVSTAD. Excuse me, Doctor; we may as well tell you the whole truth first as last——

(*Enter* MRS. STOCKMANN.)

MRS. STOCKMANN (*seeing the* DOCTOR). Ah! just as I thought!

HOVSTAD (*going towards her*). Mrs. Stockmann, too?

DR. STOCKMANN. What the devil have you come here for, Katrine?

MRS. STOCKMANN. You must know well enough what I've come for.

HOVSTAD. Won't you sit down? Or perhaps——?

MRS. STOCKMANN. Thanks; please don't trouble. And you mustn't blame me for coming here after Stockmann, for you must remember I'm the mother of three children.

DR. STOCKMANN. Stuff and nonsense! We all know that well enough!

MRS. STOCKMANN. It doesn't look as if you thought very much about your wife and children to-day, or you wouldn't be so ready to plunge us all into misfortune.

DR. STOCKMANN. Are you quite mad, Katrine? Mayn't a man with a wife and children proclaim the truth? Mayn't he do his utmost to be an active and useful citizen? Mayn't he do his duty by the town he lives in?

MRS. STOCKMANN. Everything in moderation, Thomas.

ASLAKSEN. That's just what I say. Moderation in everything.

MRS. STOCKMANN. You're doing us a great wrong, Mr. Hovstad, in enticing my husband away from house and home, and befooling him in this way——

HOVSTAD. I have befooled no one——

DR. STOCKMANN. Befooled! Do you think I should let myself be befooled?

MRS. STOCKMANN. Yes, but you do. I know very well that you're the cleverest man in the town; but you're so easily made a fool of, Thomas. (*To* HOVSTAD.) Remember he's to lose his post at the Baths if you print what he's written——

ASLAKSEN. What!

HOVSTAD. Well, really, Doctor——

DR. STOCKMANN (*laughing*). Ha ha! just let them try! No no, my dear, they'll think twice about that! I have the compact majority behind me, you see.

MRS. STOCKMANN. That's just the misfortune, that you should have such a horrid thing behind you.

DR. STOCKMANN. Nonsense, Katrine;—you go home and look after your house, and let me take care of society. How can you be in such a fright when you see me so confident and happy? (*Rubbing his hands and walking up and down.*) Truth and the People must win the day; of that you may be sure. Ah! I can see the whole democracy arrayed as one triumphant host——! (*Stopping by a chair.*) Why, what the devil is that?

ASLAKSEN (*looking at it*). Oh Lord!

HOVSTAD (*the same*). Hm!

DR. STOCKMANN. Why, here's the top-knot of authority!

(*He takes the* BURGOMASTER'S *official cap carefully between the tips of his fingers and holds it up.*)

MRS. STOCKMANN. The Burgomaster's cap!

DR. STOCKMANN. And here's the staff of office, too! But how in the devil's name did they——?

HOVSTAD. Well then——

DR. STOCKMANN. Ah! I understand. He's been here to talk you over. Ha ha! He brought his pigs to the wrong market! And when he caught sight of me in the printing-room—(*bursts out laughing*)—he took to his heels, eh, Mr. Aslaksen?

ASLAKSEN (*hurriedly*). Exactly; he took to his heels, Doctor.

DR. STOCKMANN. Made off without his stick and—— Fiddle-faddle! Peter never left anything behind him. But where the devil have you stowed him? Ah!—in there, of course. Now you shall see, Katrine!

MRS. STOCKMANN. Thomas—I beg you——!

ASLAKSEN. Take care, Doctor!

(DR. STOCKMANN *has put on the* BURGOMASTER'S *cap and grasped his stick; he now goes up to the door, throws it open, and makes a military salute. The* BURGOMASTER *enters, red with anger. Behind him comes* BILLING.)

BURGOMASTER. What's the meaning of this folly?

DR. STOCKMANN. Respect, my good Peter! Now, it's I that am in power in this town.

(*He struts up and down.*)

MRS. STOCKMANN (*almost crying*). Oh, Thomas——!

BURGOMASTER (*following him*). Give me my cap and stick!

DR. STOCKMANN (*as before*). You may be Chief of Police, but I'm Burgomaster. I'm master of the whole town, I tell you!

BURGOMASTER. Put down my cap, I say. Remember it's an official cap, as by law prescribed.

DR. STOCKMANN. Pshaw! Do you think the awakening lion of the democracy will let itself be scared by a uniform cap? There's to be a revolution in the town to-morrow, let me tell you. You threatened me with dismissal; but now I dismiss you—dismiss you from all your offices of trust. You think I can't do it?—Oh yes, I can! I have the irresistible forces of society with me. Hovstad and Billing will thunder in the *People's Messenger*, and Aslaksen will take the field at the head of the whole Householders' Association——

ASLAKSEN. I shall not, Doctor.

DR. STOCKMANN. Surely you will——

BURGOMASTER. Aha! Perhaps Mr. Hovstad would like to join the agitation after all?

HOVSTAD. No, Burgomaster.

ASLAKSEN. No, Mr. Hovstad isn't such a fool as to ruin both himself and the paper for the sake of fancy.

DR. STOCKMANN (*looking about him*). What does all this mean?

HOVSTAD. You have presented your case in a false light, Doctor; therefore I'm unable to give you my support.

BILLING. And after what the Burgomaster has been so kind as to explain to me, I——

DR. STOCKMANN. In a false light! Well, I'm responsible for that. Just you print my article, and you'll see I'll prove it up to the hilt.

HOVSTAD. I shall not print it. I cannot, and will not, and dare not print it.

DR. STOCKMANN. You dare not? What nonsense! You're editor; and I suppose it's the editor that directs a paper.

ASLAKSEN. No, it's the readers, Doctor.

BILLING. Luckily, it is.

ASLAKSEN. It's public opinion, the intelligent majority, the householders, and all the rest. It's they who direct a paper.

DR. STOCKMANN (*calmly*). And all these powers I have against me?

ASLAKSEN. Yes, you have. It would be absolute ruin for the town if your article were inserted.

DR. STOCKMANN. Indeed!

BURGOMASTER. My hat and stick! (DR. STOCKMANN *takes off the cap and lays it on the table along with the stick. The* BURGOMASTER *takes them both.*) Your term of office has come to an untimely end.

DR. STOCKMANN. The end is not yet. (*To* HOVSTAD.) So it's quite impossible to print my paper in the *Messenger?*

HOVSTAD. Quite impossible; for the sake of your family, if for no other reason.

MRS. STOCKMANN. Oh, please leave his family out of the question, Mr. Hovstad.

BURGOMASTER (*takes a manuscript from his pocket*). When this appears, the public will be in possession of all necessary information; it's an authentic statement. Here it is.

HOVSTAD (*taking the MS.*). Good! It shall certainly be inserted.

DR. STOCKMANN. And not mine! You imagine you can kill me and the truth by a conspiracy of silence! But it won't be so easy as you think. Mr Aslaksen, will you be good enough to print my article at once, as a pamphlet? I'll pay for it and be my own publisher. I'll have five hundred copies—no, I'll have six hundred.

ASLAKSEN. No. If you offered me its weight in gold I shouldn't dare to lend my press to such a purpose, Doctor. I daren't fly in the face of public opinion. You won't get it printed anywhere in the whole town.

DR. STOCKMANN. Then give it me back.

HOVSTAD (*handing him the MS.*). By all means.

DR. STOCKMANN (*taking up his hat and cane*). It shall be made public all the same. I'll read it at a mass meeting; all my fellow-citizens shall hear the voice of truth!

BURGOMASTER. Not a single society in the town would let you their hall for such a purpose.

ASLAKSEN. Not one, I'm quite certain.

BILLING. No, strike me dead if they would!

MRS. STOCKMANN. That would be too disgraceful! But why is every one against you like this?

DR. STOCKMANN (*angrily*). Ah, I'll tell you. It's because in this town all the men are old women—like you. They all think of nothing but their families, not of the general good.

MRS. STOCKMANN (*taking his arm*). Then I'll show them that an—an old woman can be a man, for once in a way. For *now* I'll stand by you, Thomas.

DR. STOCKMANN. Bravely said, Katrine! My word for it, the truth shall out! If they won't let me a hall, I'll hire a drum and march through the town with it; and I'll read my paper at every street corner.

BURGOMASTER. Surely you're not such a raving lunatic as that?

DR. STOCKMANN. I am.

ASLAKSEN. You wouldn't get a single man in the whole town to go with you.

BILLING. No, strike me dead if you would.

MRS. STOCKMANN. Don't give in, Thomas. I'll send the boys with you.

DR. STOCKMANN. That's a splendid idea!

MRS. STOCKMANN. Morten 'll be delighted; and Eilif 'll go too, I'm sure.

DR. STOCKMANN. Yes, and so will Petra. And you yourself, Katrine!

MRS. STOCKMANN. No no, not I. But I'll stand at the window and watch you—that I will.

DR. STOCKMANN (*throwing his arms about her and kissing her*). Thanks, thanks! Now, my good sirs, we're ready for the fight! Now we'll see if your poltroonery can close the mouth of the patriot who would purge society.

(*He and his wife go out together by the door in the back, left.*)

BURGOMASTER (*shaking his head dubiously*). Now he's driven *her* mad too!

Act Fourth.

(*A large old-fashioned room in* CAPTAIN HORSTER'S *house. An open folding-door in the background leads to an anteroom. Three windows, left. About the middle of the opposite wall is a platform, and on it a small table, two candles, a water-bottle and glass, and a bell. The rest of the room is lighted by sconces placed between the windows. In front, on the left, is a table with a candle on it, and by it a chair. In front, to the right, a door, and near it a few chairs.*)

(*Large meeting of all classes of townsfolk. In the crowd are a few women and school-boys. More and more people gradually stream in from the back until the room is quite full.*)

1ST CITIZEN (*to another standing near him*). So you're here too, Lamstad?

2ND CITIZEN. I always go to every meeting.

A BYSTANDER. I suppose you've brought your whistle?

2ND CITIZEN. Of course I have; haven't you?

3RD CITIZEN. Rather. And Skipper Evensen said he'd bring a great big horn.

2ND CITIZEN. He's a good one, is Evensen! (*Laughter in the group.*)

4TH CITIZEN (*joining them*). I say, what's it all about? What's going on here to-night?

2ND CITIZEN. Why, it's Dr. Stockmann that's going to lecture against the Burgomaster.

4TH CITIZEN. But the Burgomaster's his brother.

1ST CITIZEN. That doesn't matter. Dr. Stockmann's not afraid of him.

3RD CITIZEN. But he's all wrong; the *People's Messenger* says so.

2ND CITIZEN. Yes, he must be wrong this time; for neither the Householders' Association nor the Citizens' Club would let him have a hall.

1ST CITIZEN. They wouldn't even let him have the hall at the Baths.

2ND CITIZEN. No, you may be sure they wouldn't.

A MAN (*in another group*). Now, who's the one to follow in this business, eh?

ANOTHER MAN (*in the same group*). Just keep your eye on Aslaksen, and do as he does.

BILLING (*with a writing-case under his arm, makes his way through the crowd*). Excuse me, gentlemen. Will you allow me to pass? I'm here to report for the *People's Messenger*. Many thanks.

(*Sits by the table on the left.*)

A WORKING-MAN. Who's he?

ANOTHER WORKING-MAN. Don't you know him? It's that fellow Billing, that writes for Aslaksen's paper.

(CAPTAIN HORSTER *enters by the right-hand door, escorting* MRS. STOCKMANN *and* PETRA. EILIF *and* MORTEN *follow them.*)

HORSTER. This is where I thought you might sit; you can so easily slip out if anything should happen.

MRS. STOCKMANN. Do you think there'll be any disturbance?

HORSTER. One can never tell—with such a crowd But there's no need to be anxious.

MRS. STOCKMANN (*sitting down*). How kind it was of you to offer Stockmann this room!

HORSTER. As no one else would, I——

PETRA (*who has also seated herself*). And it was brave too, Horster.

HORSTER. Oh, I don't see that it needed much courage.

(HOVSTAD *and* ASLAKSEN *enter at the same moment, but make their way through the crowd separately.*)

ASLAKSEN (*going towards* HORSTER). Hasn't the Doctor come yet?

HORSTER. He's waiting in there.

(*A movement at the door in the background.*)

HOVSTAD (*to* BILLING). There's the Burgomaster look!

BILLING. Yes, strike me dead if he hasn't come to the fore after all!

(BURGOMASTER STOCKMANN *makes his way blandly through the meeting, bowing politely to both sides, and takes his stand by the wall on the left. Immediately afterwards,* DR. STOCKMANN *enters by the door on the right. He wears a black frock-coat and white necktie. Faint applause, met by a subdued hissing. Then silence.*)

DR. STOCKMANN (*in a low tone*). How do you feel, Katrine?

MRS. STOCKMANN. Oh, I'm all right. (*In a low voice.*) Now do keep your temper, Thomas.

DR. STOCKMANN. Oh, I'll keep myself well in hand. (*Looks at his watch, ascends the platform, and bows.*) It's a quarter past the hour, so I'll begin——

(*Takes out his MS.*)

ASLAKSEN. But I suppose a chairman must be elected first.

DR. STOCKMANN. No; there's no necessity.

SEVERAL GENTLEMEN (*shouting*). Yes, yes.

BURGOMASTER. I should certainly say that a chairman ought to be elected.

DR. STOCKMANN. But I've called this meeting to give a lecture, Peter!

BURGOMASTER. Dr. Stockmann's lecture may possibly lead to differences of opinion.

SEVERAL VOICES IN THE CROWD. A chairman! a chairman!

HOVSTAD. The general voice of the meeting seems to be for a chairman.

DR. STOCKMANN (*controlling himself*). Very well then; let the meeting have its way.

ASLAKSEN. Will not the Burgomaster take the chair?

THREE GENTLEMEN (*clapping*). Bravo! Bravo!

BURGOMASTER. For reasons you will easily understand, I must decline. But, fortunately, we have among us one whom I think we can all accept. I allude to the president of the Householders' Association, Mr. Aslaksen.

MANY VOICES. Yes, yes! Long live Aslaksen! Hurrah for Aslaksen!

(DR. STOCKMANN *takes his MS. and descends from the platform.*)

ASLAKSEN. If my fellow-citizens call upon me, I cannot refuse to——

(*Applause and cheers.* ASLAKSEN *ascends the platform.*)

BILLING (*writing*) So—"Mr. Aslaksen was elected by acclamation——"

ASLAKSEN. And now, as I have been called to the chair, I take the liberty of saying a few brief words. I am a quiet, peace-loving man; I am in favour of discreet moderation, and of—and of moderate discretion. Every one who knows me, knows that.

MANY VOICES. Yes, yes, Aslaksen!

ASLAKSEN. I have learnt in the school of life and of experience that moderation is the virtue in which the individual citizen finds his best advantage——

BURGOMASTER. Hear, hear!

ASLAKSEN. ——and it is discretion and moderation, too, that best serve the community. I will therefore beg our respected fellow-citizen, who has called this meeting, to keep within the bounds of moderation.

A MAN (*by the door*). Three cheers for the Temperance Society!

A VOICE. Go to the devil!

VOICES. Hush! hush!

ASLAKSEN. No interruptions, gentlemen! Does any one wish to offer any observations?

BURGOMASTER. Mr. Chairman!

ASLAKSEN. Burgomaster Stockmann will address the meeting.

BURGOMASTER. On account of my close relationship—of which you are probably aware—to the present medical officer of the Baths, I should have preferred not to speak here this evening. But my position with regard to the Baths, and my care for the most important interests of this town, force me to move a resolution. I may doubtless assume that not a single citizen here present thinks it desirable that untrustworthy and exaggerated statements should get abroad as to the sanitary condition of the Baths and of our town.

MANY VOICES. No, no! Certainly not! We protest!

BURGOMASTER. I therefore beg to move, "That this meeting declines to hear the proposed lecture or speech on the subject by the medical officer of the Baths."

DR. STOCKMANN (*flaring up*). Declines to hear! What do you mean?

MRS. STOCKMANN (*coughing*). Hm! hm!

DR. STOCKMANN (*controlling himself*). So I'm not to be heard?

BURGOMASTER. In my statement in the *People's Messenger* I have made the public acquainted with the essential facts, so that all well-disposed citizens can easily draw their own conclusions. From that statement you will see that the medical officer's proposal—besides amounting to a vote of censure against the leading men of the town—at bottom only means saddling the ratepayers with an unnecessary expense of at least a hundred thousand crowns.

(*Protestations and some hissing.*)

ASLAKSEN (*ringing the bell*). Order, gentlemen! I must beg leave to support the Burgomaster's resolution. I quite agree with him that there is something beneath the surface of the Doctor's agitation. In all his talk about the Baths, it is really a revolution he is aiming at; he wants to effect a redistribution of power. No one doubts the excellence of Dr. Stockmann's intentions—of course there can't be two opinions as to that. I, too, am in favour of self-government by the people, if only it doesn't cost the ratepayers too much. But in this case it would do so; and therefore I—confound it all—I beg your pardon—I cannot go with Dr. Stockmann upon this occasion. You can buy even gold too dear; that's my opinion.

(*Loud applause on all sides.*)

HOVSTAD. I also feel bound to explain my attitude. In the beginning, Dr. Stockmann's agitation seemed to find favour in several quarters, and I supported it as impartially as I could. But then we found we had been misled by a false statement——

DR. STOCKMANN. False——!

HOVSTAD. Well then, an untrustworthy statement. This the Burgomaster's report has proved. I trust no one here present doubts my liberal principles; the attitude of the *Messenger* on all great political questions is well known to you all. But I have learned from experienced and thoughtful men that in purely local matters a paper must observe a certain amount of caution.

ASLAKSEN. I quite agree with the speaker.

HOVSTAD. And in the matter under discussion it is evident that Dr. Stockmann has public opinion against him. But, gentlemen, what is the first and foremost duty of an editor? Is it not to work in harmony with his readers? Has he not in some sort received a tacit mandate to further assiduously and unweariedly the interests of his constituents? Or am I mistaken in this?

MANY VOICES. No, no, no! Hovstad is right!

HOVSTAD. It has cost me a bitter struggle to break with a man in whose house I have of late been a frequent guest—with a man who up to this day has enjoyed the universal goodwill of his fellow-citizens—with a man whose only, or, at any rate, whose chief fault is that he consults his heart rather than his head.

A FEW SCATTERED VOICES. That's true! Hurrah for Dr. Stockmann!

HOVSTAD. But my duty towards the community has forced me to break with him. Then, too, there is another consideration that impels me to oppose him, and, if possible, to bar the fatal path upon which he is entering: consideration for his family——

DR. STOCKMANN. Keep to the water-works and sewers!

HOVSTAD. ——consideration for his wife and his unprotected[1] children.

MORTEN. Is that us, mother?

MRS. STOCKMANN. Hush!

ASLAKSEN. I will now put the Burgomaster's resolution to the vote.

DR. STOCKMANN. It's not necessary. I shan't say anything this evening of all the filth at the Baths. No! You shall hear something quite different.

BURGOMASTER (*half aloud*). What next, I wonder?

[1] Literally, "unprovided-for."

A DRUNKEN MAN (*at the main entrance*). I'm a ratepayer, so I've a right to my opinion! It's my full, firm, incomprehensible opinion that——

SEVERAL VOICES. Silence, up there!

OTHERS. He's drunk! Turn him out!

(*The drunken man is turned out.*)

DR. STOCKMANN. Can I speak?

ASLAKSEN (*ringing the bell*). Dr. Stockmann will address the meeting.

DR. STOCKMANN. A few days ago I should have liked to see any one venture upon such an attempt to gag me as has been made here to-night! I would have fought like a lion for my sacred rights. But now I scarcely care, for now I have more important things to speak of. (*The people crowd closer round him.* MORTEN KIIL *comes in sight among the bystanders.* DR. STOCKMANN *continues.*) During the last few days I have been thinking and thinking of so many things, that at last my head seemed to be in a whirl——

BURGOMASTER (*coughing*). Hm!

DR. STOCKMANN. ——but presently my ideas clarified, and I soon got the hang of the whole matter. That's why I stand here this evening. I am about to make great revelations, my fellow-citizens! I am going to announce to you a far more important discovery than the trifling fact that our water-works are poisoned, and that our health-resort is built on pestilential ground.

MANY VOICES (*shouting*). Don't speak about the Baths! We won't listen to that! No more of that!

DR. STOCKMANN. I have said I would speak of

the great discovery I have made within the last few days—the discovery that all our sources of spiritual life are poisoned, and that our whole society rests upon a pestilential basis of falsehood.

SEVERAL VOICES (*in astonishment and half aloud*). What's he saying?

BURGOMASTER. Such an insinuation——

ASLAKSEN (*with his hand on the bell*). I must call upon the speaker to moderate his expressions.

DR. STOCKMANN. I have loved my native town as dearly as man could love the home of his childhood. I was young when I left our town, and distance, home-sickness, and memory threw, as it were, a glamour over the place and its people. (*Some clapping and shouts of approval.*) Then for years I was imprisoned in a horrible hole, far away in the north. As I went about among the people scattered here and there over the stony wilderness, it seemed to me, many a time, that these poor degraded creatures ought to have had a cattle-doctor to attend them rather than a man like me.

(*Murmurs in the room.*)

BILLING (*laying down his pen*). Strike me dead if I've ever heard——!

HOVSTAD. What an insult to a worthy peasantry!

DR. STOCKMANN. Wait a moment!— I don't think any one can reproach me with forgetting my native town up there. I sat brooding like an eider-duck, and what I hatched was—the plan of the Baths. (*Applause and interruptions.*) And when, at last, fate ordered things so happily that I could come home again—then, fellow-citizens, it seemed to me that I hadn't another desire in the world. Yes, one desire I had: an eager, constant, burning desire to be of service to my birthplace, and to its people.

BURGOMASTER (*looking into vacancy*). A strange method to select—hm!

DR. STOCKMANN. So I went about revelling in my happy illusions. But yesterday morning—no, it was really two nights ago—my mind's eyes were opened wide, and the first thing I saw was the extraordinary stupidity of the authorities——

(*Noise, cries, and laughter.* MRS. STOCKMANN *coughs emphatically.*)

BURGOMASTER. Mr. Chairman!

ASLAKSEN (*ringing his bell*). In virtue of my position——!

DR. STOCKMANN. It's petty to catch me up on a word, Mr. Aslaksen. I only meant that I became alive to the extraordinary muddle the leading men had been guilty of down at the Baths. I detest leading men—I've seen enough of them in my time. They're like goats in a young plantation: they do harm everywhere; they block the path of a free man wherever he turns—and I should be glad if we could exterminate them like other noxious animals——

(*Uproar in the room.*)

BURGOMASTER. Mr. Chairman, are such expressions permissible?

ASLAKSEN (*with his hand on the bell*). Doctor Stockmann——!

DR. STOCKMANN. I can't conceive how it is that I've only now seen through these gentry; for haven't

I had a magnificent example before my eyes here every day—my brother Peter—slow of understanding, tenacious in prejudice——

(*Laughter, noise, and whistling.* MRS. STOCKMANN *coughs.* ASLAKSEN *rings violently.*)

THE DRUNKEN MAN (*who has come in again*). Is it me you're alluding to? Sure enough, my name's Pettersen; but devil take me if——

ANGRY VOICES. Out with that drunken man! Turn him out!

(*The man is again turned out.*)

BURGOMASTER. Who is that person?

A BYSTANDER. I don't know him, Burgomaster.

ANOTHER. He doesn't belong to the town.

A THIRD. I believe he's a timber-merchant from——

(*The rest is inaudible.*)

ASLAKSEN. The man was evidently intoxicated. Continue, Dr. Stockmann; but do strive to be moderate.

DR. STOCKMANN. Well, fellow-citizens, I'll say no more about our leading men. If any one imagines, from what I've just said, that I want to make short work of these gentlemen to-night, he's mistaken—altogether mistaken. For I cherish the comforting belief that these laggards, these relics of a decaying order of thought, are diligently cutting their own throats. They need no doctor to hasten their end. And these are not the people that constitute the most serious danger to society; it is not they who are most active in poisoning our spiritual life and making a plague-spot of the ground beneath our feet; it is not they who are the most dangerous enemies of truth and freedom in our society.

CRIES FROM ALL SIDES. Who, then? Who is it? Name, name!

DR. STOCKMANN. Yes, you may be sure I'll name them! For *this* is the great discovery I made yesterday! (*In a louder tone.*) The most dangerous foe to truth and freedom in our midst is the compact majority. Yes, it's the confounded, compact, liberal majority! There, I've told you!

(*Immense disturbance in the room. Most of the audience are shouting, stamping, and whistling. Several elderly gentlemen exchange furtive glances and seem to be enjoying the scene.* MRS. STOCKMANN *rises nervously.* EILIF *and* MORTEN *advance threateningly towards the school-boys, who are making a noise.* ASLAKSEN *rings the bell and calls for order.* HOVSTAD *and* BILLING *both speak, but nothing can be heard. At last quiet is restored.*)

ASLAKSEN. I request the speaker to withdraw his ill-considered expressions.

DR. STOCKMANN. Never, Mr. Aslaksen! For it's this very majority that robs me of my freedom, and wants to forbid me to speak the truth.

HOVSTAD. Right is always on the side of the majority.

BILLING. Yes, and truth too, strike me dead!

DR. STOCKMANN. The majority is never right. Never, I say! That's one of the social lies a free, thinking man is bound to rebel against. Who make up the majority in any given country? Is it the wise men or the fools? I think we must agree that the fools are in a terrible, overwhelming majority, all the wide world over. But how the deuce can it ever be right for the fools to rule over the wise men? (*Noise and shouts.*) Yes yes, you can shout me down, but you cannot gainsay me. The majority has might—unhappily—but right it has not. I and the few, the individuals, are right. The minority is always right.

(*Renewed disturbances.*)

HOVSTAD. Ha ha! So Dr. Stockmann has turned aristocrat since the day before yesterday.

DR. STOCKMANN. I have said that I won't waste a word on the little, narrow-chested, short-winded crew that lie in our wake. Pulsating life has nothing more to do with them. I will rather speak of the few individuals among us who have made all the new, germinating truths their own. These men stand, as it were, at the outposts, so far in the van that the compact majority has not yet reached them—and *there* they fight for truths that are too lately born into the world's consciousness to have won over the majority.

HOVSTAD. So the Doctor's a revolutionist now.

DR. STOCKMANN. Yes, by Heaven, I am, Mr. Hovstad! I'm going to revolt against the lie that truth resides in the majority. What sort of truths do the majority rally round? Truths that are decrepit with age. When a truth is so old as that it's in a fair way to become a lie, gentlemen. (*Laughter and jeers.*) Yes yes, you may believe me or not, as you please; but truths are by no means the wiry Methusalehs some people think them. A normally-constituted truth lives—let me say—as a rule, seventeen or eighteen years; at the outside twenty; seldom longer. And truths so stricken in years are always shockingly thin; yet it's not till then that the majority takes them up and recommends them to society as wholesome food. I can assure you there's not much nutriment in that sort of fare; you may take my word as a doctor for that. All these majority-truths are like last year's salt pork; they're like rancid, mouldy ham, producing all the moral scurvy that devastates society.

ASLAKSEN. It seems to me that the honourable speaker is wandering rather far from the subject.

BURGOMASTER. I beg to endorse the Chairman's remark.

DR. STOCKMANN. Why you're surely mad, Peter! I'm keeping as closely to my text as I possibly can, for my text is just this—that the masses, the majority, that confounded compact majority—it's that, I say, that's poisoning our spiritual life at its source, and making a plague-spot of the ground beneath our feet.

HOVSTAD. And you make this charge against the great, independent majority, just because they're sensible enough to accept only certain and acknowledged truths?

DR. STOCKMANN. Ah, my dear Mr. Hovstad, don't talk about certain truths! The truths acknowledged by the masses, the multitude, were certain truths to the vanguard in our grandfathers' days. We, the vanguard of to-day, don't acknowledge them any longer; and I don't believe there's any other certain truth but this—that no society can live a healthy life upon such old, marrowless truths as these.

HOVSTAD. But instead of all this vague talk, suppose you were to give us some specimens of these old marrowless truths that we're living upon.

(*Approval from several quarters.*)

DR. STOCKMANN. Oh, I can't go over the whole rubbish-heap; so, for the present, I'll keep to one acknowledged truth, which is a hideous lie at bottom, but which Mr. Hovstad, and the *Messenger*, and all adherents of the *Messenger*, live on all the same.

HOVSTAD. And that is——?

DR. STOCKMANN. That is the doctrine you've inherited from our forefathers, and go on heedlessly proclaiming far and wide—the doctrine that the multitude, the vulgar herd, the masses, are the pith of the people—that they *are* the people—that the common man, the ignorant, undeveloped member of society, has the same right to condemn and to sanction, to counsel and to govern, as the intellectually distinguished few.

BILLING. Well, now, strike me dead——!

HOVSTAD (*shouting at the same time*). Citizens, please note that!

ANGRY VOICES. Ho-ho! Aren't we the people? Is it only the grand folks that are to govern?

A WORKING MAN. Turn out the fellow that talks like that!

OTHERS. Turn him out!

A CITIZEN (*shouting*). Now for your horn, Evensen.

(*The deep notes of a horn are heard; whistling, and terrific noise in the room.*)

DR. STOCKMANN (*when the noise has somewhat

subsided). Now do be reasonable! Can't you bear to hear the voice of truth for once? I don't ask you all to agree with me straight away. But I certainly should have thought that Mr. Hovstad would have backed me up, when he'd collected himself a bit. Mr. Hovstad calls himself a free-thinker——

SEVERAL VOICES (*subdued and wondering*). Free-thinker, did he say? What? Mr. Hovstad a free-thinker?

HOVSTAD (*shouting*). Prove it, Dr. Stockmann! When have I said so in print?

DR. STOCKMANN (*reflecting*). No, on my soul you're right there; you've never had the frankness to do that. Well, I won't get you into a scrape, Mr. Hovstad. Let me be the free-thinker then. And now I'll make it clear to you all, and on scientific grounds, that the *Messenger* is leading you shamefully by the nose, when it tells you that you, the masses, the crowd, are the true pith of the people. You see that's only a newspaper lie. The masses are nothing but the raw material that must be fashioned into the People. (*Murmurs, laughter, and disturbance in the room.*) Is it not so with all other living creatures? What a difference between a cultivated and an uncultivated breed of animals! Only look at a common barn-door hen. What meat do you get from such a skinny carcase? Not much, I can tell you! And what sort of eggs does she lay? A decent crow or raven can lay nearly as good. Then take a cultivated Spanish or Japanese hen, or take a fine pheasant or turkey—ah! then you'll see the difference. And now look at the dog, our near relation. Think first of an ordinary vulgar cur—I mean one of those wretched, ragged, low mongrels that haunt the gutters, and soil the side-walks. Then place such a mongrel by the side of a poodle-dog, descended through many generations from an aristocratic strain, who has lived on delicate food, and has heard harmonious voices and music. Do you think the brain of the poodle hasn't developed quite differently from that of the mongrel? Yes, you may be sure it has! It's well-bred poodle-pups like this that jugglers train to perform the most extraordinary tricks. A common peasant-cur could never learn anything of the sort—not if he tried till doomsday.

(*Noise and laughter are heard all round.*)

A CITIZEN (*shouting*). Do you want to make dogs of us now?

ANOTHER MAN. We're not animals, Doctor.

DR. STOCKMANN. Yes, on my soul, but we are animals, my good sir! We're one and all of us animals, whether we like it or not. But truly there aren't many aristocratic animals among us. Ah! there's a terrible difference between men-poodles and men-mongrels. And the ridiculous part of it is, that Mr. Hovstad quite agrees with me so long as it's four-legged animals we're talking of——

HOVSTAD. Oh, let them alone.

DR. STOCKMANN. All right—but so soon as I apply the law to two-legged animals, Mr. Hovstad stops short; then he daren't hold his own opinions, or think out his own thoughts; then he turns all his knowledge topsy-turvy, and proclaims in the *People's Messenger* that barn-door hens and gutter mongrels are precisely the finest specimens in the menagerie. But that's always the way, so long as you haven't worked the commonness out of your system, and fought your way up to spiritual distinction.

HOVSTAD. I make no pretensions to any sort of distinction. I come of simple peasant stock, and I'm proud that my root lies deep down among the common people, who are now being jeered at.

SEVERAL WORKMEN. Hurrah for Hovstad! Hurrah! hurrah!

DR. STOCKMANN. The sort of common people I'm speaking of are not found among the lower classes alone; they crawl and swarm all around us—up to the very summits of society. Just look at your own smug, respectable Burgomaster! Why, my brother Peter belongs as clearly to the common people as any man that walks on two legs——

(*Laughter and hisses.*)

BURGOMASTER. I protest against such personalities.

DR. STOCKMANN (*imperturbably*). ——and that not because, like myself, he's descended from a good-for-nothing old pirate from Pomerania, or thereabouts—for that's our ancestry——

BURGOMASTER. An absurd tradition! Utterly groundless.

DR. STOCKMANN. ——but he is so because he thinks the thoughts and holds the opinions of his official superiors. Men who do that belong, intellectually-speaking, to the mob; and that's why my distinguished brother Peter is at bottom so undistinguished,—and consequently so illiberal.

BURGOMASTER. Mr. Chairman——

HOVSTAD. So that the distinguished people in this country are the liberals? That's quite a new light on the subject. (*Laughter.*)

DR. STOCKMANN. Yes, that's part of my new discovery. And this, too, follows, that liberality of thought is almost precisely the same thing as morality. Therefore I say it's altogether unpardonable of the *Messenger* to proclaim day after day the false doctrine that it's the masses, the multitude, the compact majority, that monopolise liberality and morality,—and that vice and corruption and all sorts of spiritual uncleanness ooze out of culture, as all that filth oozes down to the Baths from the Mill Dale tan-works! (*Noise and interruptions.* DR. STOCKMANN *goes on imperturbably, smiling in his eagerness.*) And yet this same *Messenger* can preach about raising the masses and the multitude to a higher level of life! Why, deuce take it, if the *Messenger's* own doctrine holds good, the elevation of the masses would simply mean hurling them into destruction! But, happily, it's only an old traditional lie that culture demoralises. No, it's stupidity, poverty, the ugliness of life, that do the devil's work! In a house that isn't aired and swept every day—my wife Katrine maintains that the floors ought to be scrubbed too, but we can't discuss that now;—well,—in such a house, I say, within two or three years, people lose the power of thinking or acting morally. Lack of oxygen enervates the conscience. And there seems to be precious little oxygen in many and many a house in this town, since the whole compact majority is unscrupulous enough to want to found its future upon a quagmire of lies and fraud.

ASLAKSEN. I cannot allow so gross an insult to be levelled against the whole body of citizens.

A GENTLEMAN. I move that the Chairman order the speaker to sit down.

EAGER VOICES. Yes, yes, that's right! Sit down! Sit down!

DR. STOCKMANN (*flaring up*). Then I'll proclaim the truth at every street corner! I'll write to newspapers in other towns! The whole land shall know how things go on here!

HOVSTAD. It would almost seem as if the Doctor wanted to ruin the town.

DR. STOCKMANN. Yes, I love my native town so well, I would rather ruin it than see it flourishing upon a lie.

ASLAKSEN. That's putting it strongly.

(*Noise and whistling.* MRS. STOCKMANN *coughs in vain; the* DOCTOR *no longer heeds her.*)

HOVSTAD (*shouting amid the tumult*). The man who would ruin a whole community must be an enemy to his fellow-citizens!

DR. STOCKMANN (*with growing excitement*). What does it matter if a lying community is ruined! It should be levelled to the ground, I say! All men who live upon lies should be exterminated like vermin! You'll poison the whole country in time; you'll bring it to such a pass that the whole country will deserve to perish. And if it ever comes to that, I shall say, from the bottom of my heart: Perish the country! Perish all its people!

A MAN (*in the crowd*). Why, he talks like a regular enemy of the people!

BILLING. Strike me dead but there spoke the people's voice!

THE WHOLE ASSEMBLY (*shouting*). Yes! yes! yes! He's an enemy of the people! He hates his country! He hates the people!

ASLAKSEN. Both as a citizen of this town and as a man, I am deeply shocked at what I have here had to listen to. Dr. Stockmann has unmasked himself in a manner I should never have dreamt of. I am reluctantly forced to subscribe to the opinion just expressed by some worthy citizens; and I think we ought to formulate this opinion in a resolution. I therefore beg to move, "That this meeting declares the medical officer of the Baths, Dr. Thomas Stockmann, to be an enemy of the people."

(*Thunders of applause and cheers. Many form a circle round the* DOCTOR *and hoot at him.* MRS. STOCKMANN *and* PETRA *have risen.* MORTEN *and* EILIF *fight the other school-boys, who have also been hooting. Some grown-up persons separate them.*)

DR. STOCKMANN (*to the people hooting*). Ah! fools that you are! I tell you that——

ASLAKSEN (*ringing*). The Doctor is out of order in speaking. A formal vote must be taken; but out of consideration for personal feelings, it will be taken in writing and without names. Have you any blank paper, Mr. Billing?

BILLING. Here's both blue and white paper——

ASLAKSEN. That'll do; we can manage more

quickly this way. Tear it up. That's it. (*To the meeting.*) Blue means no, white means yes. I myself will go round and collect the votes.

(*The* BURGOMASTER *leaves the room.* ASLAKSEN *and a few others go round with pieces of paper in hats.*)

A GENTLEMAN (*to* HOVSTAD). What can be the matter with the Doctor? What does it all mean?

HOVSTAD. Why, you know how irrepressible he is.

ANOTHER GENTLEMAN (*to* BILLING). I say, you're often at his house. Have you ever noticed if the fellow drinks?

BILLING. Strike me dead if I know what to say. Toddy's always on the table when any one looks in.

A THIRD GENTLEMAN. No, I should rather say he was subject to fits of insanity.

FIRST GENTLEMAN. I wonder if madness runs in the family?

BILLING. I shouldn't be surprised.

A FOURTH GENTLEMAN. No, it's pure malice. He wants to be revenged for something.

BILLING. He was certainly talking about a rise in his salary the other day; but he didn't get it.

ALL THE GENTLEMEN (*together*). Ah! that explains everything.

THE DRUNKEN MAN (*in the crowd*). I want a blue one, I do! And I'll have a white one too!

SEVERAL PEOPLE. There's the tipsy man again! Turn him out!

MORTEN KIIL (*approaching the* DOCTOR). Well, Stockmann, you see now what this tomfoolery leads to!

DR. STOCKMANN. I've done my duty.

MORTEN KIIL. What was that you said about the Mill Dale tanneries?

DR. STOCKMANN. Why, you heard what I said—that all the filth comes from them.

MORTEN KIIL. From my tannery as well?

DR. STOCKMANN. Unfortunately, yours is about the worst of all.

MORTEN KIIL. Are you going to put that into the papers too?

DR. STOCKMANN. I can't keep anything back.

MORTEN KIIL. That may cost you dear, Stockmann!

(*He goes out.*)

A FAT GENTLEMAN (*goes up to* HORSTER, *without bowing to the ladies*). Well, Captain, so you lend your house to enemies of the people?

HORSTER. I suppose I can do as I please with my own, Sir.

THE GENTLEMAN. Then of course you can have no objection if I follow your example?

HORSTER. What do you mean, Sir?

THE GENTLEMAN. You shall hear from me to-morrow.

(*Turns away and goes out.*)

PETRA. Wasn't that the owner of your ship?

HORSTER. Yes, that was Mr. Vik.

ASLAKSEN (*with the voting papers in his hands, ascends the platform and rings*). Gentlemen! I have now to announce the result of the vote. All, with one exception——

A YOUNG GENTLEMAN. That's the tipsy man!

ASLAKSEN. With the exception of one intoxicated person, this meeting of citizens declares the medical officer of the Baths, Dr. Thomas Stockmann, to be an enemy of the people. (*Cheers and applause.*) Three cheers for our fine old municipality! (*Cheers.*) Three cheers for our able and energetic Burgomaster, who has so loyally put aside the claims of kindred! (*Cheers.*) The meeting is dissolved. (*He descends.*)

BILLING. Three cheers for the Chairman!

ALL. Hurrah for Aslaksen!

DR. STOCKMANN. My hat and coat, Petra! Captain, have you room for passengers to the new world?

HORSTER. For you and yours, Doctor, we'll make room.

DR. STOCKMANN (*while* PETRA *helps him on with his coat*). Good! Come, Katrine! come, boys!

(*He gives his wife his arm.*)

MRS. STOCKMANN (*in a low voice*). Dear Thomas, let us go out by the back way.

DR. STOCKMANN. No back ways, Katrine! (*In a loud voice.*) You shall hear from the enemy of the people before he shakes the dust from his feet! I'm not so good-natured as a certain person; I don't say: I forgive you, for you know not what you do.

ASLAKSEN (*shouts*). That is a blasphemous comparison, Dr. Stockmann!

BILLING. Strike me—— That's more than a serious man can stand!

A COARSE VOICE. And he threatens us into the bargain!

ANGRY CRIES. Let's smash his windows! Duck him in the fiord!

A MAN (*in the crowd*). Blow your horn, Evensen! Blow man, blow!

(*Horn-blowing, whistling, and wild shouting. The* DOCTOR, *with his family, goes towards the door.* HORSTER *clears the way for them.*)

ALL (*shouting after them as they go out*). Enemy of the people! Enemy of the people! Enemy of the people!

BILLING. Strike me dead if I'd care to drink toddy at Stockmann's to-night.

(*The people throng towards the door; the noise passes gradually farther away; from the street are heard cries of "Enemy of the people! Enemy of the people!"*)

Act Fifth.

(DR. STOCKMANN'S *Study. Bookshelves and glass cases with various collections along the walls. In the back, a door leading to the anteroom; in front, on the left, a door to the sitting-room. In the wall to the right are two windows, all the panes of which are smashed. In the middle of the room is the* DOCTOR'S *writing-table, covered with books and papers. The room is in disorder. It is forenoon.*)

(DR. STOCKMANN, *in dressing-gown, slippers, and skull-cap, is bending down and raking with an umbrella under one of the cabinets; at last he rakes out a stone.*)

DR. STOCKMANN (*speaking through the sitting-room doorway*). Katrine, I've found another!

MRS. STOCKMANN (*in the sitting-room*). Oh, you'll find plenty more.

DR. STOCKMANN (*placing the stone on a pile of others on the table*). I shall keep these stones as sacred relics. Eilif and Morten shall see them every day, and when I die they shall be heirlooms. (*Poking under the bookcase.*) Hasn't—what the devil is her name?—the girl—hasn't she been for the glazier yet?

MRS. STOCKMANN (*coming in*). Yes, but he said he didn't know whether he'd be able to come to-day.

DR. STOCKMANN. You'll see he daren't come.

MRS. STOCKMANN. Well, Randine had an idea he was afraid to come, because of the neighbours.

(*Speaks through the sitting-room doorway.*) What is it, Randine?—All right. (*Goes out and returns immediately.*) Here's a letter for you, Thomas.

DR. STOCKMANN. Let's see. (*Opens the letter and reads.*) Aha!

MRS. STOCKMANN. Who's it from?

DR. STOCKMANN. From the landlord. He gives us notice.

MRS. STOCKMANN. Is it possible? Such a nice man as that——

DR. STOCKMANN (*looking at the letter*). He daren't do otherwise, he says. He's very loath to do it; but he daren't do otherwise—on account of his fellow-citizens—out of respect for public opinion—is in a dependent position—doesn't dare to offend certain influential men——

MRS. STOCKMANN. There, you see, Thomas.

DR. STOCKMANN. Yes yes, I see well enough; they're all cowards, every one of them, in this town; no one dares do anything for fear of all the rest. (*Throws the letter on the table.*) But it's all the same to us, Katrine. We'll be off to the new world, and then——

MRS. STOCKMANN. But are you sure this idea of going abroad is altogether wise, Thomas?

DR. STOCKMANN. Would you have me stay here where they have pilloried me as an enemy of the people, branded me, smashed my windows! And look here, Katrine, they've torn a hole in my black trousers.

MRS. STOCKMANN. Oh dear. and they're your best too!

DR. STOCKMANN. One should never put on his best trousers to go out to battle for freedom and truth. Of course, I don't care much about the trousers; you can always patch them up for me. But that the mob should dare to attack me as if they were my equals—*that's* what I can't stomach, for the life of me.

MRS. STOCKMANN. Yes, they've behaved abominably to you here, Thomas; but is that any reason for leaving the country altogether?

DR. STOCKMANN. Do you think the plebeians aren't just as insolent in other towns? Oh yes, they are, my dear; they're pretty much of a muchness everywhere. Well, never mind, let the curs snap; *that's* not the worst; the worst is that every one, all over the country, is the slave of his party. Not that I suppose—very likely it's no better in the free West either; the compact majority, and enlightened public opinion, and all the other devil's trash is rampant there too. But you see the conditions are larger there than here; they may kill you, but they don't slow-torture you; they don't put the screw on a free soul there, as they do at home here. And then, if need be, you can hold aloof from it all. (*Walks up and down.*) If I only knew of any primeval forest, or a little South Sea island to be sold cheap——

MRS. STOCKMANN. Yes, but the boys, Thomas.

DR. STOCKMANN (*comes to a standstill*). What an extraordinary woman you are, Katrine! Would you prefer the boys to grow up in such a society as ours? Why, you saw yourself yesterday evening that one-half of the population is stark mad, and if the other half hasn't lost its reason, that's only because they're hounds who haven't any reason to lose.

MRS. STOCKMANN. But really, my dear Thomas, you do say such imprudent things!

DR. STOCKMANN. Well, but isn't it the truth that I tell them? Don't they turn all ideas upside down? Don't they stir up right and wrong in one hotch-potch? Don't they call lies what I know to be truth? But the maddest thing of all is to see crowds of grown men, calling themselves Liberals, go about persuading themselves and others that they are friends of freedom! Did you ever hear anything like it, Katrine?

MRS. STOCKMANN. Yes, yes, no doubt it's all wrong together. But—— (PETRA *enters from the sitting-room.*) Back from school already?

PETRA. Yes; I've been dismissed.

MRS. STOCKMANN. Dismissed?

DR. STOCKMANN. You too!

PETRA. Mrs. Busk gave me notice, and so I thought it best to leave there and then.

DR. STOCKMANN. Quite right, my girl!

MRS. STOCKMANN. Who could have thought Mrs. Busk was such a bad woman?

PETRA. Oh mother, Mrs. Busk isn't bad at all; I saw clearly how much it pained her. But she didn't dare to do otherwise, she said; and so I'm dismissed.

DR. STOCKMANN (*laughing and rubbing his hands*). She dared not do otherwise. Just like the rest! Oh, it's delicious.

MRS. STOCKMANN. Oh well, after that frightful uproar last night——

PETRA. It wasn't only that. What do you think, father——?

DR. STOCKMANN. Well?

PETRA. Mrs. Busk showed me no fewer than three letters she had received this morning——

DR. STOCKMANN. Anonymous, of course?

PETRA. Yes.

DR. STOCKMANN. They've never the courage to give their names, Katrine——!

PETRA. And two of them stated that a gentleman who is often at our house said at the club last night that I held extremely advanced opinions upon various things——

DR. STOCKMANN. Of course you didn't deny it.

PETRA. Of course not. You know Mrs. Busk herself is pretty advanced in her opinions when we're alone together; but now that this has come out about me she dared not keep me on.

MRS. STOCKMANN. Some one that's often at our house, too! There, you see, Thomas, what comes of all your hospitality.

DR. STOCKMANN. We won't live any longer in such a pig-stye! Pack up as quickly as you can, Katrine; let's get away—the sooner the better.

MRS. STOCKMANN. Hush! I think there's some one in the passage. Just see, Petra.

PETRA (*opening the door*). Ah! is it you, Captain Horster? Please come in.

HORSTER (*from the anteroom*). Good morning. I thought I must just look in and see how you're getting on.

DR. STOCKMANN (*shaking his hand*). Thanks; that's very good of you.

MRS. STOCKMANN. And thanks for your escort home last night, Captain Horster.

PETRA. How did you ever get back again?

HORSTER. Oh, that was all right. You know I'm pretty strong, and those fellows' bark is worse than their bite.

DR. STOCKMANN. Isn't it marvellous, this piggish cowardice? Come here, I want to show you something! Look, here are all the stones they threw in at us. Only look at them! Upon my soul there aren't more than two decent-sized lumps in the whole heap; the rest are nothing but pebbles—mere gravel. They stood down there, and yelled, and swore they'd do me an injury;—but as for really doing it—no, there's mighty little fear of that in this town!

HORSTER. You may thank your stars for that this time, anyhow, Doctor.

DR. STOCKMANN. So I do, of course. But it's depressing all the same; for if it ever came to a serious national struggle, you'd see that public opinion would be for taking to its heels, and the compact majority would scamper for their lives like a flock of sheep, Captain Horster. That's what's so sad to think of; it grieves me to the heart.—But deuce take it—it's foolish of me to feel anything of the sort! They've called me an enemy of the people; well then, I'll *be* an enemy of the people!

MRS. STOCKMANN. That you'll never be, Thomas.

DR. STOCKMANN. You'd better not take your oath of it, Katrine. A bad name may act like a pin-scratch in the lung. And that confounded word—I can't get rid of it; it has sunk deep into my heart—and there it lies gnawing and sucking like an acid. And no magnesia can cure me.

PETRA. Pshaw! You should only laugh at them, father.

HORSTER. People will think differently yet, Doctor.

MRS. STOCKMANN. Yes, Thomas, that's as certain as that you're standing here.

DR. STOCKMANN. Yes, perhaps, when it's too late. Well, as they make their bed so they must lie! Let them go on wallowing here in the mire, and learn to repent having driven a patriot into exile. When do you sail, Captain Horster?

HORSTER. Hm—that's really what I came to speak to you about——

DR. STOCKMANN. Has anything gone wrong with the ship?

HORSTER. No; but the fact is, I'm not going with it.

PETRA. Surely you've not been dismissed?

HORSTER (*smiling*). Yes, I have.

PETRA. You too!

MRS. STOCKMANN. There, you see, Thomas.

DR. STOCKMANN. And for the truth's sake! Oh, if I could possibly have imagined such a thing——

HORSTER. You mustn't take it to heart; I shall soon get a berth with some other company, elsewhere.

DR. STOCKMANN. And this is Mr. Vik! A wealthy man, independent of any one! Good heavens——!

HORSTER. Oh, for that matter, he's a very well-meaning man; and he says himself he would gladly have kept me on if only he dared.

DR. STOCKMANN. But he didn't dare—of course not!

HORSTER. It isn't easy, he says, when you belong to a party——

DR. STOCKMANN. My gentleman has hit it there! A party is like a sausage-machine; it grinds all the brains together in one mash; and that's why we see nothing but porridge-heads and pulp-heads all around!

MRS. STOCKMANN. Now really, Thomas!

PETRA (*to* HORSTER). If only you hadn't seen us home, perhaps it wouldn't have come to this.

HORSTER. I don't regret it.

PETRA (*gives him her hand*). Thank you for that!

HORSTER (*to* DR. STOCKMANN). What I wanted to say to you was this: if you're really determined to go abroad, I've thought of another way——

DR. STOCKMANN. That's good—if only we can get off——

MRS. STOCKMANN. Hush! Isn't that a knock?

PETRA. I'm sure that's uncle.

DR. STOCKMANN. Aha! (*Calls.*) Come in.

MRS. STOCKMANN. My dear Thomas, now do for once promise me——

(*The* BURGOMASTER *enters from the anteroom*).

BURGOMASTER (*in the doorway*). Oh! you're engaged. Then I'd better——

DR. STOCKMANN. No no; come in.

BURGOMASTER. But I wanted to speak with you alone.

MRS. STOCKMANN. We'll go into the sitting-room.

HORSTER. And I'll look in again presently.

DR. STOCKMANN. No no; go with the ladies, Captain Horster; I must have further information——

HORSTER. All right, then I'll wait.

(*He follows* MRS. STOCKMANN *and* PETRA *into the sitting-room. The* BURGOMASTER *says nothing, but casts glances at the windows.*)

DR. STOCKMANN. Perhaps you find it rather draughty here to-day? Put on your cap.

BURGOMASTER. Thanks, if I may (*does so*). I fancy I caught cold yesterday evening. I stood there shivering—

DR. STOCKMANN. Really? On my soul, I found it quite warm enough.

BURGOMASTER. I regret that it was not in my power to prevent these nocturnal excesses.

DR. STOCKMANN. Have you anything else in particular to say to me?

BURGOMASTER (*producing a large letter*). I have this document for you from the Directors of the Baths.

DR. STOCKMANN. I'm dismissed?

BURGOMASTER. Yes; from to-day. (*Places the letter on the table.*) We're very sorry—but, frankly, we dared not do otherwise on account of public opinion.

DR. STOCKMANN (*smiling*). Dared not? I've heard that phrase already to-day.

BURGOMASTER. I beg you to realise your position clearly. For the future, you can't count upon any sort of practice in the town.

DR. STOCKMANN. Deuce take the practice! But how can you be so sure of that?

BURGOMASTER. The Householders' Association is sending round a circular from house to house, in which all well-disposed citizens are called upon not to employ you; and I dare swear that not a single father of a family will venture to refuse his signature; he simply *dare* not.

DR. STOCKMANN. Well well; I don't doubt that. But what then?

BURGOMASTER. If I might advise you, I should say—leave the town for a time.

DR. STOCKMANN. Yes, I've been thinking of leaving the town.

BURGOMASTER. Good. And when six months or so have elapsed, if, after mature deliberation, you could make up your mind to acknowledge your error, with a few words of regret——

DR. STOCKMANN. I might perhaps be reinstated, you think?

BURGOMASTER. Perhaps; it's not quite out of the question.

DR. STOCKMANN. Yes, but how about public opinion? You daren't, on account of public opinion.

BURGOMASTER. Opinion is extremely variable. And, to speak candidly, it's of the greatest importance for us to have such an admission under your own hand.

DR. STOCKMANN. Then you may whistle for it! Surely you remember what I've said to you before about such foxes' tricks!

BURGOMASTER. At that time your position was infinitely more favourable; at that time you thought you had the whole town at your back——

DR. STOCKMANN. Yes, and now I've the whole town *on* my back—— (*Flaring up.*) But no—not if I had the devil and his dam on my back—never—never, I tell you!

BURGOMASTER. The father of a family has no right[1] to act as you are doing; you have no right to, Thomas.

DR. STOCKMANN. I have no right! There's only one thing in the world that a free man has no right to do; and do you know what that is?

BURGOMASTER. No.

DR. STOCKMANN. Of course not; but I'll tell you. A free man has no right to wallow in filth like a cur; he has no right to act so that he ought to spit in his own face.

BURGOMASTER. That sounds extremely plausible; and if there were not another explanation of your obstinacy—but we all know there is——

DR. STOCKMANN. What do you mean by that?

BURGOMASTER. You understand well enough. But as your brother, and as a man of common sense, I warn you not to build too confidently upon prospects and expectations that may very likely come to nothing.

[1] "Has no right" represents the Norwegian "tör ikke"—the phrase which, elsewhere in this scene, is translated "dare not." The latter rendering should perhaps have been adhered to throughout; but in this passage the Norwegian words convey a shade of meaning which is best represented by "has no right."—W. A.

DR. STOCKMANN. Why, what on earth are you driving at?

BURGOMASTER. Do you really want me to believe that you're ignorant of the terms of old Morten Kiil's will?

DR. STOCKMANN. I know that the little he has is to go to a home for old and needy artizans. But what's that got to do with me?

BURGOMASTER. To begin with, "the little he has" is no trifle. Morten Kiil is a tolerably wealthy man.

DR. STOCKMANN. I've never had the least notion of that——!

BURGOMASTER. Hm! Really? Then I suppose you had no notion that a not inconsiderable part of his fortune is to go to your children, you and your wife having a life-interest in it. Hasn't he told you that?

DR. STOCKMANN. No, on my soul! On the contrary, he's done nothing but grumble to me because he was so preposterously over-taxed. But are you really sure of this, Peter?

BURGOMASTER. I have it from a thoroughly trustworthy source.

DR. STOCKMANN. Why, good heavens, then Katrine's safe!—and the children too! Oh! I must tell her—— (*Calls.*) Katrine, Katrine!

BURGOMASTER (*holding him back*). Hush! don't say anything about it yet.

MRS. STOCKMANN (*opening the door*). What is it?

DR. STOCKMANN. Nothing, my dear; go in again. (MRS. STOCKMANN *closes the door. He walks up and down.*) Provided for! Only think—all of them provided for! And for life! After all it's a blessed feeling to know that you're secure!

BURGOMASTER. Yes, but that's just what you're not. Morten Kiil can revoke his will any day or hour he chooses.

DR. STOCKMANN. But he won't, my good Peter. The Badger is only too delighted to see me attack you and your wiseacre friends.

BURGOMASTER (*starts and looks searchingly at him*). Aha! that throws a new light on a good many things.

DR. STOCKMANN. What things?

BURGOMASTER. So the whole affair has been a carefully concocted intrigue. Your recklessly violent onslaught—in the name of truth—upon the leading men of the town——

DR. STOCKMANN. Well, what of it?

BURGOMASTER. It was nothing but a preconcerted return for that vindictive old Morten Kiil's will.

DR. STOCKMANN (*almost speechless*). Peter—you're the most abominable plebeian I've ever known in my life.

BURGOMASTER. All is over between us. Your dismissal is irrevocable—for now we have a weapon against you.

(*He goes out.*)

DR. STOCKMANN. Shame! shame! shame! (*Calls.*) Katrine! The floor must be scrubbed after him! Tell her to come here with a pail—what's her name? confound it—the girl with the sooty nose——

MRS. STOCKMANN (*in the sitting-room doorway*). Hush, hush! Thomas!

PETRA (*also in the doorway*). Father, here's grandfather; he wants to know if he can speak to you alone.

DR. STOCKMANN. Yes, of course he can. (*By the door.*) Come in, father-in-law. (MORTEN KIIL *enters.* DR. STOCKMANN *closes the door behind him.*) Well, what is it? Sit down.

MORTEN KIIL. I won't sit down. (*Looking about him.*) It looks cheerful here to-day, Stockmann.

DR. STOCKMANN. Yes, doesn't it?

MORTEN KIIL. Sure enough it does; and you've plenty of fresh air too; you've surely got enough of that oxygen you were talking about yesterday. You must have an awfully good conscience to-day, I should think.

DR. STOCKMANN. Yes, I have.

MORTEN KIIL. So I should suppose. (*Tapping himself on the breast.*) But do you know what I've got here?

DR. STOCKMANN. A good conscience too, I hope.

MORTEN KIIL. Pshaw! No; something far better than that.

(*Takes out a large pocket-book, opens it, and shows* STOCKMANN *a bundle of papers.*)

DR. STOCKMANN (*looking at him in astonishment*). Shares in the Baths!

MORTEN KIIL. They weren't difficult to get to-day.

DR. STOCKMANN. And you've gone and bought these up——?

MORTEN KIIL. All I could possibly pay for.

DR. STOCKMANN. Why, my dear sir,—just when the Baths are in such a desperate condition——

MORTEN KIIL. If you behave like a reasonable creature, the Baths will soon be all right again.

DR. STOCKMANN. Well, you can see for yourself I'm doing all I can. But the people of this town are mad!

MORTEN KIIL. You said yesterday that the worst filth came from my tannery. Now, if that's true, then my grandfather, and my father before me, and I myself, have for ever so many years been poisoning the town, like three destroying angels. Do you think I'll sit quiet under such a reproach?

DR. STOCKMANN. Unfortunately, you can't help it.

MORTEN KIIL. No, thanks. I mean to stand up for my good name. I've heard that people call me "the Badger." Well, a badger's a sort of pig, I know; but I want to give them the lie. I will live and die a clean man.

DR. STOCKMANN. And how will you manage *that?*

MORTEN KIIL. You shall make me clean, Stockmann.

DR. STOCKMANN. I!

MORTEN KIIL. Do you know with what money I've bought these shares? No, you can't know; but now I'll tell you. It's the money Katrine and Petra and the boys are to have after my death. For, you see, I've laid by something after all.

DR. STOCKMANN (*flaring up*). And you've taken Katrine's money for this!

MORTEN KIIL. Yes; the whole of it is invested in the Baths now. And now I want to see if you're really stark, staring mad, Stockmann. If you go on making out that these beasts and other filthy things dribble down from my tannery, it'll be just as if you were to flay broad stripes of Katrine's skin—and Petra's too, and the boys. No decent father would ever do that—unless he were a madman.

DR. STOCKMANN (*walking up and down*). Yes, but I *am* a madman; I *am* a madman!

MORTEN KIIL. You surely can't be so raving mad where your wife and children are concerned.

DR. STOCKMANN (*stopping in front of him*). Why couldn't you have spoken to me before you went and bought all that rubbish?

MORTEN KIIL. What's done can't be undone.

DR. STOCKMANN (*walking restlessly about*). If only I weren't so certain about the affair——! But I'm absolutely convinced that I'm right!

MORTEN KIIL (*weighing the pocket-book in his hand*). If you stick to this madness, these aren't worth much.

(*Puts the book into his pocket.*)

DR. STOCKMANN. But, deuce take it! surely science must be able to find some antidote, some sort of prophylactic——

MORTEN KIIL. Do you mean something to kill the animals?

DR. STOCKMANN. Yes, or at least to make them harmless.

MORTEN KIIL. Can't you try rat's-bane?

DR. STOCKMANN. Oh, nonsense, nonsense!—But since every one declares it's nothing but fancy, why fancy let it be! Let them have their own way!

Haven't the ignorant, narrow-hearted curs reviled me as an enemy of the people?—and weren't they on the point of tearing the clothes off my back?

MORTEN KIIL. And they've smashed all your windows for you too!

DR. STOCKMANN. Then, too, one's duty to one's family! I must talk it over with Katrine; her judgment is so sound in matters of this sort.

MORTEN KIIL. That's right! You just follow the advice of a sensible woman.

DR. STOCKMANN (*going at him angrily*). How could you act so preposterously! Staking Katrine's money and getting me into this horrible dilemma! When I look at you, I seem to see the devil himself——!

MORTEN KIIL. Then I'd better be off. But I must hear from you, yes or no, by two o'clock. If it's *no*, all the shares go to the Charity—and that this very day.

DR. STOCKMANN. And what does Katrine get?

MORTEN KIIL. Not a rap. (*The door of the anteroom opens.* HOVSTAD *and* ASLAKSEN *are seen outside it.*) Hullo! look at these two.

DR. STOCKMANN (*staring at them*). What! They actually dare to come here!

HOVSTAD. Why, of course we do.

ASLAKSEN. You see, we've something to say to you.

MORTEN KIIL (*whispers*). Yes or no—by two o'clock.

ASLAKSEN (*with a glance at* HOVSTAD). Aha!

(MORTEN KIIL *goes out.*)

DR. STOCKMANN. Well, what do you want with me? Be brief.

HOVSTAD. I can well understand that you resent our conduct at the meeting yesterday——

DR. STOCKMANN. Your conduct, you say! Yes, it was pretty conduct! I call it misconduct—old-womanish cowardice. Shame upon you!

HOVSTAD. Call it what you will; but we *could* not act otherwise.

DR. STOCKMANN. You *dared* not, I suppose? Isn't that so?

HOVSTAD. Yes, if you like to put it that way.

ASLAKSEN. But why didn't you let us into the secret beforehand? Just the merest hint to Mr. Hovstad or to me?

DR. STOCKMANN. A hint? What about?

ASLAKSEN. About what was at the bottom of it.

DR. STOCKMANN. I don't in the least understand you.

ASLAKSEN (*nods confidentially*). Oh yes, you do, Dr. Stockmann.

HOVSTAD. It's no good making a mystery of it any longer.

DR. STOCKMANN (*looking from one to the other*). Why, what in the devil's name——!

ASLAKSEN. May I ask—isn't your father-in-law going about the town buying up all the shares in the Baths?

DR. STOCKMANN. Yes, he's been buying shares in the Baths to-day; but——

ASLAKSEN. It would have been more prudent to

let somebody else do that—some one not so closely connected with you.

HOVSTAD. And then you oughtn't to have appeared in the matter under your own name. No one need have known that the attack on the Baths came from you. You should have taken me into your counsels, Dr. Stockmann.

DR. STOCKMANN (*stares straight in front of him; a light seems to break in upon him, and he looks thunder-struck*). Is this possible? Can such things be?

ASLAKSEN (*smiling*). It's plain enough that they can. But they ought to be managed delicately, you understand.

HOVSTAD. And there ought to be other people in it; for the responsibility always falls more lightly when there are several to share it.

DR. STOCKMANN (*calmly*). In one word, gentlemen, what is it you want?

ASLAKSEN. Mr. Hovstad can best——

HOVSTAD. No, you explain, Aslaksen.

ASLAKSEN. Well, it's this: now that we know how the matter really stands, we believe we can venture to place the *People's Messenger* at your disposal.

DR. STOCKMANN. You can venture to now, eh? But how about public opinion? Aren't you afraid of bringing down a storm upon us?

HOVSTAD. We must manage to ride out the storm.

ASLAKSEN. And you must keep all your wits about you, Doctor. As soon as your attack has produced its effect——

DR. STOCKMANN. As soon as my father-in-law

and I have bought up the shares at a discount, you mean——?

HOVSTAD. No doubt it's mainly on scientific grounds that you want to take the management of the Baths into your own hands.

DR. STOCKMANN. Of course; it was on scientific grounds that I set the old Badger to work. And then we'll tinker up the water-works a little, and potter about a bit down at the beach, without its costing the town sixpence. Don't you think that'll do, eh?

HOVSTAD. I think so—if you have the *Messenger* to back you up.

ASLAKSEN. In a free society the press is a power, Doctor.

DR. STOCKMANN. Yes indeed, and so is public opinion; and you, Mr. Aslaksen—I suppose you'll be answerable for the Householders' Association?

ASLAKSEN. Both for the Householders' Association and the Temperance Society. You may rely upon that.

DR. STOCKMANN. But gentlemen—really I'm quite ashamed to mention such a thing—but—what return——?

HOVSTAD. Of course, we should prefer to give you our support for nothing. But the *Messenger* is not very firmly established; it's not getting on as it ought to; and I should be very sorry to have to stop the paper just now, when there's so much to be done in general politics.

DR. STOCKMANN. Naturally; that would be very hard for a friend of the people like you. (*Flaring up.*) But I—I am an enemy of the people!

(*Striding about the room.*) Where's my stick? Where the devil's my stick?

HOVSTAD. What do you mean?

ASLAKSEN. Surely you don't mean to——

DR. STOCKMANN (*standing still*). And suppose I don't give you a single farthing out of all my shares? You must remember we rich folk don't like parting with our money.

HOVSTAD. And *you* must remember that this business of the shares can be represented in two ways.

DR. STOCKMANN. Yes, you're the man for that; if I don't come to the rescue of the *Messenger*, you'll manage to put a vile complexion on the affair; you'll hunt me down, I suppose—bait me—try to throttle me as a dog throttles a hare.

HOVSTAD. That's a law of nature—every animal must fight for itself.

ASLAKSEN. And must take its food where it can find it, you know.

DR. STOCKMANN. Then see if you can't find some out in the gutter; (*striding about the room*) for now, by heaven! we'll see which is the strongest animal of us three. (*Finds his umbrella and brandishes it.*) Now, look here——!

HOVSTAD. You surely don't mean to assault us!

ASLAKSEN. I say, take care of that umbrella!

DR. STOCKMANN. Out at the window with you, Mr. Hovstad!

HOVSTAD (*by the anteroom door*). Are you quite mad?

DR. STOCKMANN. Out at the window, Mr. Aslaksen! Jump, I tell you! Be quick about it!

ASLAKSEN (*running round the writing-table*). Moderation, Doctor; I'm delicate; I can't stand much. (*Screams.*) Help! help!

(MRS. STOCKMANN, PETRA, *and* HORSTER *enter from sitting-room.*)

MRS. STOCKMANN. Good heavens, Thomas! what ever is the matter?

DR. STOCKMANN (*brandishing the umbrella*). Jump, I tell you! Out into the gutter!

HOVSTAD. An unprovoked assault! I call you to witness, Captain Horster.

(*Rushes off through the anteroom.*)

ASLAKSEN (*bewildered*). If one only knew the local situation——!

(*He slinks out by the sitting-room door.*)

MRS. STOCKMANN (*holding back the* DOCTOR). Now, do restrain yourself, Thomas!

DR. STOCKMANN (*throwing down the umbrella*). On my soul, they've got off after all.

MRS. STOCKMANN. But what did they want with you?

DR. STOCKMANN. I'll tell you afterwards; I've other things to think of now. (*Goes to the table and writes on a visiting-card.*) Look here, Katrine, what's written here?

MRS. STOCKMANN. Three big *Noes;* what does that mean?

DR. STOCKMANN. That I'll tell you afterwards, too. (*Handing the card.*) There, Petra; let the girl run to the Badger's with this as fast as she can. Be quick!

(PETRA *goes out through the anteroom with the card.*)

DR. STOCKMANN. Well, if I haven't had visits to-day from all the emissaries of the devil! But now I'll sharpen my pen against them till it becomes a goad; I'll dip it in gall and venom; I'll hurl my ink-stand straight at their skulls.

MRS. STOCKMANN. Yes, but aren't we going away, Thomas?

(PETRA *returns.*)

DR. STOCKMANN. Well!

PETRA. All right.

DR. STOCKMANN. Good. Going away, do you say? No, I'll be damned if we do; we stay where we are, Katrine.

PETRA. Stay!

MRS. STOCKMANN. Here in the town?

DR. STOCKMANN. Yes, here; the field of battle is here; here the fight must be fought; here I will conquer! As soon as my trousers are mended, I'll go out into the town and look after a house; we must have a roof over our heads for the winter.

HORSTER. That you can have with me.

DR. STOCKMANN. Can I?

HORSTER. Yes, indeed you can. I've room enough, and, besides, I'm hardly ever at home.

MRS. STOCKMANN. Oh, how kind of you, Horster.

PETRA. Thank you.

DR. STOCKMANN (*shaking his hand*). Thanks, thanks! So that's off my mind. And this very day I shall set to work in earnest. Ah! there's a rare lot to be done here, Katrine! It's a good thing I've all my time at my disposal now; for you know I've had notice from the Baths——

MRS. STOCKMANN (*sighing*). Oh yes, I was expecting that.

DR. STOCKMANN. ——And now they want to take away my practice as well. But let them! The poor I shall keep anyhow—those that can't pay; and, good Lord! it's they that need me most. But by heaven! I'll make them hear me; I'll preach to them in season and out of season, as it's written somewhere.

MRS. STOCKMANN. My dear Thomas, I think you've seen what good preaching does.

DR. STOCKMANN. You really are ridiculous, Katrine. Am I to let myself be beaten off the field by public opinion, and the compact majority, and such devilry? No, thank you. Besides, my point is so simple, so clear and straightforward. I only want to drive into the heads of these curs that the Liberals are the worst foes of free men; that party-programmes wring the necks of all young and vital truths; that considerations of expediency turn justice and morality upside down, until life is simply hideous. Come, Captain Horster, don't you think I shall be able to make the people understand *that?*

HORSTER. Maybe; I don't know much about these things myself.

DR. STOCKMANN. Well then—listen! It's the party-leaders that must be got rid of. For, you see, a party-leader is just like a wolf—like a starving wolf; he must devour a certain number of small animals a year, if he's to exist at all. Just look at Hovstad and Aslaksen! How many small animals they polish off; or else they mangle and maim them, so that they're fit for nothing else but to be householders and subscribers to the *People's Messenger.* (*Sits on the edge of the table.*) Just come here, Katrine; see how bravely the sun shines to-day! And how the blessed fresh spring air blows in upon me!

MRS. STOCKMANN. Yes, if only we could live on sunshine and spring air, Thomas!

DR. STOCKMANN. Well, you'll have to pinch and save where you can—and we'll get on all right. That's my least concern. Now what *does* trouble me is, that I don't see any man with enough independence and nobility of character to dare to take up my work after me.

PETRA. Oh! don't bother about that, father; you have time before you.—Why, see, there are the boys already.

(EILIF *and* MORTEN *enter from the sitting-room.*)

MRS. STOCKMANN. Have you had a holiday to-day?

MORTEN. No; but we had a fight with the other fellows in play-time——

EILIF. That's not true; it was the other fellows that fought us.

MORTEN. Yes, and then Mr. Rörlund said we'd better stop at home for a few days.

DR. STOCKMANN (*snapping his fingers and springing down from the table*). Now I have it, now I have it, on my soul! You shall never set foot in school again!

THE BOYS. Never go to school!

MRS. STOCKMANN. Why, Thomas——

DR. STOCKMANN. Never, I say. I'll teach you

myself—that's to say, I won't teach you any blessed thing——

MORTEN. Hurrah!

DR. STOCKMANN. —— ——but I'll try to make free, noble-minded men of you.—Look here, you'll have to help me, Petra.

PETRA. Yes father, you may be sure I will.

DR. STOCKMANN. And we'll have our school in the room where they reviled me as an enemy of the people. But we must have more pupils. I must have at least twelve boys to begin with.

MRS. STOCKMANN. You'll never get them in this town.

DR. STOCKMANN. We shall see! (*To the boys.*) Don't you know any street urchins—any regular ragamuffins——?

MORTEN. Yes father, I know lots!

DR. STOCKMANN. That's all right; bring me a few of them. I want to experiment with the street-curs for once; there are sometimes excellent heads among them.

MORTEN. But what are we to do when we've become free and noble-minded men?

DR. STOCKMANN. Drive all the wolves out to the far west, boys.

(EILIF *looks rather doubtful;* MORTEN *jumps about, shouting "Hurrah!"*)

MRS. STOCKMANN. If only the wolves don't drive you out, Thomas.

DR. STOCKMANN. Are you quite mad, Katrine! Drive *me* out! now that I'm the strongest man in the town!

MRS. STOCKMANN. The strongest—now?

DR. STOCKMANN. Yes, I venture to say this: that now I'm one of the strongest men upon earth.

MORTEN. I say, father!

DR. STOCKMANN (*in a subdued voice*). Hush! you mustn't speak about it yet; but I've made a great discovery.

MRS. STOCKMANN. What, again?

DR. STOCKMANN. Yes, certainly. (*Gathers them about him, and speaks confidentially.*) This is what I've discovered, you see: the strongest man upon earth is he who stands most alone.

MRS. STOCKMANN (*shakes her head, smiling*). Ah! Thomas——!

PETRA (*grasping his hands encouragingly*). Father!

THE WILD DUCK.

(1884.)

Characters.

WERLE, *a merchant, manufacturer, etc.*
GREGERS WERLE, *his son.*
OLD EKDAL.
HIALMAR EKDAL, *his son, a photographer.*
GINA EKDAL, *Hialmar's wife.*
HEDVIG, *their daughter, fourteen years old.*
MRS. SÖRBY, *Werle's housekeeper.*
RELLING, *a doctor.*
MOLVIK, *ex-student of theology.*
GRÅBERG, *Werle's bookkeeper.*
PETTERSEN, *Werle's servant.*
JENSEN, *a hired waiter.*
A FLABBY GENTLEMAN.
A THIN-HAIRED GENTLEMAN.
A SHORT-SIGHTED GENTLEMAN.
Six other gentlemen, dinner-guests at Werle's.
Several hired waiters.

The first act passes in Werle's house, the four following acts at Hialmar Ekdal's.

[PRONUNCIATION.—Gregers Werle = *Grayghers Verlĕ;* Hialmar Ekdal = *Yalmar Aykdal;* Gina = *Gheena;* Gråberg = *Groberg;* Jensen = *Yensen.*]

THE WILD DUCK.

PLAY IN FIVE ACTS.

Act First.

(*At* WERLE'S *house. A richly and comfortably furnished study; bookcases and upholstered furniture; a writing-table, with papers and documents, in the centre of the room; lighted lamps with green shades casting a dim light. In the background, open folding doors with curtains drawn back. Within is seen a large and elegant room brilliantly lighted with lamps and branching candlesticks. In front, on the right* (*in the study*), *a small baize door leads into* WERLE'S *office. On the left, in front, a fireplace with a glowing coal fire, and farther back a folding door leading into the dining-room.*)

(WERLE'S *servant*, PETTERSEN, *in livery, and* JENSEN, *the hired waiter, in black, are putting the study in order. In the large room, two or three other hired waiters are moving about arranging things and lighting more candles. From the dining-room, the hum of conversation and laughter of many voices are heard; a glass is tapped with a knife; silence follows, and a toast is proposed; shouts of "Bravo!" and then again a buzz of conversation.*)

PETTERSEN (*lights a lamp on the chimney-piece and sets a shade over it*). Just listen, Jensen; now the old man's on his legs proposing Mrs. Sörby's health in a long speech.

JENSEN (*pushing forward an arm-chair*). Is it true, what people say, that there's something between them?

PETTERSEN. Lord knows.

JENSEN. I'm told he's been a lively customer in his day.

PETTERSEN. May be.

JENSEN. It's in honour of his son that he's giving this dinner-party, they say.

PETTERSEN. Yes. His son came home yesterday.

JENSEN. I never knew till now that Mr. Werle *had* a son.

PETTERSEN. Oh yes, he has a son. But he's always up at the Höidal works. He's never once come to town all the years I've been in service here.

A WAITER (*in the doorway of the other room*). Pettersen, here's an old fellow wanting——

PETTERSEN (*mutters*). The devil—who's this now?

(OLD EKDAL *appears from the right, in the inner room. He is dressed in a threadbare overcoat with a high collar; he wears woollen mittens, and carries in his hand a stick and a fur cap. Under his arm, a brown paper parcel. Dirty red-brown wig and small grey moustache.*)

PETTERSEN (*goes towards him*). Good Lord—what do *you* want here?

EKDAL (*at the door*). Must get into the office, Pettersen.

PETTERSEN. The office was closed an hour ago, and——

EKDAL. So they told me at the door. But

Gråberg's in there still. Let me slip in this way, Pettersen; there's a good fellow. (*Points towards the baize door.*) I've been in this way before.

PETTERSEN. Well, you may pass. (*Opens the door.*) But mind you go out again the proper way, for we've got company.

EKDAL. I know—hm. Thanks, Pettersen, good old friend! Thanks! (*Mutters softly.*) Ass! (*He goes into the office;* PETTERSEN *shuts the door after him.*)

JENSEN. Is he one of the office people?

PETTERSEN. No, he's only an outsider that does odd jobs of copying. But he's been a gentleman in his time, has old Ekdal.

JENSEN. You can see he's been through a lot.

PETTERSEN. Yes; he was a lieutenant, you know.

JENSEN. The devil he was!

PETTERSEN. No mistake about it. But afterwards he went into the timber trade or something of that sort. They say he once played Mr. Werle a very nasty trick. They were in partnership at the Höidal works at the time. Oh, I know old Ekdal well, I do. Many's the glass of bitters and bottle of ale we two have drunk at Madam Eriksen's.

JENSEN. He can't have much to stand treat with.

PETTERSEN. Why, bless you, Jensen, it's me that stands treat. You see I always think one must be a bit civil to folks that have seen better days.

JENSEN. Did he go bankrupt then?

PETTERSEN. No, worse than that. He went to prison.

JENSEN. To prison!

PETTERSEN. Or perhaps it was the Penitentiary —(*listens*). Hush, they're leaving the table.

(*The dining-room door is thrown open from inside, by a couple of waiters.* MRS. SÖRBY *comes out conversing with two gentlemen. Gradually the whole company follows, amongst them* WERLE. *Last come* HIALMAR EKDAL *and* GREGERS WERLE.)

MRS. SÖRBY (*in passing, to the servant*). Pettersen, we'll have the coffee in the music-room.

PETTERSEN. Very well, Mrs. Sörby.

(*She goes with the two Gentlemen into the inner room, and thence out to the right.* PETTERSEN *and* JENSEN *go out the same way.*)

A FLABBY GENTLEMAN (*to a* THIN-HAIRED GENTLEMAN). Whew! What a dinner!—It was a stiff bit of work!

THE THIN-HAIRED GENTLEMAN. Oh, with a little good-will one can get through an astonishing lot in three hours.

THE FLABBY GENTLEMAN. Yes, but afterwards, afterwards, my dear Chamberlain!

A THIRD GENTLEMAN. I hear the coffee and maraschino are to be served in the music-room.

THE FLABBY GENTLEMAN. Bravo! Perhaps Mrs. Sörby will play us something.

THE THIN-HAIRED GENTLEMAN (*in a low voice*). If only Mrs. Sörby doesn't play us a tune we don't like!

THE FLABBY GENTLEMAN. Oh no, not she! Bertha will never turn against her old friends.

(*They laugh and pass into the inner room.*)

WERLE (*in a low voice, dejectedly*). I don't think anybody noticed it, Gregers.

GREGERS (*looks at him*). Noticed what?

WERLE. Didn't you notice it either?

GREGERS. Why, what do you mean?

WERLE. We were thirteen at table.

GREGERS. Indeed? Were there thirteen of us?

WERLE (*glances towards* HIALMAR EKDAL). Twelve is our ordinary party. (*To the others.*) This way, gentlemen! (WERLE *and the others, all except* HIALMAR *and* GREGERS, *go out by the back, to the right.*)

HIALMAR (*who has overheard the conversation*). You oughtn't to have invited me, Gregers.

GREGERS. What! Not ask my best and only friend to a party supposed to be in my honour——!

HIALMAR. But I don't think your father likes it. You see I'm quite outside his set.

GREGERS. So I hear. But I wanted to see you and talk with you, for I certainly shan't be staying long. Ah, we two old schoolfellows have drifted far apart from each other. It must be sixteen or seventeen years since we met.

HIALMAR. Is it so long?

GREGERS. It is indeed. Well, how goes it with you? You look well. You've grown stout and almost portly.

HIALMAR. Hm, "portly" you can scarcely call it; but I daresay I look a little more of a man than I did.

GREGERS. Yes, you do; your outer man's in first-rate condition.

HIALMAR. Ah, but the inner man! That's another matter, I can tell you! Of course you know of the terrible catastrophe that has befallen me and mine since we last met.

GREGERS (*more softly*). How is your father getting on now?

HIALMAR. Don't let's talk of it, old fellow. Of course my poor unhappy father lives with me. You see he hasn't another soul in the world to care for him. But you can understand that this is a miserable subject for me. Tell me how you've been getting on up at the works.

GREGERS. I've had a delightfully lonely time of it; plenty of leisure to reflect on things in general. Come over here; let's make ourselves comfortable.

(*He seats himself in an arm-chair by the fire and pulls* HIALMAR *down into another alongside of it.*)

HIALMAR (*sentimentally*). After all, Gregers, I thank you for inviting me to your father's table; for I take it as a sign that you've got over your feeling against me.

GREGERS (*surprised*). How could you imagine I had any feeling against you?

HIALMAR. You had at first, you know.

GREGERS. How at first?

HIALMAR. After the great misfortune. It was natural enough that you should. Your father was within an ace of being drawn into that—well, that terrible business.

GREGERS. Why should that give me any feeling against you? Who put that into your head?

HIALMAR. I know it did, Gregers; your father told me so himself.

GREGERS (*starts*). My father! Oh indeed. Hm—was that why you never let me hear from you—not a single word.

HIALMAR. Yes.

GREGERS. Not even when you took to photography?

HIALMAR. Your father said I'd better not write you about anything.

GREGERS (*looking straight before him*). Well well, perhaps he was right. But tell me now, Hialmar: are you pretty well satisfied with your present position?

HIALMAR (*with a little sigh*). Oh yes, I am; I've really no cause to complain. At first, you know, I felt it a little strange. It was such a totally new state of things for me. But of course my whole circumstances were totally changed. Father's utter, irretrievable ruin,—the shame and disgrace of it, Gregers——

GREGERS (*affected*). Yes, yes; I understand.

HIALMAR. I couldn't think of remaining at college; there wasn't a shilling to spare; on the contrary, there were debts; principally to your father I believe——

GREGERS. Hm——

HIALMAR. Well, you see, I thought it best to break once for all with my old surroundings and associations. It was your father that specially urged me to it; and since he interested himself so much in me——

GREGERS. Father did?

HIALMAR. Yes, you knew that, didn't you? Where do you suppose I got the money to learn photography, and to furnish a studio and make a start? All that costs a pretty penny, I can tell you.

GREGERS. And my father provided the money?

HIALMAR. Yes, my dear fellow, didn't you know? I understood him to say he had written to you about it.

GREGERS. Not a word about *his* part in the business. He must have forgotten it. Our correspondence has always been purely a business one. So it was my father that——!

HIALMAR. Yes, certainly. He didn't wish it to be generally known; but he it was. And of course it was he too that put me in a position to marry. Don't you—don't you know about that either?

GREGERS. No, I haven't heard a word of it. (*Shakes him by the arm.*) But, my dear Hialmar, I can't tell you what pleasure all this gives me—and regret too. I've perhaps done my father injustice after all—in some things. This proves that there's some good in his nature. It shows a sort of compunction——

HIALMAR. Compunction——?

GREGERS. Yes, or whatever you like to call it. Oh, I can't tell you how glad I am to hear this of father.—And so you're married, Hialmar! That's further than I shall ever get. Well, I hope you're happy in your married life?

HIALMAR. Yes, thoroughly happy, She's as good

a wife as a man could wish for. And she's by no means without education.

GREGERS (*rather surprised*). No, surely not.

HIALMAR. You see, life is itself an education. Her daily intercourse with me—— And then we know one or two rather remarkable men, who come a good deal about us. I assure you you'd hardly know Gina again.

GREGERS. Gina?

HIALMAR. Yes; have you forgotten that her name's Gina?

GREGERS. Whose name? I really don't know——

HIALMAR. Don't you remember that she used to be in service here?

GREGERS (*looks at him*). Is it Gina Hansen ——?

HIALMAR. Yes, of course it's Gina Hansen.

GREGERS. ——who kept house for us during the last year of my mother's illness?

HIALMAR. Yes, exactly. But, my dear friend, I'm quite sure your father wrote you that I was married.

GREGERS (*who has risen*). Oh yes, he mentioned it; but not that—(*walking about the room*). Stay—perhaps after all—now that I think of it. My father always writes such short letters (*half seats himself on the arm of the chair*). Now, tell me, Hialmar—this interests me—how did you come to know Gina—your wife?

HIALMAR. The simplest thing in the world. Gina didn't stay here long; everything was so much upset at that time, with your mother's illness and so forth, that Gina wasn't equal to it all, and so she gave notice and left. That was the year before your mother died—or perhaps it was the same year.

GREGERS. It was the same year. I was up at the works then. But afterwards?

HIALMAR. Then Gina lived for a year at home with her mother, a Madam Hansen, an excellent hard-working woman, who kept a little eating-house. She had a room to let too; a very pretty comfortable room.

GREGERS. And I suppose you were lucky enough to secure it?

HIALMAR. Yes; it was your father that recommended it to me. So you see it was there I really came to know Gina.

GREGERS. And then you got engaged?

HIALMAR. Yes. It doesn't take young people long to fall in love——; hm——

GREGERS (*gets up and walks about a little*). Tell me, was it after your engagement—was it then that my father—I mean was it then that you began to take up photography?

HIALMAR. Yes, precisely. I wanted to get on and be able to set up house as soon as possible; and your father and I agreed that this photography business was the readiest way. Gina thought so too. Oh, and there was another thing in its favour, you know: it happened, luckily, that Gina had learnt to retouch.

GREGERS. That chimed in marvellously.

HIALMAR (*pleased, rises*). Yes, didn't it? Quite marvellously, you know!

GREGERS. Yes, no doubt. My father seems to have been almost a kind of providence for you.

HIALMAR (*with emotion*). He didn't forsake his old friend's son in the hour of his need. He has a good heart, you see.

MRS. SÖRBY (*enters, arm-in-arm with* WERLE). Nonsense, my dear Mr. Werle; you mustn't stop there any longer staring at the lights. It's not good for you.

WERLE (*lets go her arm and passes his hand over his eyes*). I believe you're right.

(PETTERSEN *and* JENSEN *come round with refreshment trays.*)

MRS. SÖRBY (*to the Guests in the other room*). This way, gentlemen; if any one wants a glass of punch, he must be so good as to come in here.

THE FLABBY GENTLEMAN (*comes up to* MRS. SÖRBY). Surely it isn't possible that you've suspended our cherished tobacco-privileges?

MRS. SÖRBY. Yes. No smoking in Mr. Werle's quarters, Chamberlain.

THE THIN-HAIRED GENTLEMAN. When did you enact these stringent amendments on the cigar law, Mrs. Sörby?

MRS. SÖRBY. After the last dinner, Chamberlain, when certain persons permitted themselves to overstep the mark.

THE THIN-HAIRED GENTLEMAN. And may one never overstep the mark a little bit, Madame Bertha? Not the least little bit?

MRS. SÖRBY. Not in any way, Mr. Balle.

(*Most of the Guests have assembled in the study; servants hand round glasses of punch.*)

WERLE (*to* HIALMAR, *who is standing beside a table*). What are you studying there, Ekdal?

HIALMAR. Only an album, Mr. Werle.

THE THIN-HAIRED GENTLEMAN (*who is wandering about*). Ah, photographs! They're quite in your line of course.

THE FLABBY GENTLEMAN (*in an arm-chair*). Haven't you brought any of your own with you?

HIALMAR. No, I haven't.

THE FLABBY GENTLEMAN. You ought to have; looking at pictures is good for the digestion.

THE THIN-HAIRED GENTLEMAN. And it contributes to the entertainment, you know.

A SHORT-SIGHTED GENTLEMAN. And all contributions are thankfully received.

MRS. SÖRBY. The Chamberlains mean that when one is invited out one should do something to earn one's dinner, Mr. Ekdal.

THE FLABBY GENTLEMAN. Where one dines so well, that duty should be a pleasure.

THE THIN-HAIRED GENTLEMAN. And of course when it's a question of the struggle for life——

MRS. SÖRBY. I quite agree with you!

(*They continue the conversation, with laughter and joking.*)

GREGERS (*softly*). You must join in, Hialmar.

HIALMAR (*writhing*). What am I to talk about?

THE FLABBY GENTLEMAN. Don't you think, Mr. Werle, that Tokay may be considered a tolerably safe wine—from the medical point of view, I mean.

WERLE (*by the fire*). I can answer for the Tokay you had to-day, at any rate; it's of one of the very finest seasons. Of course you would notice that.

THE FLABBY GENTLEMAN. Yes, it had a remarkably delicate flavour.

HIALMAR (*shyly*). Is there any difference in the seasons?

THE FLABBY GENTLEMAN (*laughs*). Come! That's good!

WERLE (*smiles*). It really doesn't pay to set fine wine before you.

THE THIN-HAIRED GENTLEMAN. Tokay is like photographs, Mr. Ekdal; it must have sunshine. Isn't that so?

HIALMAR. Yes, it's largely a question of light.

MRS. SÖRBY. And it's exactly the same with Chamberlains—they, too, need sunshine,[1] as the saying is.

THE THIN-HAIRED GENTLEMAN. Oh fie! That's a very stale sarcasm!

THE SHORT-SIGHTED GENTLEMAN. Mrs. Sörby is coming out.

THE FLABBY GENTLEMAN. ——and at our expense. (*Threatening her.*) Oh, Madame Bertha, Madame Bertha!

MRS. SÖRBY. Yes, and there's not the least doubt that the seasons differ greatly. The old vintages are the finest.

THE SHORT-SIGHTED GENTLEMAN. Do you reckon me amongst the old?

MRS. SÖRBY. Oh, far from it.

[1] The "sunshine" of Court favour.

THE THIN-HAIRED GENTLEMAN. There now! But *me*, dear Mrs. Sörby——?

THE FLABBY GENTLEMAN. Yes, and me? What vintage do you think we belong to?

MRS. SÖRBY. I think you belong to the sweet vintages, gentlemen. (*She sips a glass of punch. The gentlemen laugh and flirt with her.*)

WERLE. Mrs. Sörby can always find a loop-hole —when she wants to. Fill your glasses, gentlemen! Pettersen, will you attend to——! Gregers, suppose we have a glass together. (GREGERS *does not move.*) Won't you join us, Ekdal? I couldn't find a chance of drinking with you at table.

(GRÅBERG, *the Bookkeeper, looks in through the baize door.*)

GRÅBERG. Excuse me, sir, but I can't get out.

WERLE. Have you been locked in again?

GRÅBERG. Yes, and Flakstad has gone away with the keys.

WERLE. Well, you can pass out this way.

GRÅBERG. But there's some one else——

WERLE. All right; come through, both of you. Don't be afraid.

(GRÅBERG *and* OLD EKDAL *come out of the office.*)

WERLE (*involuntarily*). Ugh! Pah!

(*The laughter and talk among the Guests cease.* HIALMAR *shrinks back at the sight of his father, puts down his glass, and turns towards the fireplace.*)

EKDAL (*does not look up, but makes little bows to both sides as he passes, murmuring*) Beg pardon, come the wrong way. Door locked—door locked. Beg pardon.

(*He and* GRÅBERG *go out by the back, to the right.*)

WERLE (*between his teeth*). Confound that Gråberg!

GREGERS (*open-mouthed and staring, to* HIALMAR). Why surely that wasn't——!

THE FLABBY GENTLEMAN. What's that? Who was it?

GREGERS. Oh, nobody; only the bookkeeper and some one with him.

THE SHORT-SIGHTED GENTLEMAN (*to* HIALMAR). Did you know that man?

HIALMAR. I don't know—I didn't notice——

THE FLABBY GENTLEMAN. What the deuce is the matter?

(*He goes over to some others who are talking softly.*)

MRS. SÖRBY (*whispers to the Servant*). Give him something outside;—something good, mind.

PETTERSEN (*nods*). I'll see to it. (*Goes out.*)

GREGERS (*softly and with emotion, to* HIALMAR). So that was really he!

HIALMAR. Yes.

GREGERS. And yet you could stand there and deny that you knew him!

HIALMAR (*whispers vehemently*). But how could I——

GREGERS. ——acknowledge your own father?

HIALMAR (*with pain*). Oh, if you were in my place——

(*The conversation amongst the Guests, which has been carried on in a low tone, now swells into constrained boisterousness.*)

THE THIN-HAIRED GENTLEMAN (*approaching* HIALMAR *and* GREGERS *in a friendly manner*). Aha! Reviving old college memories, eh? Don't you smoke, Mr. Ekdal? Have a light? Oh, by-the-bye, we mustn't——

HIALMAR. No, thank you, I won't——

THE FLABBY GENTLEMAN. Haven't you a nice little poem you could recite for us, Mr. Ekdal? You used to recite so charmingly.

HIALMAR. I'm sorry I can't remember anything.

THE FLABBY GENTLEMAN. Oh, that's a pity. Well, what shall we do, Balle?

(*Both Gentlemen move away and pass into the other room.*)

HIALMAR (*gloomily*). I'm going, Gregers! When one has felt the crushing hand of Fate on one's head, you know—— Say good-bye to your father for me.

GREGERS. Yes, yes. Are you going straight home?

HIALMAR. Yes. Why?

GREGERS. Oh, because I may perhaps look in on you later.

HIALMAR. No, you mustn't do that. You mustn't come to my home. Mine is a melancholy dwelling, Gregers; especially after a splendid banquet like this. We can always meet somewhere in the town.

MRS. SÖRBY (*who has approached softly*). Are you going, Ekdal?

HIALMAR. Yes.

MRS. SÖRBY. Remember me to Gina.

HIALMAR. Thanks.

MRS. SÖRBY. And say I'm coming up to see her one of these days.

HIALMAR. Yes, thank you. (*To* GREGERS.) Stay here, I'll slip out unobserved.

(*He saunters away, then into the other room, and so out to the right.*)

MRS. SÖRBY (*softly to the Servant, who has come back*). Well, did the old man get something to take with him?

PETTERSEN. Yes; I gave him a bottle of cognac.

MRS. SÖRBY. Oh, you might have thought of something better than that.

PETTERSEN. Oh no, Mrs. Sörby; cognac is what he likes best in the world.

THE FLABBY GENTLEMAN (*in the doorway, with a sheet of music in his hand*). Shall we have a little music, Mrs. Sörby?

MRS. SÖRBY. Yes, by all means, let us.

THE GUESTS. Bravo, bravo!

(*She goes with all the Guests through the back room, out to the right.* GREGERS *remains standing by the fire.* WERLE *is looking for something on the writing-table, and appears to wish that* GREGERS *would go; as* GREGERS *does not move,* WERLE *goes towards the door.*)

GREGERS. Father, won't you stop a moment?

WERLE (*stops*). What is it?

GREGERS. I must have a word with you.

WERLE. Can't it wait till we're alone?

GREGERS. No, it can't; for perhaps we'll never be alone together.

WERLE (*comes nearer*). What do you mean?

(*During the following, pianoforte music is heard from the distant music-room.*)

GREGERS. How has that family been allowed to go so miserably to the wall?

WERLE. I suppose you mean the Ekdals.

GREGERS. Yes, I mean the Ekdals. Lieutenant Ekdal and you once stood in such close relations.

WERLE. Unfortunately our relations were too close; that I have felt to my cost for many a year. It's thanks to him that I, yes *I*, have had a kind of slur cast upon my reputation.

GREGERS (*softly*). Are you sure that he alone was to blame?

WERLE. Who else do you suppose——?

GREGERS. You and he acted together in that affair of the forests——

WERLE. But wasn't it Ekdal that drew up the map of the forest tracts—that fraudulent map! It was he who cut down timber illegally on Government ground. In fact, the whole management was in his hands. I was quite in the dark as to what Lieutenant Ekdal was doing.

GREGERS. Lieutenant Ekdal seems to have been in the dark himself as to what he was doing.

WERLE. That may be. But the fact remains that he was found guilty and I acquitted.

GREGERS. Yes, of course I know that nothing was proved against you.

WERLE. Acquittal is acquittal. Why do you rake up these old troubles that turned my hair grey before its time? Is that the sort of thing you've been going and brooding over all these years? I can assure you, Gregers, here in the town the story's been forgotten long ago—so far as I am concerned.

GREGERS. But that unhappy Ekdal family!

WERLE. What would you have had me do for the people? When Ekdal came out of prison he was a broken-down man, fit for nothing. There are people in the world who sink to the bottom the moment they get a couple of shot in their body, and never come to the surface again. You may take my word for it, Gregers, I've done all I could without positively exposing myself, and giving rise to all sorts of suspicion and gossip——

GREGERS. Suspicion——? Oh yes, I see.

WERLE. I've given Ekdal copying to do from the office, and I pay him far, far more for it than his work is worth——

GREGERS (*without looking at him*). Hm, I don't doubt that.

WERLE. You laugh? Perhaps you doubt me? Well, I certainly can't refer you to my books, for I never enter payments of that sort.

GREGERS (*smiles coldly*). No, there are certain payments it's best not to keep any account of.

WERLE (*starts*). What do you mean by that?

GREGERS (*mustering up courage*). Have you entered what it cost you to have Hialmar Ekdal taught photography?

WERLE. I? How entered it?

GREGERS. I've learnt that it was you who paid for it. And I've learnt, too, that it was you who generously enabled him to make a start in life.

WERLE. Well, and yet you say I've done nothing

for the Ekdals! I can assure you these people have cost me enough in all conscience.

GREGERS. Have you entered any of these expenses in your books?

WERLE. Why do you ask?

GREGERS. Oh, I have my reasons. Now tell me: when you interested yourself so warmly in your old friend's son—wasn't that just when he was going to get married?

WERLE. Why, how the deuce—after all these years, how can I——?

GREGERS. You wrote me a letter about that time—a business letter, of course; and in a postscript you mentioned—quite briefly—that Hialmar Ekdal had married a Miss Hansen.

WERLE. Yes, that was quite right. That was her name.

GREGERS. But you didn't tell me that this Miss Hansen was Gina Hansen, our former housekeeper.

WERLE (*with a forced laugh of derision*). Well, upon my word, it didn't occur to me that you were so particularly interested in our former housekeeper.

GREGERS. No more I was. But (*lowers his voice*) there were others in this house who were particularly interested in her.

WERLE. What do you mean by that? (*Flaring up.*) You can't be alluding to me?

GREGERS (*softly but firmly*). Yes, I am alluding to you.

WERLE. And you dare——you presume to——! How can he—that thankless hound—that photographer fellow—how dare he go making such insinuations?

GREGERS. Hialmar has never hinted a word of it. I don't believe he has the faintest suspicion of such a thing.

WERLE. Then where have you got it from? Who can have told you anything of the kind?

GREGERS. My poor unfortunate mother told me, and that the very last time I saw her.

WERLE. Your mother! I might have known as much! You and she—you always held together. It was she who first turned you against me.

GREGERS. No, it was all the suffering she had to go through, until she broke down and came to such a pitiful end.

WERLE. Oh, she had no suffering to go through; not more than most people, at all events. But there's no getting on with morbid, overstrained creatures. I've found that often enough. And so you could go and nurse such a suspicion—go and burrow into all sorts of old rumours and slanders against your own father! I must say, Gregers, I really think that at your age you might be doing something more useful.

GREGERS. Yes, it's high time.

WERLE. Then perhaps your mind would be easier than it seems to be now. What can be your object in remaining up at the works, year out and year in, drudging away like a common clerk, and not receiving a farthing more than the ordinary monthly wage? It's absolute folly.

GREGERS. Ah, if I were only sure of that.

WERLE. I understand you well enough. You

want to be independent, and not beholden to me for anything. Now there just happens to be an opportunity for you to become independent, your own master in everything.

GREGERS. Indeed? In what way.

WERLE. When I wrote you insisting on your coming to town at once—hm——

GREGERS. Yes, what do you really want me for? I've been waiting all day to know.

WERLE. I propose to offer you a partnership in the firm.

GREGERS. I! In your firm? As partner?

WERLE. Yes. It wouldn't involve our being constantly together. You could look after the business here, and I should move up to the works.

GREGERS. *You* would?

WERLE. Yes. You see I'm not so fit for work as I once was. I'm obliged to spare my eyes, Gregers; they've begun to be rather weak.

GREGERS. They've always been so.

WERLE. Not as they are now. And besides—circumstances might possibly make it desirable for me to live up there—for a time, at any rate.

GREGERS. I could never have imagined such a thing.

WERLE. Listen, Gregers: there are many things that form a barrier between us; but we're father and son after all. It seems to me we might manage to come to some sort of understanding with each other.

GREGERS. Outwardly, you mean, of course?

WERLE. Well, even that would be something. Think it over, Gregers. Don't you think we might, eh?

GREGERS (*looking at him coldly*). There's something behind all this.

WERLE. How so?

GREGERS. You want to make use of me in some way.

WERLE. In such a close relationship as ours, each can always be useful to the other.

GREGERS. Yes, people say so.

WERLE. I want to have you at home with me for a time now. I'm a lonely man, Gregers; I've always felt lonely, all my life through; but most of all now that I'm getting up in years. I need to have somebody beside me——

GREGERS. You have Mrs. Sörby.

WERLE. Yes, I have her; and she has become, so to speak, almost indispensable to me. She is bright and even-tempered; she enlivens the house; and that's such a great thing for me.

GREGERS. Well then, you have everything just as you wish.

WERLE. Yes, but I'm afraid it can't last. A woman so placed may easily find herself in a false position, in the eyes of the world. For that matter, it does a man no good either.

GREGERS. Oh, when a man gives such dinners as you give, he can risk a great deal.

WERLE. Yes, but she, Gregers? I'm afraid she won't accept the situation much longer; and even if she did—even if, out of attachment to me, she were to disregard gossip and scandal and all that——? Do you think, Gregers—you with your highly-developed sense of justice——

GREGERS (*interrupts him*). Tell me in one word: are you thinking of marrying her?

WERLE. Suppose I were thinking of it? What then?

GREGERS. That's what I say: what then?

WERLE. Would you be inflexibly opposed to it?

GREGERS. Not at all. Not by any means.

WERLE. I didn't know whether your devotion to your mother's memory——

GREGERS. I am not overstrained.

WERLE. Well, whatever you may or may not be, at all events you've lifted a great weight from my mind. I'm extremely pleased that I can reckon on your concurrence in this matter.

GREGERS (*looking intently at him*). Now I see what you want to do with me.

WERLE. To do with you? What an expression!

GREGERS. Oh, don't let us be nice in our choice of words—not when we're alone together, at any rate. (*With a short laugh.*) Well well! This is the reason why I had to come to town in person. For the sake of Mrs. Sörby, we're to get up a pretence at family life in the house—a tableau of filial affection. That'll be something new indeed.

WERLE. How dare you speak in that tone!

GREGERS. Was there ever any family life here? Never since I can remember. But now I suppose you require something of the sort. No doubt it'll have an excellent effect when it's reported that the son has hastened home, on the wings of filial piety, to the grey-haired father's wedding-feast. What'll remain of all the rumours as to the wrongs the poor dead mother had to put up with? Not a vestige. Her son annihilates them at one stroke.

WERLE. Gregers—I believe there's no one in the world you dislike as much as me.

GREGERS (*softly*). I've seen you at too close quarters.

WERLE. You've seen me with your mother's eyes. (*Lowers his voice a little.*) But you should remember that her vision was clouded now and then.

GREGERS (*trembling*). I see what you're hinting at. But who was to blame for mother's unfortunate weakness? Why you, and all these——! The last of them was that woman that you palmed off upon Hialmar Ekdal, when you no longer—— Ugh!

WERLE (*shrugs his shoulders*). Word for word as if it were your mother speaking!

GREGERS (*without heeding*). And there he sits now, with his great confiding, childlike mind, in the midst of the deception—lives under the same roof with such a creature, and does not know that what he calls his home is built upon a lie! (*Comes a step nearer.*) When I look back upon your past, I seem to see a battle-field with shattered lives on every hand.

WERLE. I almost think the chasm that divides us is too wide.

GREGERS (*bowing, with self-command*). So I have observed; and therefore I take my hat and go.

WERLE. You're going! out of the house?

GREGERS. Yes, for at last I see my mission in life.

WERLE. What mission?

GREGERS. You would only laugh if I told you.

WERLE. A lonely man doesn't laugh so easily, Gregers.

GREGERS (*pointing towards the background*). Look, father,—the Chamberlains are playing blind-man's-buff with Mrs. Sörby. Good-night and good-bye.

(*He goes out by the back to the right. Sounds of laughter and merriment from the Company, who appear in the outer room.*)

WERLE (*muttering contemptuously after* GREGERS). Ha——! Poor wretch—and he says he's not overstrained!

Act Second.

(HIALMAR EKDAL'S *studio, a good-sized room at the top of the house. On the right, a sloping roof of large panes of glass, half covered by a blue curtain. In the right-hand corner, at the back, the entrance door; further forward, on the same side, a door leading to the sitting-room. Two corresponding doors on the opposite side, and between them an iron stove. At the back a wide double sliding-door. The studio is plainly but comfortably fitted up and furnished. Between the doors on the right, standing out a little from the wall, a sofa with a table and some chairs; on the table a lighted lamp with a shade; beside the stove an old arm-chair. Photographic instruments and apparatus of different kinds lying about the room. Against the back wall, to the left of the double door, stands a bookcase containing a few books, boxes, and bottles of chemicals, instruments, tools, and other objects. Photographs and small articles, such as camel's-hair pencils, paper, and so forth, lie on the table.*)

(GINA EKDAL *sits on a chair by the table, sewing.* HEDVIG *is sitting on the sofa with her hands shading her eyes and her thumbs in her ears, reading a book.*)

GINA (*glances once or twice at* HEDVIG, *as if with secret anxiety; then says*) Hedvig! (HEDVIG *does not hear.* GINA *repeats more loudly*) Hedvig!

HEDVIG (*takes away her hands and looks up*). Yes, mother?

GINA. Hedvig dear, you mustn't sit reading any longer now.

HEDVIG. Oh mother, mayn't I read a little more? Just a little bit?

GINA. No no, you must put away your book now. Your father doesn't like it; he never reads himself in the evening.

HEDVIG (*shuts the book*). No, father doesn't care much about reading.

GINA (*puts aside her sewing and takes up a lead pencil and a little account-book from the table*). Can you remember how much we paid for the butter to-day?

HEDVIG. It was one crown sixty-five.

GINA. That's right. (*Puts it down.*) It's terrible what a lot of butter we get through in this house. Then there was the smoked sausage, and the cheese—let me see—(*writes*)—and the ham—hm. (*Adds up.*) Yes, that makes just——

HEDVIG. And then the beer.

GINA. Yes, of course. (*Writes.*) How it mounts up! But we can't do with less.

HEDVIG. But then you and I didn't need anything hot for dinner, as father was out.

GINA. No, that was a good thing. And then I took eight crowns fifty for photographs.

HEDVIG. Really! So much as that?

GINA. Exactly eight crowns fifty.

(*Silence.* GINA *takes up her sewing again.* HEDVIG *takes paper and pencil and begins to draw, shading her eyes with her left hand.*)

HEDVIG. Isn't it jolly to think that father's at Mr. Werle's big dinner party?

GINA. You can't say that he's exactly Mr. Werle's

guest. It was the son that invited him. (*After a pause.*) We've nothing to do with that Mr. Werle.

HEDVIG. I'm longing for father to come home. He promised to ask Mrs. Sörby for something nice for me.

GINA. Yes, there are plenty of good things going in that house, I can tell you.

HEDVIG (*continues drawing*). I believe I'm rather hungry too.

(OLD EKDAL, *with the paper parcel under his arm and another parcel in his coat pocket, comes in through the entrance door.*)

GINA. How late you are to-day, grandfather!

EKDAL. They'd closed the office. Had to wait in Gråberg's room. And then they let me through—hm.

HEDVIG. Did you get some fresh copying, grandfather?

EKDAL. This whole packet. Just look.

GINA. That's capital.

HEDVIG. And you've got another parcel in your pocket.

EKDAL. Eh? Oh nonsense, that's nothing. (*Puts his stick away in a corner.*) This work'll keep me a long time, Gina. (*Opens one of the sliding-doors in the back wall a little.*) Hush! (*Peeps into the room for a moment, then pushes the door carefully to again.*) Hee-hee! They're fast asleep, all the lot of them. And she's gone into the basket herself. Hee-hee!

HEDVIG. Are you sure she's not cold in that basket, grandfather?

EKDAL. Not a bit of it! Cold? With all that straw? (*Goes towards the further door on the left.*) There are matches in here, I suppose.

GINA. The matches are on the drawers. (EKDAL *goes into his room.*)

HEDVIG. It's nice that grandfather's got all that copying.

GINA. Yes, poor old father; it means a bit of pocket-money for him.

HEDVIG. And he won't be able to sit the whole forenoon down at that horrid Madam Eriksen's.

GINA. No more he will. (*Short silence.*)

HEDVIG. Do you suppose they're still at the dinner-table?

GINA. Goodness knows; very likely

HEDVIG. Think of all the delicious things father's having to eat! I'm certain he'll be in splendid spirits when he comes. Don't you think so, mother?

GINA. Yes; and if only we could tell him that we'd got the room let——

HEDVIG. But we don't need that this evening.

GINA. Oh, we'd be none the worse of it, I can tell you. It's no use to us as it is.

HEDVIG. I meant that we don't need it this evening, for father'll be in a good humour anyhow. We'd better save up the room for another time.

GINA (*looks across at her*). Are you glad when you've some good news to tell father when he comes home in the evening?

HEDVIG. Yes; for then we have a pleasanter time.

GINA (*thinking to herself*). Yes, there's something in that.

(OLD EKDAL *comes in again and is going out by the foremost door to the left.*)

GINA (*half turning in her chair*). Do you want something out of the kitchen, grandfather?

EKDAL. Yes, I do, yes. Don't you trouble. (*Goes out.*)

GINA. He's not raking away at the fire, is he? (*Waits a moment.*) Hedvig, go and see what he's about.

(EKDAL *comes in again with a small jug of steaming hot water.*)

HEDVIG. Are you getting some hot water, grandfather?

EKDAL. Yes, I am. Want it for something. Want to write, and the ink has got as thick as porridge,—hm.

GINA. But you ought to have supper first, grandfather. It's laid in there.

EKDAL. Can't be bothered with supper, Gina. Very busy, I tell you. No one's to come to my room. No one—hm.

(*He goes into his room;* GINA *and* HEDVIG *look at each other.*)

GINA (*softly*). Can you imagine where he's got money from?

HEDVIG. From Gråberg, I daresay.

GINA. Not a bit of it. Gråberg always sends the money to me.

HEDVIG. Then he must have got a bottle on credit somewhere.

GINA. Poor grandfather, who'd give him credit?

(HIALMAR EKDAL, *in an overcoat and grey felt hat, comes in from the right.*)

GINA (*throws down her sewing and rises*). Why, Ekdal, are you here already?

HEDVIG (*at the same time, jumping up*). Fancy your coming so soon, father!

HIALMAR (*taking off his hat*). Yes, most of the people were coming away.

HEDVIG. So early?

HIALMAR. Yes, it was a dinner-party, you know. (*Is taking off his overcoat.*)

GINA. Let me help you

HEDVIG. Me too.

(*They draw off his coat;* GINA *hangs it up on the back wall.*)

HEDVIG. Were there many there, father?

HIALMAR. Oh no, not many. We were about twelve or fourteen at table.

GINA. And you had some talk with them all?

HIALMAR. Oh yes, a little; but Gregers took me up most of the time.

GINA. Is Gregers as ugly as ever?

HIALMAR. Well, he's not very much to look at. Hasn't the old man come home?

HEDVIG. Yes, grandfather's in his room, writing.

HIALMAR. Did he say anything?

GINA. No, what should he say?

HIALMAR. Didn't he say anything about——? I fancy I heard that he'd been with Gråberg. I'll go in to him for a moment.

GINA. No no, better not.

HIALMAR. Why not? Did he say he didn't want me to go in?

GINA. He doesn't want to see anybody this evening——

HEDVIG (*making signs*). Hm—hm!

GINA (*not noticing*). ——he's been in to fetch hot water——

HIALMAR. Aha! Then he's——?

GINA. Yes, I suppose so.

HIALMAR. Oh God! my poor old white-haired father!—Well well; there let him sit and get all the enjoyment he can.

(OLD EKDAL, *in an indoor coat and with a lighted pipe, comes from his room.*)

EKDAL. Got home? Thought it was you I heard talking.

HIALMAR. Yes, I've just come.

EKDAL. You didn't see me, did you?

HIALMAR. No; but they said you'd passed through—so I thought I'd follow you.

EKDAL. Hm, kind of you, Hialmar. Who were they, all those fellows?

HIALMAR. Oh, all sorts of people. There was Chamberlain Flor, and Chamberlain Balle, and Chamberlain Kaspersen, and Chamberlain—this, that, and the other—I don't know who all——

EKDAL (*nodding*). Hear that, Gina! He's been with nothing but Chamberlains.

GINA. Yes, I hear they're terribly genteel in that house nowadays.

HEDVIG. Did the Chamberlains sing, father? Or did they read aloud?

HIALMAR. No, they only chattered. They wanted me to recite something for them; but I knew better than that.

EKDAL. Didn't you do it?

GINA. Oh, you might have done it.

HIALMAR. No; one mustn't be at everybody's beck and call. (*Walks about the room.*) I won't, at any rate.

EKDAL. No no; Hialmar's not to be had for the asking.

HIALMAR. I don't see why I should bother myself to entertain people on the rare occasions when I go into society. Let the others exert themselves. These fellows go from one great dinner-table to the next and gorge and guzzle day out and day in. It's for them to bestir themselves and do something in return for all the good food they get.

GINA. But you didn't say that?

HIALMAR (*humming*). Ho-ho-ho——; faith I gave them a bit of my mind.

EKDAL. Not the Chamberlains!

HIALMAR. Oh, why not? (*Lightly.*) We got into a little dispute about Tokay afterwards.

EKDAL. Tokay! There's a fine wine for you?

HIALMAR (*comes to a standstill*). It may be a fine wine. But of course you know the vintages differ; it all depends on how much sunshine the grapes have got.

GINA. Why, you know everything, Ekdal.

EKDAL. And did they dispute that?

HIALMAR. They tried to; but they didn't much like being told that it was just the same with

Chamberlains—that with them, too, different batches were of different qualities.

GINA. What things you think of!

EKDAL. Hee-hee! So they got that in their pipes too.

HIALMAR. Right to their faces.

EKDAL. Do you hear that, Gina? He said it right to the Chamberlains' faces.

GINA. Just think——! Right to their faces!

HIALMAR. Yes, but I don't want it talked about. One doesn't speak of such things. The whole affair passed off in all friendliness of course. They were nice, genial fellows; I didn't want to wound them—not I!

EKDAL. Right to their faces!

HEDVIG (*caressingly*). How nice it is to see you in a dress-coat! It suits you, father.

HIALMAR. Yes, doesn't it? And this one really sits to perfection. It fits almost as if it had been made for me;—a little tight in the arm-holes perhaps;—help me, Hedvig. (*Takes off the coat.*) I think I'll put on my jacket. Where's my jacket, Gina?

GINA. Here it is. (*Brings the jacket and helps him.*)

HIALMAR. That's it! Don't forget to send the coat back to Molvik first thing to-morrow morning.

GINA (*laying it away*). I'll be sure and see to it.

HIALMAR (*stretching himself*). After all, this is more comfortable. A free-and-easy indoor costume suits my whole personality better. Don't you think so, Hedvig?

HEDVIG. Yes, father.

HIALMAR. When I loosen my necktie into a pair of flowing ends—like this—eh?

HEDVIG. Yes, that goes so well with your moustache and the sweep of your curls.

HIALMAR. I shouldn't call them curls exactly; I'd rather say locks.

HEDVIG. Yes, but they're really big curls.

HIALMAR. No, locks.

HEDVIG (*after a pause, twitching his jacket*). Father!

HIALMAR. Well, what is it?

HEDVIG. Oh, you know very well.

HIALMAR. No, really I don't——

HEDVIG (*half laughing, half whimpering*). Oh yes, father; now don't tease me any longer!

HIALMAR. Why, what do you mean?

HEDVIG (*shaking him*). Oh nonsense; come, where are they, father? All the good things you promised me, you know?

HIALMAR. Oh—if I haven't forgotten all about them!

HEDVIG. Now you're only making game of me, father! Oh, it's a shame! Where have you put them?

HIALMAR. No, I positively forgot to get anything. But wait a little! I've got something else for you, Hedvig. (*Goes and searches in the coat pockets.*)

HEDVIG (*skipping and clapping her hands*). Oh mother, mother!

GINA. There, you see; if only you give him time——

HIALMAR (*with a paper*). Look, here it is.

HEDVIG. That? Why, that's only a paper.

HIALMAR. That's the bill of fare, the whole bill of fare. Here you see: "Menu"—that means bill of fare.

HEDVIG. Haven't you anything else?

HIALMAR. I forgot the other things, I tell you. But you may take my word for it, these dainties are very unsatisfying. Sit down at the table and read the bill of fare, and then I'll describe to you how the dishes taste. Here you are, Hedvig.

HEDVIG (*gulping down her tears*). Thank you.

(*She seats herself, but does not read;* GINA *makes signs to her;* HIALMAR *notices it.*)

HIALMAR (*walking up and down the room*). No one knows how much the father of a family has to think of; and if he forgets the slightest thing, he's treated to sour faces at once. Well well, one gets used to that too. (*Stops near the stove, by the old man's chair.*) Have you peeped in there this evening, father?

EKDAL. Yes, to be sure I have. She's gone into the basket.

HIALMAR. Ah, she's gone into the basket! Then she's beginning to get used to it.

EKDAL. Yes; just as I prophesied. But you know there are still a few little things——

HIALMAR. A few improvements, yes.

EKDAL. They're quite necessary, you know.

HIALMAR. Yes. Let's have a talk about the improvements, father. Come, and we'll sit on the sofa.

EKDAL. All right. Hm, let me fill my pipe first.

Must just clean it too. Hm. (*He goes into his room.*)

GINA (*smiling to* HIALMAR). His pipe!

HIALMAR. Oh yes yes, Gina; let him alone——; the poor shipwrecked old man.—Yes, these improvements—we'd better get them out of hand to-morrow.

GINA. You'll hardly have time to-morrow, Ekdal.

HEDVIG (*interposing*). Oh yes he will, mother!

GINA. ——for remember those copies that have to be retouched; they've sent for them time after time.

HIALMAR. Oh, bother the copies. I'll soon get them finished. Have any new orders come in?

GINA. No, worse luck; to-morrow I've nothing but those two sittings, you know.

HIALMAR. Nothing else? Oh no, when one doesn't set about things with a will——

GINA. But what more can I do? Don't I advertise in the papers as much as we can afford.

HIALMAR. Yes, the papers, the papers; you see how much good *that* does. And I suppose no one has been to see the room either?

GINA. No, not yet.

HIALMAR. That was only to be expected. Unless one's on the alert—— The thing is to make a real effort, Gina.

HEDVIG (*going towards him*). Shall I fetch you the flute, father?

HIALMAR. No; no flute for me; *I* want no pleasures in this world. (*Walking about.*) Yes, I'll work to-morrow; you'll see if I don't. You may be sure I'll work as long as my strength holds out.

GINA. But my dear good Ekdal, I didn't mean it in that way.

HEDVIG. Father, shall I bring in a bottle of beer?

HIALMAR. No, certainly not. I require nothing, nothing——(*comes to a standstill*). Beer? Were you talking about beer?

HEDVIG (*cheerfully*). Yes, father; beautiful fresh beer.

HIALMAR. Well—since you insist upon it, you may bring in a bottle.

GINA. Yes, do; and we'll be nice and cosy. (HEDVIG *runs towards the kitchen door.*)

HIALMAR (*by the stove, stops her, looks at her, puts his arm round her neck, and presses her to him*). Hedvig, Hedvig!

HEDVIG (*joyfully and in tears*). My dear, kind father!

HIALMAR. No, don't call me that. Here have I been revelling at the rich man's table,—been sitting and gorging myself at the groaning board——! And I couldn't even——!

GINA (*sitting at the table*). Oh nonsense, nonsense, Ekdal.

HIALMAR. Oh, but you mustn't be too hard upon me. You know that I love you for all that.

HEDVIG (*throwing her arms round him*). And we love you, oh so dearly, father!

HIALMAR. And if I'm unreasonable sometimes —why then—you must remember that I'm a man beset by a host of cares. There there! (*Drys his eyes.*) No beer at such a moment as this. Give me the flute. (HEDVIG *runs to the bookcase and fetches it.*) Thanks! That's right. With my flute in my hand and you two at my side—ah——!

(HEDVIG *seats herself at the table near* GINA; HIALMAR *wanders up and down, then sets energetically to work and plays a Bohemian peasant dance, but in a slow plaintive tempo, and with sentimental expression.*)

HIALMAR (*breaking off the melody, holds out his left hand to* GINA, *and says with emotion*). Our roof may be poor and humble, Gina; but it is home. And with all my heart I say: here dwells my happiness. (*He begins to play again; almost immediately after, a knocking is heard at the entrance door.*)

GINA (*rising*). Hush, Ekdal,—I think there's somebody coming.

HIALMAR (*laying the flute in the bookcase*). There! Again! (GINA *goes and opens the door.*)

GREGERS WERLE (*in the passage*). Excuse me——

GINA (*starting back slightly*). Oh!

GREGERS. ——Doesn't Mr. Ekdal, the photographer, live here?

GINA. Yes, he does.

HIALMAR (*going towards the door*). Gregers! You here after all? Well, come in then.

GREGERS (*coming in*). I told you I would come and look you up.

HIALMAR. But this evening——? Have you left the party?

GREGERS. I've left both the party and my father's house—— Good evening, Mrs. Ekdal. I don't know whether you recognise me?

GINA. Oh yes; it's not difficult to know young Mr. Werle again.

GREGERS. No, I'm like my mother; and of course you remember her.

HIALMAR. Have you left the house, do you say?

GREGERS. Yes, I've gone to a hotel.

HIALMAR. Indeed. Well, since you've come, take off your coat and sit down.

GREGERS. Thanks. (*He draws off his overcoat. He is now dressed in a plain grey suit of a countrified cut.*)

HIALMAR. Here, on the sofa. Make yourself comfortable. (GREGERS *seats himself on the sofa;* HIALMAR *takes a chair at the table.*)

GREGERS (*looking around him*). So these are your quarters, Hialmar—this is your home.

HIALMAR. This is the studio, as you see——

GINA. But it's the largest of our rooms, so we generally sit here.

HIALMAR. We used to live in a better place; but this flat has one great advantage: there are such capital outer rooms——

GINA. And we have a room on the other side of the passage, that we can let.

GREGERS (*to* HIALMAR). Ah, so you have lodgers too?

HIALMAR. No, not yet. They're not so easy to find, you see; you've got to keep your eyes about you. (*To* HEDVIG.) What about that beer?

(HEDVIG *nods and goes out into the kitchen.*)

GREGERS. Your daughter, I suppose?

HIALMAR. Yes, that's Hedvig.

GREGERS. And she's your only child?

HIALMAR. Yes, the only one. She's the joy of our lives, and—(*lowering his voice*)—at the same time our deepest sorrow, Gregers.

GREGERS. What do you mean?

HIALMAR. She's in danger of losing her eyesight.

GREGERS. Becoming blind?

HIALMAR. Yes. Only the first symptoms have appeared as yet, and she may not feel it much for some time. But the doctor has warned us. It's coming, inexorably.

GREGERS. What an awful misfortune! How do you account for it?

HIALMAR (*sighs*). Hereditary, no doubt.

GREGERS (*starting*). Hereditary?

GINA. Ekdal's mother had weak eyes.

HIALMAR. Yes, so my father says; I can't remember her.

GREGERS. Poor child! And how does she take it?

HIALMAR. Oh, you can imagine we haven't the heart to tell her of it. She suspects no danger. Gay and careless and chirping like a little bird, she's fluttering into the eternal night of her life. (*Overcome.*) Oh, it's cruelly hard for me, Gregers.

(HEDVIG *brings a tray with beer and glasses which she sets upon the table.*)

HIALMAR (*stroking her hair*). Thanks, thanks, Hedvig.

(HEDVIG *puts her arm round his neck and whispers in his ear.*)

HIALMAR. No, no bread and butter just now. (*Looks up.*) But perhaps you'd like some, Gregers.

GREGERS (*with a gesture of refusal*). No, no thank you.

HIALMAR (*still melancholy*). Well, you can bring in a little all the same. If you have a crust, that's all I want. And put plenty of butter on it, mind.

(HEDVIG *nods gaily and goes out into the kitchen again.*)

GREGERS (*who has been following her with his eyes*). She seems quite strong and healthy otherwise.

GINA. Yes. In other ways there's nothing amiss with her, thank goodness.

GREGERS. She promises to be very like you, Mrs. Ekdal. How old is she now?

GINA. Hedvig will soon be exactly fourteen; her birthday is the day after to-morrow.

GREGERS. She's pretty tall for her age.

GINA. Yes, she's shot up wonderfully this last year.

GREGERS. It makes one realise one's own age to see these young people growing up.—How long is it now since you were married?

GINA. We've been married—let me see—nearly fifteen years.

GREGERS. Is it so long as that?

GINA (*becomes attentive; looks at him*). Yes, it is indeed.

HIALMAR. Yes, so it is. Fifteen years all but a few months. (*Changing his tone.*) They must have been long years for you, up at the works, Gregers.

GREGERS. They seemed long while I was living them; now they're over, I hardly know how the time has gone.

(OLD EKDAL *comes from his room without his pipe, but with his old-fashioned uniform cap on his head; his gait is somewhat unsteady.*)

EKDAL. There, Hialmar, now we can have a good talk about this—hm—what was it again?

HIALMAR (*going towards him*). Father, we've a visitor here—Gregers Werle.—I don't know if you remember him.

EKDAL (*looking at* GREGERS, *who has risen*). Werle? Is that the son? What does he want with me?

HIALMAR. Nothing; it's me he's come to see.

EKDAL. Oh! Then there's nothing wrong?

HIALMAR. No, of course not.

EKDAL (*swinging his arms*). Not that I'm afraid, you know; but——

GREGERS (*goes over to him*). Let me give you a greeting from your old hunting-grounds, Lieutenant Ekdal.

EKDAL. Hunting-grounds?

GREGERS. Yes, up in Höidal, about the works, you know.

EKDAL. Oh, up there. Yes, I knew all those places well in the old times.

GREGERS. You were a great sportsman then.

EKDAL. So I was, I don't deny it. You're looking at my uniform cap. I don't ask anybody's leave to wear it in the house. So long as I don't go out in the streets with it——

(HEDVIG *brings a plate of bread and butter, which she puts upon the table.*)

HIALMAR. Sit down, father, and have a glass of beer. Help yourself, Gregers.

(EKDAL *mutters and stumbles over to the sofa.* GREGERS *seats himself on the chair nearest to him,* HIALMAR *on the other side of* GREGERS. GINA *sits a little way from the table, sewing;* HEDVIG *stands beside her father.*)

GREGERS. Can you remember, Lieutenant Ekdal, how Hialmar and I used to come up and visit you in the summer and at Christmas?

EKDAL. Did you? No, no, no; I don't remember it. But sure enough I've been a great sportsman. I've shot bears too. I've shot nine of them.

GREGERS (*looking sympathetically at him*). And now you never get any shooting?

EKDAL. Can't say that, sir. Get a shot now and then perhaps. Of course not in the old way. For the woods you see—the woods, the woods——! (*Drinks.*) Are the woods fine up there now?

GREGERS. Not so fine as in your time. They've been thinned a good deal.

EKDAL. Thinned? (*More softly, and as if afraid.*) It's dangerous work that. Bad things come of it. The woods avenge themselves.

HIALMAR (*filling up his glass*). Come—a little more, father.

GREGERS. How can a man like you—such a man for the open air—live in the midst of a stuffy town, boxed within four walls?

EKDAL (*laughs quietly and glances at* HIALMAR). Oh, it's not so bad here. Not at all so bad.

GREGERS. But don't you miss all that you used to be so fond of—the cool sweeping breezes, the free life in the woods and on the uplands, amongst beasts and birds——?

EKDAL (*smiling*). Hialmar, shall we let him see it?

HIALMAR (*hastily and a little embarrassed*). Oh no no father; not this evening.

GREGERS. What does he want to show me?

HIALMAR. Oh, it's only something—you can see it another time.

GREGERS (*continues, to the old man*). You see I've been thinking, Lieutenant Ekdal, that you should come up with me to the works; I'm sure to be going back soon. You could probably get some copying there too. And here, you have nothing on earth to interest you—nothing to liven you up.

EKDAL (*stares in astonishment at him*). Have *I* nothing on earth to——!

GREGERS. Of course you have, Hialmar; but then he has his own family. And a man like you, who has always had such a passion for what is free and wild——

EKDAL (*thumps the table*). Hialmar, he *shall* see it!

HIALMAR. Oh but, father, is it worth while? It's all dark.

EKDAL. Nonsense; it's moonlight. (*Rises.*) He *shall* see it, I tell you. Let me pass! Come and help me, Hialmar!

HEDVIG. Oh yes, do, father!

HIALMAR (*rising*). Very well then.

GREGERS (*to* GINA). What is it?

GINA. Oh you mustn't think it's anything so very wonderful.

(EKDAL *and* HIALMAR *have gone to the back wall and are each pushing back a side of the sliding door;* HEDVIG *helps the old man;* GREGERS *remains standing by the sofa;* GINA *sits still and sews. Through the open doorway a large, deep irregular garret is seen with odd nooks and corners; a couple of stove-pipes running through it, from rooms below. There are skylights through which clear moonlight shines in on some parts of the great room; others lie in deep shadow.*)

EKDAL (*to* GREGERS). You may come right in if you like.

GREGERS (*going over to them*). But what is it?

EKDAL. Come and see. Hm.

HIALMAR (*somewhat embarrassed*). This belongs to father, you understand.

GREGERS (*at the door, looks into the garret*). Why, you keep poultry, Lieutenant Ekdal!

EKDAL. Should think we did keep poultry. They've gone to roost now. But you should just see our fowls by daylight!

HEDVIG. And there's a——

EKDAL. Hush—hush; don't say anything about it yet.

GREGERS. And you've got pigeons too, I see.

EKDAL. Oh yes, haven't we got pigeons! They have their nests up there under the roof-tree; for pigeons like to roost high, you see.

HIALMAR. They aren't all common pigeons.

EKDAL. Common! Should think not indeed! We have tumblers, and a pair of pouters too. But come here! Can you see that hutch down there by the wall?

GREGERS. Yes; what do you use it for?

EKDAL. That's where the rabbits sleep, sir.

GREGERS. Dear me, so you've rabbits too?

EKDAL. Yes, I believe you, we have rabbits! He's asking if we have rabbits, Hialmar! Hm. But now comes *the* thing, you must know; here we have it; move away, Hedvig. Stand here; that's right,—and now look down there. Don't you see a basket with straw in it?

GREGERS. Yes. And I see there's a fowl in the basket.

EKDAL. Hm—"a fowl"——

GREGERS. Isn't it a duck?

EKDAL (*hurt*). Yes, of course it's a duck.

HIALMAR. But what *kind* of duck, do you think?

HEDVIG. It's not just a common duck.

EKDAL. Hush!

GREGERS. And it's not a Turkish duck either.

EKDAL. No, Mr.—Werle; it's not a Turkish duck; for it's a wild duck!

GREGERS. No, is it really? A wild duck?

EKDAL. Yes, it is. That "fowl" as you call it —is the wild duck. It's our wild duck, sir.

HEDVIG. *My* wild duck. She belongs to me.

GREGERS. And can it live up here in the garret? Does it thrive?

EKDAL. Of course it has a trough of water to splash about in, you know.

HIALMAR. Fresh water every other day.

GINA (*turning towards* HIALMAR). But my dear Ekdal, it's getting icy cold here.

EKDAL. Hm, let's shut up then. It's as well not to disturb their night's rest, too. Close up, Hedvig.

(HIALMAR *and* HEDVIG *push the garret doors together.*)

EKDAL. Another time you shall see her properly. (*Seats himself in the arm-chair by the stove.*) Oh, they're curious things, these wild ducks, I can tell you.

GREGERS. How did you manage to catch it, Lieutenant Ekdal?

EKDAL. I didn't catch it. There's a certain man in this town whom we have to thank for it.

GREGERS (*starts slightly*). That man wasn't my father, was he?

EKDAL. You've hit it. Your father and no one else. Hm.

HIALMAR. It was odd that you should guess that, Gregers.

GREGERS. You were telling me that you owed such a lot of things to my father; and so I thought perhaps——

GINA. But we didn't get the duck from Mr. Werle himself——

EKDAL. It's Håkon Werle we have to thank for her, all the same, Gina. (*To* GREGERS.) He was out in a boat, you see, and he shot her. But your father's sight is pretty bad now. Hm; he only wounded her.

GREGERS. Ah! She got a couple of shot in her body, I suppose.

HIALMAR. Yes, two or three.

HEDVIG. She was hit under the wing, so that she couldn't fly.

GREGERS. And so she dived to the bottom, eh?

EKDAL (*sleepily, in a thick voice*). Of course. Wild ducks always do that. They shoot to the bottom as deep as they can get, sir, and bite themselves fast in the tangle and seaweed and all the confounded stuff that grows down there. And they never come up again.

GREGERS. But your wild duck came up again, Lieutenant Ekdal.

EKDAL. Your father had such an extraordinarily clever dog. And that dog—he dived in after the duck and fished her up again.

GREGERS (*who has turned to* HIALMAR). And then you took her in here!

HIALMAR. Not at once; at first she was taken home to your father's house; but she wouldn't thrive there; so Pettersen was told to put an end to her.

EKDAL (*half asleep*). Hm—yes—Pettersen—that ass——

HIALMAR (*speaking more softly*). That's how we got her, you see; for father knows Pettersen a little; and when he heard about the wild duck he got him to hand her over to us.

GREGERS. And she thrives all right in the garret there?

HIALMAR. Yes, wonderfully well. She's got fat. You see she's been in there so long now that she's forgotten her natural wild life; and it all depends on that.

GREGERS. You're right there, Hialmar. Only

never let her get a glimpse of the sky and the sea—— But I mustn't stop any longer; I think your father's asleep.

HIALMAR. Oh, as for that——

GREGERS. But, by-the-bye—you said you had a room to let—a spare room?

HIALMAR. Yes; what then? Do you know of anybody——?

GREGERS. Can I have that room?

HIALMAR. You?

GINA. Oh no, Mr. Werle, *you*——

GREGERS. May I have the room? If so, I'll take possession first thing to-morrow morning.

HIALMAR. Yes, with the greatest pleasure——

GINA. But, Mr. Werle, it's not at all the sort of room for *you*.

HIALMAR. Gina! how can you say that?

GINA. Well, the room's neither large enough nor light enough, and——

GREGERS. That doesn't matter, Mrs. Ekdal.

HIALMAR. I call it quite a nice room, and not badly furnished either.

GINA. But remember the two that live underneath.

GREGERS. What two?

GINA. Oh, one of them has been a tutor——

HIALMAR. He's a Mr. Molvik.

GINA. And then there's a doctor called Relling.

GREGERS. Relling? I know him a little; he practised for a time up in Höidal.

GINA. They're a pair of regular ne'er-do-wells. They're often out on the loose in the evenings, and then they come home very late, and they're not always quite——

GREGERS. One soon gets accustomed to that sort of thing. I hope I'll be like the wild duck——

GINA. Hm; I think you ought to sleep upon it first, all the same.

GREGERS. You seem very unwilling to have me in the house, Mrs. Ekdal.

GINA. Oh no! how can you think so?

HIALMAR. Well, you really behave strangely about it, Gina. (*To* GREGERS) Then you're thinking of staying in the town for the present?

GREGERS (*putting on his overcoat*). Yes, now I'm thinking of remaining here.

HIALMAR. And yet not at your father's? What do you propose to do?

GREGERS. Ah, if I only knew that, I shouldn't be so badly off! But when one has the misfortune to be called Gregers—! "Gregers"—and then "Werle" after it; did you ever hear anything so hideous?

HIALMAR. Oh, I don't think so at all.

GREGERS. Ugh! Bah! I feel as if I should like to spit upon the fellow that answers to such a name. When one has the misfortune to be Gregers—Werle in this world, as I am——

HIALMAR (*laughs*). Ha ha! If you weren't Gregers Werle, what would you like to be?

GREGERS. If I could choose, I should like best to be a clever dog.

GINA. A dog!

HEDVIG (*involuntarily*). Oh no!

GREGERS. Yes, an extraordinarily clever dog; one that goes to the bottom after wild ducks when they dive and bite themselves fast in tangle and sea-weed, down among the ooze.

HIALMAR. Look here now, Gregers—I don't understand a word of all this.

GREGERS. Oh well, I daresay it's not worth understanding. Then I'll move in early to-morrow morning. (*To* GINA) I won't give you any trouble, for I do everything for myself. (*To* HIALMAR) We'll leave the rest till to-morrow. Good-night, Mrs. Ekdal. (*Nods to* HEDVIG.) Good-night.

GINA. Good-night, Mr. Werle.

HEDVIG. Good-night.

HIALMAR (*who has lighted a candle*). Stop a minute, I must show you a light; it's sure to be dark on the stairs.

(GREGERS *and* HIALMAR *go out through the passage door.*)

GINA (*looking straight before her, with her sewing in her lap*). Wasn't that strange talk about his wanting to be a dog!

HEDVIG. Do you know, mother, I believe he meant something quite different by that.

GINA. What should he mean?

HEDVIG. Oh, I don't know; but it seemed to me he meant something different from what he said, all the time.

GINA. Do you think so? Yes, it was strange.

HIALMAR (*comes back*). The lamp was still burning. (*Puts out the candle and sets it down.*) Ah, now one can get a mouthful of food at last. (*Begins to eat the bread and butter.*) Well, you see, Gina—if you just keep your eyes open——

GINA. How, keep your eyes open?

HIALMAR. Why, aren't we lucky to have got the room let at last? And just think—to a person like Gregers—a good old friend.

GINA. I don't know what to say about it.

HEDVIG. Oh mother, you'll see; it'll be such fun!

HIALMAR. You're very strange. You were so bent upon letting the room before, and now you don't like it.

GINA. Yes I do, Ekdal; if it had only been to some one else—— But what do you suppose Mr. Werle will say?

HIALMAR. Old Werle? It doesn't concern him.

GINA. But surely you can see that something's gone wrong between them again, as the young man's leaving home. You know very well how matters stand between those two.

HIALMAR. Yes, that's very likely, but——

GINA. And now Mr. Werle may think that it's you who have egged him on——

HIALMAR. Let him think so, then! Mr. Werle has done a great deal for me; far be it from me to deny it. But that doesn't make me everlastingly dependent upon him.

GINA. But, my dear Ekdal, mayn't grandfather suffer for it? Perhaps he'll lose the little bit of work he gets from Gråberg now.

HIALMAR. I'm inclined to say: so much the better! Isn't it humiliating for a man like me to see his grey-haired father going about as a pariah? But the fulness of time will soon come now, I trust. (*Takes a fresh piece of bread and butter.*) As sure as I've a mission in life, I mean to fulfil it now.

HEDVIG. Oh yes, father, do!

GINA. Hush, don't wake him!

HIALMAR (*more softly*). I *will* fulfil it, I say. The day will come when—— And therefore it's a good thing that we've let the room, for that makes me more independent. The man who has a mission in life must be independent. (*By the arm-chair, with emotion.*) Poor old white-haired father! Rely on your Hialmar. He has broad shoulders—strong shoulders, at any rate. You shall yet wake up some fine day and—— (*To* GINA.) Don't you believe it?

GINA (*rising*). Yes, of course I do; but in the meantime let's see about getting him to bed.

HIALMAR. Yes, come.

(*They take hold of the old man carefully.*)

Act Third.

(HIALMAR EKDAL'S *studio. It is morning; the daylight shines through the large window in the slanting roof; the curtain is drawn back.*)

(HIALMAR *is sitting at the table, busy retouching a photograph; several others lie before him. Presently* GINA, *in her hat and cloak, enters by the passage door; she has a covered basket on her arm.*)

HIALMAR. Back already, Gina?

GINA. Oh yes, one has to look sharp. (*Sets her basket on a chair, and takes off her things.*)

HIALMAR. Did you look in at Gregers' room?

GINA. Yes, I did. It's a rare sight, I can tell you; he's begun by making a pretty mess of it.

HIALMAR. Indeed?

GINA. He was determined to do everything for himself, he said; so when he set to work to light the stove, he must needs screw the damper round until the whole room was full of smoke. Ugh! It smelt like——

HIALMAR. Well, really!

GINA. But that's not the worst of it; for then he wanted to put out the fire, and poured all the water from his ewer into the stove, so that the floor was swimming like a pig-sty.

HIALMAR. How annoying!

GINA. I've got the porter's wife to clear up after him, pig that he is! But the room won't be habitable till the afternoon.

HIALMAR. What's he doing with himself in the meantime?

GINA. He said he was going out for a little while.

HIALMAR. I looked in upon him too, for a moment—after you had gone.

GINA. So I heard. You've asked him to lunch.

HIALMAR. Just to a little bit of early lunch, you know. It's his first day—we can hardly do less. You've got something in the house, I suppose?

GINA. I'll have to find something or other.

HIALMAR. And don't be too sparing, for I think Relling and Molvik are coming up too. I just met Relling on the stairs, you see; so I had to——

GINA. Oh, are we to have those two as well?

HIALMAR. Good Lord—a couple more or less can't make any difference.

OLD EKDAL (*opens his door and looks in*). I say, Hialmar——(*sees* GINA). Oh!

GINA. Do you want anything, grandfather?

EKDAL. Oh no, it doesn't matter. Hm! (*Retires again.*)

GINA (*takes up the basket*). Be sure you see that he doesn't go out.

HIALMAR. All right, all right.—And, Gina, it wouldn't be amiss if you had a little herring-salad; Relling and Molvik were out on the loose again last night.

GINA. If only they don't come up too soon for me——

HIALMAR. No, of course they won't; take your own time.

GINA. Very well; and meanwhile you can be working a bit.

HIALMAR. Well, I *am* working! I'm working as hard as I can!

GINA. Then you'll have that job off your hands, you see.

(*She goes out to the kitchen with her basket.*)

(HIALMAR *sits for a time working at the photograph; he does it lazily and listlessly.*)

EKDAL (*peeps in, looks round the studio and says softly*). Are you busy?

HIALMAR. Yes, I'm toiling away at these pictures——

EKDAL. Well well, of course,—since you're so busy—hm!

(*He goes out again; the door stands open.*)

HIALMAR (*continues for some time in silence; then he lays down his brush and goes over to the door*). Are *you* busy, father?

EKDAL (*in a grumbling tone, inside*). If you're busy, I'm busy too. Hm!

HIALMAR. Oh, all right. (*Goes to his work again.*)

EKDAL (*presently, coming to the door again*). Hm; I say, Hialmar, I'm not so very busy, you know.

HIALMAR. I thought you were writing.

EKDAL. Oh, devil take it! can't Gråberg wait a day or two? It's not a matter of life and death, I should think.

HIALMAR. No; and you're not his slave either.

EKDAL. And about that other business in there——

HIALMAR. Just what I was thinking of. Do you want to go in? Shall I open the door for you?

EKDAL. Well, it wouldn't do any harm.

HIALMAR (*rises*). Then we'd have that off our hands.

EKDAL. Yes, exactly. It's got to be ready first thing to-morrow. It *is* to-morrow, isn't it? Hm?

HIALMAR. Yes, of course it's to-morrow.

(HIALMAR *and* EKDAL *push aside the sliding door. The morning sun is shining in through the skylights; some doves are flying about; others are perched, cooing, upon the rafters; the hens cackle now and then, further back in the garret.*)

HIALMAR. There, now you can get to work, father.

EKDAL (*goes in*). Aren't you coming too?

HIALMAR. Well really, do you know——; I almost think—— (*Sees* GINA *at the kitchen door.*) I? No; I haven't time; I must work.—But now for our new dodge——

(*He pulls a cord; a curtain slips down inside, the lower part consisting of a piece of sailcloth, the upper part of a stretched net. The floor of the garret is thus no longer visible.*)

HIALMAR (*goes to the table*). There! Now I can sit in peace for a little while.

GINA. Is he rampaging in there again?

HIALMAR. Would you have preferred him to slip down to Madam Eriksen's? (*Seats himself.*) Do you want anything? You were saying——

GINA. I was only going to ask if you think we can lay the lunch-table here?

HIALMAR. Yes; nobody has made any early appointment, I suppose?

GINA. No, we've no one to-day except those two sweethearts that are to be taken together.

HIALMAR. Why the deuce couldn't they be taken together another day!

GINA. But my dear Ekdal, I told them to come in the afternoon, when you're having your nap.

HIALMAR. Oh, that's capital. Very well, we'll have lunch here then.

GINA. All right; but there's no hurry about laying the cloth; you can have the table for an hour yet.

HIALMAR. Do you think I'm not sticking at my work? I'm at it as hard as I can!

GINA. Then you'll be free later, you know.

(*Goes out into the kitchen again. Short pause.*)

EKDAL (*in the garret doorway, behind the net*). Hialmar!

HIALMAR. Well?

EKDAL. Afraid we'll have to move the water-trough, after all.

HIALMAR. That's what I've been saying all along.

EKDAL. Hm—hm—hm. (*Goes away from the door again.*)

(HIALMAR *goes on working a little; glances towards the garret and half rises.* HEDVIG *comes in from the kitchen.*)

HIALMAR (*sits down again hurriedly*). What do you want?

HEDVIG. I only wanted to come in beside you, father.

HIALMAR (*after a pause*). It seems to me you go poking your nose everywhere. Are you set to watch me?

HEDVIG. No, not at all.

HIALMAR. What's mother doing out there?

HEDVIG. Oh, mother's in the middle of making the herring-salad. (*Goes to the table.*) Isn't there any little thing I could help you with, father?

HIALMAR. Oh no. I must bear the whole burden—so long as my strength holds out. You needn't trouble, Hedvig; if only your father keeps his health——

HEDVIG. Oh no, father! You shan't talk in that horrible way.

(*She wanders about a little, stops by the doorway and looks into the garret.*)

HIALMAR. What's he doing?

HEDVIG. I think he's making a new path to the water-trough.

HIALMAR. He'll never manage it by himself! And I'm doomed to sit here——!

HEDVIG (*goes to him*). Let me take the brush, father; I know how to do it.

HIALMAR. Oh nonsense; you'll only hurt your eyes.

HEDVIG. Not a bit. Give me the brush.

HIALMAR (*rising*). Well, it'll only take a minute or two.

HEDVIG. Pooh, what harm can it do then? (*Takes the brush.*) There! (*Seats herself.*) And here's one I can begin upon.

HIALMAR. But mind you don't hurt your eyes!

Do you hear? *I* won't be answerable; you must take the responsibility upon yourself—so I tell you!

HEDVIG (*retouching*). Yes yes, all right.

HIALMAR. You're quite clever at it, Hedvig. Only a minute or two, you know. (*He slips through by the edge of the curtain into the garret.* HEDVIG *sits at her work.* HIALMAR *and* EKDAL *are heard disputing inside.*)

HIALMAR (*appears behind the net*). I say, Hedvig—give me those pincers that are lying on the shelf. And the chisel. (*Turns away inside.*) Now you shall see, father. Just let me show you what I mean.

(HEDVIG *has fetched the required tools from the shelf, and hands them in to him.*)

HIALMAR. Ah, thanks. He couldn't have got on without me.

(*Goes in again; they are heard carpentering and talking inside.* HEDVIG *stands looking in at them. A moment later there is a knock at the passage door; she does not notice it.*)

GREGERS WERLE (*bareheaded, in indoor dress, enters and stops near the door*). Hm——!

HEDVIG (*turns and goes towards him*). Good morning. Please come in.

GREGERS. Thank you. (*Looks towards the garret.*) You seem to have workpeople in the house.

HEDVIG. No, it's only father and grandfather. I'll tell them you are here.

GREGERS. No no, don't do that; I'd rather wait a little.

(*Seats himself on the sofa.*)

HEDVIG. It's so untidy here. (*Begins to clear away the photographs.*)

GREGERS. Oh, don't move them. Are those pictures that have to be finished?

HEDVIG. Yes, they're a few I was helping father with.

GREGERS. Don't let me disturb you at all.

HEDVIG. Oh no. (*She gathers the things to her and sits down to work;* GREGERS *looks at her, meanwhile, in silence.*)

GREGERS. Did the wild duck sleep well last night?

HEDVIG. Yes, I think so, thanks.

GREGERS (*turning towards the garret*). It looks quite different by day from what it did last night in the moonlight.

HEDVIG. Yes, it varies so much. It looks different in the morning and in the afternoon; and it's different on rainy days from what it is in fine weather.

GREGERS. Have you noticed that?

HEDVIG. Yes, how could I help it?

GREGERS. Are *you* fond of being in there with the wild duck?

HEDVIG. Yes, when I can manage it——

GREGERS. Perhaps you haven't much leisure; you go to school, I daresay?

HEDVIG. No, not now; father's afraid of me hurting my eyes.

GREGERS. Oh; then he reads with you himself?

HEDVIG. Father has promised to read with me; but he hasn't had time yet.

GREGERS. Then is there nobody else that helps you a little?

HEDVIG. Yes, Mr. Molvik; but he's not always exactly—quite——

GREGERS. Sober?

HEDVIG. Yes, I suppose that's it!

GREGERS. Ah, then you've time for anything you please. And in there I suppose it's a sort of world by itself?

HEDVIG. Oh yes, quite. And there are such lots of wonderful things.

GREGERS. Indeed?

HEDVIG. Yes, there are big cupboards full of books, and a great many of the books have pictures in them.

GREGERS. Aha!

HEDVIG. And there's an old bureau with drawers and flaps, and a big clock with figures that come out. But it doesn't go now.

GREGERS. So time has come to a standstill in there—in the wild duck's domain.

HEDVIG. Yes. And there's an old paint-box and things of that sort; and all the books.

GREGERS. And you read the books, I suppose?

HEDVIG. Oh yes, when I get the chance. Most of them are English though, and I don't understand English. But then I look at the pictures.—There's one great big book called "Harryson's History of London."[1] It must be a hundred years old; and there are such heaps of pictures in it. At the beginning

[1] *A New and Universal History of the Cities of London and Westminster*, by Walter Harrison. London, 1775, folio.

there's Death with an hour-glass, and a girl. I think that's horrid. But then there are all the other pictures of churches, and castles, and streets, and big ships sailing on the sea.

GREGERS. But tell me, where did all these wonderful things come from?

HEDVIG. Oh, an old sea captain once lived here, and he brought them home. They used to call him "The Flying Dutchman." That was curious, because he wasn't a Dutchman.

GREGERS. Wasn't he?

HEDVIG. No. But he disappeared at last; and so he left all these things behind him.

GREGERS. Tell me now, when you're sitting in there looking at the pictures, don't you wish you could travel and see the great world itself?

HEDVIG. Oh no! I mean always to stay at home and help father and mother.

GREGERS. To finish photographs?

HEDVIG. No, not only that. I should love above everything to learn to engrave pictures like those in the English books.

GREGERS. Hm. What does your father say to that?

HEDVIG. I don't think father likes it; he's so strange about that. Only think, he talks of my learning basket-making, and straw-plaiting! But I don't think *that* would lead to much.

GREGERS. Oh no, I don't think so either.

HEDVIG. But father was right in saying that if I had learnt basket-making I could have made the new basket for the wild duck.

GREGERS. So you could; and it was, strictly speaking, your business, wasn't it?

HEDVIG. Yes, for it's *my* wild duck.

GREGERS. Of course it is.

HEDVIG. Yes, it belongs to me. But I lend it to father and grandfather as often as they please.

GREGERS. Indeed? What do they do with it?

HEDVIG. Oh, they look after it, and build places for it, and so on.

GREGERS. No doubt; for the wild duck is by far the most distinguished inhabitant of the garret, I suppose.

HEDVIG. Yes, indeed she is; for she's a real wild fowl, you know. And she's so much to be pitied; she has no one to care for, poor thing.

GREGERS. She has no family, as the rabbits have——

HEDVIG. No. The hens too, many of them, were chickens together; but she's been taken right away from all her belongings. And then there's such a lot that's strange about the wild duck. Nobody knows her, and nobody knows where she came from either.

GREGERS. And she has been down in the depths of the sea.

HEDVIG (*with a quick glance at him, represses a smile and asks*). Why do you say "the depths of the sea"?

GREGERS. What else should I say?

HEDVIG. You could say "the bottom of the sea."[1]

[1] Gregers here uses the poetical, or at any rate old-fashioned, expression "havsens bund," while Hedvig asks him rather to use the more commonplace "havets bund" or "havbunden."

GREGERS. Oh, mayn't I just as well say the depths of the sea?

HEDVIG. Yes; but it sounds so strange to me when other people speak of the depths of the sea.

GREGERS. Why so? Tell me why?

HEDVIG. No, I won't; because it's so stupid.

GREGERS. Oh no, I'm sure it's not. Do tell me why you smiled.

HEDVIG. Well, this is the reason: whenever I come to realise suddenly—in a flash—what's in there, it always seems to me that the whole room and everything in it should be called "the depths of the sea."—But that's so stupid.

GREGERS. You mustn't say that.

HEDVIG. Yes, because it's only a garret.

GREGERS (*looks fixedly at her*). Are you so sure of that?

HEDVIG (*astonished*). That it's a garret?

GREGERS. Are you quite certain of it?

(HEDVIG *is silent, and looks at him open-mouthed.* GINA *comes in from the kitchen with the table things.*)

GREGERS (*rising*). I've come in upon you too early.

GINA. Oh, you must be somewhere; and we're nearly ready now, any way. Clear the table, Hedvig.

(HEDVIG *clears away her things; she and* GINA *lay the cloth during the following.* GREGERS *seats himself in the arm-chair, and turns over an album.*)

GREGERS. I hear you can retouch, Mrs. Ekdal.

GINA (*with a side glance*). Yes, I can.

GREGERS. That was exceedingly lucky.

GINA. How lucky?

GREGERS. Since Ekdal was to be a photographer, I mean.

HEDVIG. Mother can take photographs too.

GINA. Oh, yes. I've had to teach myself that too.

GREGERS. So it's you that really carry on the business, I suppose?

GINA. Yes, when Ekdal hasn't time himself.

GREGERS. He's a great deal taken up with his old father, no doubt.

GINA. Yes; and Ekdal isn't the sort of man to do nothing but take portraits of everyday people.

GREGERS. I quite agree with you; but having once gone in for the thing——

GINA. You know, Mr. Werle, Ekdal's not like one of your common photographers.

GREGERS. Of course not; but still——

(*A shot is fired within the garret.*)

GREGERS (*starting up*). What's that?

GINA. Ugh! Now they're firing again!

GREGERS. Have they firearms in there?

HEDVIG. They're out shooting.

GREGERS. What! (*At the door of the garret.*) Are you shooting, Hialmar?

HIALMAR (*inside the net*). Are you there? I didn't know; I was so taken up—— (*To* HEDVIG.) Why didn't you let us know? (*Comes into the studio.*)

GREGERS. Do you go shooting in the garret?

HIALMAR (*showing a double-barrelled pistol*). Oh, only with this.

GINA. Yes, you and grandfather will do yourselves an injury some day with that pigstol.

HIALMAR (*with irritation*). I believe I've told you that this kind of firearm is called a *pistol*.

GINA. Oh, that's not much better, that I can see.

GREGERS. So you've become a sportsman too, Hialmar?

HIALMAR. Only a little rabbit-shooting now and then. It's mostly to please father, you understand.

GINA. Men are so strange; they must always have something to pervert themselves with.

HIALMAR (*snappishly*). Just so; we must always have something to *divert* ourselves with.

GINA. Yes, that's exactly what I say.

HIALMAR. Hm. (*To* GREGERS.) You see the garret's luckily so situated that no one can hear us shooting. (*Lays the pistol on the top shelf of the book-case.*) Don't touch the pistol, Hedvig! One of the barrels is loaded, remember that.

GREGERS (*looking through the net*). You have a fowling-piece too, I see.

HIALMAR. That's father's old gun. It's no use now; there's something gone wrong with the lock. But it's fun to have it all the same, for we can take it to pieces now and then, and grease it and screw it together again.—Of course it's mostly father that fiddle-faddles with all that sort of thing.

HEDVIG (*beside* GREGERS). Now you can see the wild duck properly.

GREGERS. I'm just looking at her. She droops one wing rather, I think.

HEDVIG. Well, no wonder; she was wounded, you know.

GREGERS. And she trails one foot a little. Isn't that so?

HIALMAR. Perhaps a very little bit.

HEDVIG. Yes, it was by that foot the dog seized her.

HIALMAR. But otherwise she hasn't the least thing the matter with her, and that's really wonderful for a creature that's got a charge of shot in her body, and has been between a dog's teeth——

GREGERS (*with a glance at* HEDVIG)—— And that's been in the depths of the sea—so long.

HEDVIG (*smiling*). Yes.

GINA (*laying the table*). That blessed wild duck! What a lot of fuss you make over her.

HIALMAR. Hm;—is lunch nearly ready?

GINA. Yes, directly. Hedvig, you must come and help me now.

(GINA *and* HEDVIG *go out into the kitchen.*)

HIALMAR (*in a low voice*). I think you'd better not stand there looking in at father; he doesn't like it. (GREGERS *moves away from the garret door.*) I may as well shut up before the others come. (*Claps his hands to send the fowls back.*) Ssh—ssh, in with you! (*Draws up the curtain and pulls the doors together.*) All these appliances are my own invention. It's really amusing to have things of this sort to potter about, and to put to rights when they get out of order. And it's quite necessary, you see; for Gina objects to having rabbits and fowls in the studio.

GREGERS. Of course. I suppose it's *your* wife that's the ruling spirit here?

HIALMAR. I generally leave the details of business to her; for then I can take refuge in the parlour and think of more important things.

GREGERS. What things may they be, Hialmar?

HIALMAR. I wonder you haven't asked about that sooner. But perhaps you haven't heard of the invention?

GREGERS. The invention? No.

HIALMAR. Really? Haven't you? Oh no, out there in the wilderness——

GREGERS. So you've invented something, have you?

HIALMAR. I haven't quite completed it yet; but I'm working at it. You can imagine that when I resolved to give myself up to photography, it wasn't with the idea of doing nothing but take portraits of all sorts of everyday people.

GREGERS. No; your wife was saying the same thing just now.

HIALMAR. I swore that if I consecrated my powers to this handicraft I would so exalt it that it should become both an art and a science. And therefore I resolved to devote myself to this great invention.

GREGERS. And what's the nature of the invention? What is it to do?

HIALMAR. Oh, my dear fellow, you mustn't ask for details yet. It takes time, you see. And you mustn't think that my motive is vanity. It's not for my own sake that I'm working. Oh no; it's my life's mission that stands before me night and day.

GREGERS. What is your life's mission?

HIALMAR. Do you forget the old man with the silver hair?

GREGERS. Your poor father? Well, but what can you do for him?

HIALMAR. I can awaken his self-respect from the dead, by raising the name of Ekdal to honour and dignity again.

GREGERS. Then that's your life's mission?

HIALMAR. Yes. I want to save the shipwrecked man. For shipwrecked he was by the very first blast of the storm. Even while those terrible investigations were going on, he was no longer himself. That pistol there—the one we use to shoot rabbits with—has played its part in the tragedy of the house of Ekdal.

GREGERS. The pistol? Indeed?

HIALMAR. When the sentence of imprisonment was passed—he had the pistol in his hand——

GREGERS. Had he——?

HIALMAR. Yes; but he dared not use it. His courage failed him. So broken, so demoralised was he even then! Oh, can you understand it? He, a soldier; he, who had shot nine bears, and who was descended from two lieutenant-colonels—one after the other of course.—Can you understand it, Gregers?

GREGERS. Yes, I understand it well enough.

HIALMAR. I don't. And once more the pistol played a part in our family history. When he had put on the grey clothes and was under lock and key—oh, that was a terrible time for me, I can tell you. I had the blinds drawn down over both my windows.

When I peeped out I saw the sun shining as usual. I couldn't understand it. I saw the people going along the street, laughing and talking about indifferent things. I couldn't understand it. It seemed to me that the whole of existence must be at a standstill—as if under an eclipse.

GREGERS. I felt like that too, when my mother died.

HIALMAR. In that hour Hialmar Ekdal pointed the pistol at his own breast.

GREGERS. You too thought of——!

HIALMAR. Yes.

GREGERS. But you didn't fire?

HIALMAR. No. At the decisive moment I won the victory over myself. I remained in life. But I can assure you it takes some courage to choose life under those circumstances.

GREGERS. Well, that depends on how one takes it.

HIALMAR. Yes, entirely. But it was all for the best, for now I shall soon perfect my invention; and Dr. Relling thinks, as I do myself, that father will be allowed to wear his uniform again. I will ask for that as my only reward.

GREGERS. So that's what he meant about his uniform?

HIALMAR. Yes, that's what he most yearns for. You can't imagine how my heart bleeds for him. Every time we celebrate any little family festival—for example, Gina's and my wedding-day, or whatever it may be—in comes the old man in the lieutenant's uniform of happier days. But if he only hears a knock at the door—for he daren't show himself to strangers, you know—he hurries back to his room again as fast as his old legs can carry him. Oh, it's heartrending for a son to see such things!

GREGERS. How long do you think it will be before your invention is completed?

HIALMAR. Come now, you mustn't expect me to enter into particulars like that. An invention is a thing one hasn't entire control over. It depends largely on intuition—on inspiration—and it's almost impossible to predict when the inspiration may come.

GREGERS. But it's advancing?

HIALMAR. Yes, certainly, it's advancing. I turn it over in my mind every day: I'm full of it. Every afternoon, when I've had my dinner, I shut myself up in the parlour where I can ponder undisturbed. But I can't be goaded to it; it's not a bit of good; Relling says so too.

GREGERS. And don't you think that all that business in the garret draws you off and distracts you too much?

HIALMAR. No no no, quite the contrary. You mustn't say that. I can't be everlastingly absorbed in the same laborious train of thought. I must have something outside of it to fill up the pauses. The inspiration, the intuition, you see—when it comes, it comes, and there's an end of it.

GREGERS. My dear Hialmar, I almost think you have something of the wild duck in you.

HIALMAR. Something of the wild duck? How do you mean?

GREGERS. You've dived down and bitten yourself fast in the undergrowth.

HIALMAR. Are you alluding to the almost fatal shot that has broken father's wing—and mine too?

GREGERS. Not mainly to that. I don't say that you've been wounded; but you've strayed into a poisonous marsh, Hialmar; you have an insidious disease within you, and you've sunk down to die in the dark.

HIALMAR. I? To die in the dark? Look here, Gregers, you must really leave off talking such nonsense.

GREGERS. Don't be afraid; I will try to help you up again. I too have a mission in life now; I found it yesterday.

HIALMAR. That's all very well; but you'll please leave *me* out of it. I can assure you that—apart from my easily explained melancholy, of course—I am as contented as any one can wish to be.

GREGERS. Your contentment is an effect of the marsh vapours.

HIALMAR. Now, my dear Gregers, pray don't go on about disease and poison; I'm not used to that sort of talk. In my house, nobody ever speaks to me about unpleasant things.

GREGERS. Ah, I can easily believe that.

HIALMAR. It's not good for me, you see. And there aren't any marsh vapours here, as you express it. The poor photographer's roof is lowly, I know—and my circumstances are narrow. But I'm an inventor, and I'm the breadwinner of a family. That exalts me above my mean surroundings.—Ah, here comes lunch!

(GINA *and* HEDVIG *bring bottles of ale, a decanter*

of brandy, glasses, etc. At the same time, RELLING *and* MOLVIK *enter from the passage; they are both without hat or overcoat.* MOLVIK *is dressed in black.*)

GINA (*setting things upon the table*). Oh, you two have come in the nick of time.

RELLING. Molvik got it into his head that he could smell herring-salad, and then there was no holding him. Good morning again, Ekdal.

HIALMAR. Gregers, may I introduce Mr. Molvik. Doctor—— Oh, you know Relling, don't you?

GREGERS. Yes, slightly.

RELLING. Oh, Mr. Werle, junior! Yes, we two have been on each other's tracks up at the Höidal works. You've just moved in?

GREGERS. I moved in this morning.

RELLING. Molvik and I live right underneath you; so you haven't far to go for the doctor and the clergyman, if should you need them.

GREGERS. Thanks, it's not unlikely; for yesterday we were thirteen at table.

HIALMAR. Oh, come now, don't let's get upon unpleasant subjects again!

RELLING. You can make your mind easy, Ekdal; I'll be hanged if the finger of fate points to you.

HIALMAR. I hope not, for the sake of my family. But let us sit down and eat and drink and be merry.

GREGERS. Shan't we wait for your father?

HIALMAR. No, he'll have his taken in to him later. Come along!

(*The Men seat themselves at table, and eat and*

drink. GINA *and* HEDVIG *go in and out and wait upon them.*)

RELLING. Molvik was frightfully screwed yesterday, Mrs. Ekdal.

GINA. Really? Yesterday again?

RELLING. Didn't you hear him when I brought him home last night?

GINA. No, I can't say I did.

RELLING. That was a good thing, for Molvik was disgusting last night.

GINA. Is that true, Molvik?

MOLVIK. Let us blot out last night's proceedings. That sort of thing is totally apart from my better self.

RELLING (*to* GREGERS). It comes over him like a sort of possession, and then I have to go out on the loose with him. Mr. Molvik is dæmonic, you see.

GREGERS. Dæmonic?

RELLING. Molvik's dæmonic, yes.

GREGERS. Hm.

RELLING. And dæmonic natures are not made to walk straight through the world; they must meander a little now and then.—Well, so you still stick up there at those horrible grimy works?

GREGERS. I have stuck there until now.

RELLING. And did you manage to enforce that claim you went about asserting?

GREGERS. Claim? (*Understands him.*) Ah, I see.

HIALMAR. Have you been enforcing claims, Gregers?

GREGERS. Oh, nonsense.

RELLING. Faith, but he has, though! He went

round to all the cotters' cabins, presenting something he called the claim of the ideal.

GREGERS. I was young then.

RELLING. You're right; you were very young. And as for the claim of the ideal—you never got it honoured while I was up there.

GREGERS. Nor since either.

RELLING. Ah, then you've learnt to knock a little discount off, I expect.

GREGERS. Never, when I stand before a true man.

HIALMAR. Well, that's reasonable, I should say. A little butter, Gina.

RELLING. And a slice of bacon for Molvik.

MOLVIK. Ugh! not bacon!

(*A knock at the garret door.*)

HIALMAR. Open the door, Hedvig; father wants to come out.

(HEDVIG *goes over and opens the door a little way;* EKDAL *comes in with a fresh rabbit skin; she closes the door after him.*)

EKDAL. Good morning, gentlemen! Good sport to-day. Shot a big one.

HIALMAR. And you've skinned it before I came!

EKDAL. Salted it too. It's good tender meat, is rabbit; it's sweet; it tastes like sugar. Good appetite to you, gentlemen!

(*Goes into his room.*)

MOLVIK (*rising*). Excuse me——; I can't——; I must get down stairs as quickly as——

RELLING. Drink some soda water, man!

MOLVIK (*hurrying away*). Ugh—ugh!

(*Goes through the passage door.*)

RELLING (*to* HIALMAR). Let's drain a glass to the old hunter.

HIALMAR (*clinks glasses with him*). To the man of daring deeds that has looked death in the face!

RELLING. To the grey-haired——(*drinks*). I say, is his hair grey or white?

HIALMAR. Something between the two, I think; for that matter, he hasn't very many hairs left on his head.

RELLING. Well, one can get through the world with a wig. After all, you're a happy man, Ekdal; you have this noble mission to strive for——

HIALMAR. And I do strive, I can tell you.

RELLING. And you have your excellent wife, waddling[1] quietly in and out in her felt slippers, and making everything cosy and comfortable about you.

HIALMAR. Yes, Gina (*nods to her*), you're a good companion on the path of life.

GINA. Oh, don't sit there criticising me.

RELLING. And your Hedvig too, Ekdal!

HIALMAR (*affected*). The child, yes! The child before everything! Hedvig, come here to me. (*Strokes her hair.*) What day is it to-morrow, eh?

HEDVIG (*shaking him*). Oh no, you're not to say anything, father!

HIALMAR. It cuts me to the heart when I think

[1] This speech of Relling's is exceedingly difficult. We have been sorely tempted to disregard altogether the characteristic "vagger i hofterne," for which we have failed to find any natural English equivalent. The word "waddling" seems to convey Relling's meaning accurately enough. It is not complimentary to Gina's carriage; but neither is "vagger i hofterne."

how poor an affair it'll be; only a little festivity in the garret——

HEDVIG. Oh but that's just what I like!

RELLING. Just you wait till the wonderful invention sees the light, Hedvig!

HIALMAR. Yes indeed! then you shall see——! Hedvig, I've resolved to make your future secure. You shall live in comfort all your days. I will demand something or other for you. That shall be the poor inventor's sole reward.

HEDVIG (*whispering, with her arms round his neck*). Oh you dear, kind father!

RELLING (*to* GREGERS). Don't you find it delightful, for once in a way, to sit at a well-spread table in a happy family circle?

HIALMAR. Yes, I really prize these social hours.

GREGERS. For my part, I don't thrive in marsh vapours.

RELLING. Marsh vapours?

HIALMAR. Oh, don't begin with that talk again!

GINA. Heaven knows there's no bad smell here, Mr. Werle; I give the place a good airing every blessed day.

GREGERS (*leaves the table*). No airing will drive out the taint I mean.

HIALMAR. Taint!

GINA. Yes, what do you say to that, Ekdal!

RELLING. Excuse me, but haven't you yourself brought the taint from those mines up there?

GREGERS. It's like you to call what I bring into this house a taint.

RELLING (*goes up to him*). I tell you what it is,

Mr. Werle, junior: I have a strong suspicion that you're still carrying about that claim of the ideal, large as life, in your coat-tail pocket.

GREGERS. I carry it in my breast.

RELLING. Well, wherever you've got it, I advise you not to come dunning us with it here, so long as I'm on the premises.

GREGERS. And if I do it all the same?

RELLING. Then you'll go head-foremost down stairs; now I've warned you.

HIALMAR (*rising*). Oh, but Relling——!

GREGERS. Yes, just you turn me out——

GINA (*steps between them*). You mustn't do that, Relling. But I must say, Mr. Werle, that it ill becomes you to talk about swamps and taints, after all the mess you made with your stove.

(*A knock at the passage door.*)

HEDVIG. Mother, there's somebody knocking.

HIALMAR. There now, we're going to have a whole lot of people!

GINA. Let me go—— (*Goes over and opens the door, starts, and draws back.*) Oh—oh dear!

(WERLE, *in a fur coat, advances one step into the room.*)

WERLE. Excuse me; but I think my son is staying here.

GINA (*with a gulp*). Yes.

HIALMAR (*approaching him*). Won't you do us the honour to——?

WERLE. Thank you, I merely wish to speak to my son.

GREGERS. What is it? Here I am.

WERLE. I wish to speak with you in your room.

GREGERS. In my room?—well——(*is going*).

GINA. No, your room's not in a fit state to——

WERLE. Well then, out in the passage there; I want to have a few words with you alone.

HIALMAR. You can do that here, Sir. Come into the parlour, Relling.

(HIALMAR *and* RELLING *go off to the right.* GINA *takes* HEDVIG *with her into the kitchen*).

GREGERS (*after a short pause*). Well, now we're alone.

WERLE. From something you let fall last evening, and from your coming to lodge with the Ekdals, I can't help inferring that you have some hostile intention towards me.

GREGERS. I intend to open Hialmar Ekdal's eyes. He shall see his position as it really is—that is all.

WERLE. Is that the mission in life you spoke of yesterday?

GREGERS. Yes. You have left me no other.

WERLE. Is it I that have crippled your mind, Gregers?

GREGERS. You have crippled my whole life. I'm not thinking of all that about mother—but it's thanks to you that I have a guilty conscience continually pursuing and gnawing at me.

WERLE. Aha, it's your conscience that's ill at ease, is it?

GREGERS. I ought to have taken a stand against you when the trap was set for Lieutenant Ekdal. I should have cautioned him, for I had a misgiving as to what was in the wind.

WERLE. Yes, that was the time to have spoken.

GREGERS. I did not dare to, I was so cowed and spiritless. I was mortally afraid of you, not only then, but long afterwards.

WERLE. You've got over that fear now, it appears.

GREGERS. Yes, fortunately. The wrong done to old Ekdal, both by me and by—others, can never be remedied; but Hialmar I can rescue from all the falsehood and deception that are bringing him to ruin.

WERLE. Do you think that'll be doing him a kindness?

GREGERS. I firmly believe so.

WERLE. You think our friend the photographer is the sort of man to appreciate such friendly offices?

GREGERS. Yes, I do.

WERLE. Hm, we shall see.

GREGERS. Besides, if I'm to go on living, I must try and find some cure for my sick conscience.

WERLE. It will never be well. Your conscience has been sickly from childhood. That's an inheritance from your mother, Gregers—the only inheritance she left you.

GREGERS (*with a scornful half-smile*). Haven't you yet digested your resentment at your own miscalculation as to the fortune she would bring you?

WERLE. Don't let us get upon irrelevant subjects. —Then you keep to your purpose of setting young Ekdal upon what you imagine to be the right scent?

GREGERS. Yes, that's my fixed resolve.

WERLE. Well, in that case I might have spared

myself this visit; for of course it's useless to ask you to return home with me?

GREGERS. Quite useless.

WERLE. And I suppose you won't enter the firm either?

GREGERS. No.

WERLE. Very good. But as I'm thinking of marrying again, your share in the property will fall to you at once.[1]

GREGERS (*quickly*). No, I don't wish that.

WERLE. You don't wish it?

GREGERS. No, I daren't take it, for conscience' sake.

WERLE (*after a pause*). Are you going up to the works again?

GREGERS. No; I consider myself released from your service.

WERLE. But what are you going to do?

GREGERS. Only to fulfil my mission, nothing more.

WERLE. Well, but afterwards? What are you going to live upon?

GREGERS. I have laid by a little out of my salary.

WERLE. How long will *that* last?

GREGERS. I think it will last out my time.

WERLE. What do you mean?

GREGERS. I shall answer no more questions.

WERLE. Good-bye then, Gregers.

GREGERS. Good-bye. (WERLE *goes.*)

[1] By Norwegian law, before a widower can marry again, a certain proportion of his property must be settled on his children by his former marriage.

HIALMAR (*peeping in*). He's gone, isn't he?

GREGERS. Yes.

(HIALMAR *and* RELLING *enter; also* GINA and HEDVIG *from the kitchen.*)

RELLING. That lunch was a failure.

GREGERS. Put on your coat, Hialmar; I want you to come for a long walk with me.

HIALMAR. With pleasure. What was it your father wanted? Anything about me?

GREGERS. Come along. We must have a talk. I'll go and put on my overcoat.

(*Goes out by the passage door.*)

GINA. You shouldn't go out with him, Ekdal.

RELLING. No, don't you do it. Stay where you are.

HIALMAR (*gets his hat and overcoat*). Oh, nonsense! When a friend of my youth feels impelled to open his mind to me in private——

RELLING. But deuce take it—don't you see the fellow's mad, cracked, demented!

GINA. There, you hear! His mother before him had mad fits like that sometimes.

HIALMAR. The more need for a friend's watchful eye. (*To* GINA.) Be sure you have dinner ready in good time. Good-bye for the present. (*Goes out by the passage door.*)

RELLING. It's a pity the fellow didn't go to hell through one of the Höidal mines.

GINA. Good Lord! what makes you say that?

RELLING (*muttering*). Oh, I have my reasons.

GINA. Do you think young Werle is really mad?

RELLING. No, worse luck; he's no madder than

people in general. But one disease he's certainly suffering from.

GINA. What is it that's wrong with him?

RELLING. Well, I'll tell you, Mrs. Ekdal. He's suffering from chronic integrity in an acute form.

GINA. Integrity?

HEDVIG. Is that a kind of disease?

RELLING. Yes, it's a national disease; but it only appears sporadically. (*Nods to* GINA.) Thanks for your hospitality.

(*He goes out by the passage door.*)

GINA (*walking to and fro*). Ugh, that Gregers Werle—he's always been a horrible creature.

HEDVIG (*standing by the table, and looking searchingly at her*). I think all this is very strange.

Act Fourth.

(HIALMAR EKDAL'S *studio. A photograph has just been taken; a camera with the cloth over it, a pedestal, two chairs, a folding table, etc., are standing out in the room. Afternoon light; the sun is going down; a little later it begins to grow dusk.*)

(GINA *stands in the passage doorway, with a little box and a wet glass plate in her hand, and is speaking to somebody outside.*)

GINA. Yes, certainly. When I make a promise I keep it. The first dozen shall be ready on Monday. Good afternoon. (*Some one is heard going downstairs.* GINA *shuts the door, slips the plate into the box, and puts it into the covered camera.*)

HEDVIG (*comes in from the kitchen*). Are they gone?

GINA (*tidying up*). Yes, thank goodness, I've got rid of them at last.

HEDVIG. But can you imagine why father hasn't come home yet?

GINA. Are you sure he's not down in Relling's room?

HEDVIG. No, he's not; I ran down the kitchen stair and asked just now.

GINA. And I suppose his dinner's getting cold.

HEDVIG. Yes, I can't understand it. Father's always so careful to be home to dinner!

GINA. Oh, he'll be here directly, you'll see.

HEDVIG. I wish he would come; everything seems so queer to-day.

GINA (*calls out*). There he is!

(HIALMAR EKDAL *comes in at the passage door.*)

HEDVIG (*going to him*). Father! Oh what a time we've been waiting for you!

GINA (*glances at him*). You've been a long time away, Ekdal.

HIALMAR (*without looking at her*). Rather long, yes.

(*He takes off his overcoat;* GINA *and* HEDVIG *go to help him; he motions them away.*)

GINA. Perhaps you've had dinner with Werle?

HIALMAR (*hanging up his coat*). No.

GINA (*going towards the kitchen door*). Then I'll bring some in for you.

HIALMAR. No; let the dinner be. I don't want anything to eat.

HEDVIG (*going nearer to him*). Aren't you well, father?

HIALMAR. Well? Oh yes, tolerably. Gregers and I had a tiring walk?

GINA. You oughtn't to have gone so far, Ekdal; you're not used to it.

HIALMAR. Hm; there's many a thing a man must get used to in this world. (*Wanders about the room.*) Has any one been here whilst I was out?

GINA. Nobody but the two sweethearts.

HIALMAR. No new orders?

GINA. No, not to-day.

HEDVIG. There'll be some to-morrow, father, you'll see.

HIALMAR. I hope there will; for to-morrow I'm going to set to work in earnest.

HEDVIG. To-morrow! Don't you remember what day it is to-morrow?

HIALMAR. Oh yes, by-the-bye—— Well, the day after, then. Henceforth I mean to do everything myself; I'll do all the work alone.

GINA. What's the good of that, Ekdal? It'll only make life a burden to you. I can manage the photography; and you can go on working at your invention.

HEDVIG. And think of the wild duck, father,—and all the hens and rabbits and——!

HIALMAR. Don't talk to me of all that trash! From to-morrow I'll never set foot in the garret again.

HEDVIG. Oh but, father, you promised that we should have a little entertainment——

HIALMAR. Hm, true. Well then, from the day after to-morrow. I'm almost inclined to wring that cursed wild duck's neck!

HEDVIG (*shrieks*). The wild duck!

GINA. Well I never!

HEDVIG (*shaking him*). Oh no, father; you know it's my wild duck!

HIALMAR. That's why I don't do it. I haven't the heart to—for your sake, Hedvig. But in my inmost soul I feel that I ought to do it. I ought not to suffer a creature that has been in *those* hands under my roof.

GINA. Why, good gracious, because grandfather got it from that wretched Pettersen——

HIALMAR (*wandering about*). There are certain claims—what shall I call them?—let me say claims of the ideal—certain obligations, which a man cannot set aside without injury to his soul.

HEDVIG (*going after him*). But think of the wild duck,—the poor wild duck!

HIALMAR (*stops*). I tell you I'll spare it—for your sake. Not a hair of its head shall be touched,—I mean, I'll spare it. There are greater problems than that to be dealt with. But you should go out a little now, Hedvig, as usual; it's getting dusk enough for you now.

HEDVIG. No, I don't care about going out now.

HIALMAR. Yes do; it seems to me you peer about so with your eyes; all these vapours in here are bad for you. The air is heavy under this roof.

HEDVIG. Very well then, I shall run down the kitchen stair and take a little walk. My cloak and hat?—oh, they're in my own room. Father—be sure you don't do the wild duck any harm whilst I'm out.

HIALMAR. Not a feather of its head shall be touched. (*Draws her to him.*) You and I, Hedvig—we two——! Well, go along.

(HEDVIG *nods to her parents and goes out through the kitchen.*)

HIALMAR (*walks about without looking up*). Gina.

GINA. Yes?

HIALMAR. From to-morrow, or say from the day after to-morrow, I should like to keep the household account-book myself.

GINA. Do you want to keep the accounts too, now?

HIALMAR. Yes; or to put down the receipts at any rate.

GINA. Lord help us! that's soon done.

HIALMAR. One would hardly think so; at any rate you seem to make the money go a very long way. (*Stops and looks at her.*) How do you manage it?

GINA. It's because Hedvig and I need so little.

HIALMAR. Is it the case that father is very liberally paid for the copying he does for Mr. Werle?

GINA. I don't know whether the pay is so liberal. I don't know the prices for such work.

HIALMAR. Well, what does he get, about? Let me hear!

GINA. Oh, it varies; it comes to about as much as he costs us, with a little pocket-money over.

HIALMAR. As much as he costs us! And you've never told me this before!

GINA. No, I couldn't; it pleased you so much to think he got everything from you.

HIALMAR. And he gets it from Mr. Werle!

GINA. Oh yes; he has plenty and to spare, he has.

HIALMAR. Light the lamp for me, please!

GINA (*lighting the lamp*). And of course we don't know that it's Mr. Werle himself; it may be Gråberg——

HIALMAR. Why attempt such an evasion?

GINA. I don't know; I only thought——

HIALMAR. Hm!

GINA. It wasn't I that got grandfather that

writing. It was Bertha, when she used to come about us.

HIALMAR. It seems to me your voice is trembling.

GINA (*putting the lamp-shade on*). Is it?

HIALMAR. And your hands are shaking, aren't they?

GINA (*firmly*). Speak straight out, Ekdal. What has he been saying about me?

HIALMAR. Is it true—can it be true that—that there was an—an understanding between you and Mr. Werle, while you were in service there?

GINA. That's not true. Not at that time. Mr. Werle did come after me, I own it. And his wife thought there was something in it, and then she made such a hocus-pocus and hurly-burly, and she knocked and drove me about so, that I left her service.

HIALMAR. But afterwards then!

GINA. Well, then I went home. And mother—well, she wasn't the woman you took her for, Ekdal; she kept on worrying and worrying at me about one thing and another—for Mr. Werle was a widower by that time.

HIALMAR. Well, and then?

GINA. I suppose you must know it. He didn't give it up until he'd had his way.

HIALMAR (*striking his hands together*). And this is the mother of my child! How could you hide this from me?

GINA. It was wrong of me; I ought certainly to have told you long ago.

HIALMAR. You should have told me at the very first; then I should have known what you were.

GINA. But would you have married me all the same?

HIALMAR. How can you suppose so?

GINA. That's just why I didn't dare to tell you anything then. I'd come to care for you so much, you know; and I couldn't go and make myself utterly miserable——

HIALMAR (*walks about*). And this is my Hedvig's mother! And to know that all I see before me—(*kicks at a chair*)—all that I call my home—I owe to a favoured predecessor! Oh that scoundrel Werle!

GINA. Do you repent the fifteen years we've lived together?

HIALMAR. Haven't you every day, every hour, repented of the spider's-web of deceit you had spun around me? Answer me that! How could you help writhing with penitence and remorse?

GINA. My dear Ekdal, I've had plenty to do looking after the house and all the daily business——

HIALMAR. Then you never think of reviewing your past?

GINA. No; heaven knows I'd almost forgotten those old stories.

HIALMAR. Oh, that blank, callous contentment! To me there is something revolting about it. Think of it—never so much as a twinge of remorse!

GINA. But tell me, Ekdal, what would have become of you if you hadn't had a wife like me?

HIALMAR. Like you——!

GINA. Yes; for you know I've always been a little more practical and wide-awake than you. Of course I'm a year or two older.

HIALMAR. What would have become of me!

GINA. You'd got into all sorts of bad ways when first you met me; you can't deny that.

HIALMAR. So that's what you call bad ways? Oh, you don't understand what a man goes through when he's in grief and despair—especially a man of my fiery temperament.

GINA. Well, that may be so. And I don't say I've anything to boast of; for you became a moral of a husband directly you'd a house and home of your own. And now we'd got everything so nice and cosy about us; and Hedvig and I were just thinking we'd soon be able to give ourselves a little rein, in the way of both food and clothes.

HIALMAR. In the swamp of deceit, yes.

GINA. Oh, that that wretched creature had never set his foot inside our doors!

HIALMAR. And I, too, thought my home such a pleasant one. That was a delusion. Where shall I now find the elasticity of spirit to bring my invention into the world of reality? Perhaps it will die with me; and then it will be your past, Gina, that will have killed it.

GINA (*nearly crying*). You mustn't say such things, Ekdal. I've only wanted to do what was best for you all my days!

HIALMAR. I ask you, what becomes of the bread-winner's dream? When I used to lie in there on the sofa and ponder over the invention, I had a clear enough presentiment that it would sap my vitality to the last drop. I felt even then that the day when I held the patent in my hand would be the day—of my release. And then it was my dream that you should live on and be known as the deceased inventor's well-to-do widow!

GINA (*drying her tears*). No, you mustn't talk like that, Ekdal. May the Lord never let me see the day I am left a widow!

HIALMAR. Oh, the whole dream has vanished. It's all over now. All over!

(GREGERS WERLE *opens the passage-door cautiously and looks in.*)

GREGERS. May I come in?

HIALMAR. Yes, come in.

GREGERS (*comes forward, his face beaming with satisfaction, and holds out both his hands to them*). Well, dear friends——! (*Looks from one to the other, and whispers to* HIALMAR.) Haven't you done it yet?

HIALMAR (*aloud*). It *is* done.

GREGERS. It *is?*

HIALMAR. I have passed through the bitterest moments of my life.

GREGERS. But also the most ennobling, I should think.

HIALMAR. Well, we've got through it for the present.

GINA. God forgive you, Mr. Werle.

GREGERS (*in great surprise*). But I don't understand this.

HIALMAR. What don't you understand?

GREGERS. After so great a crisis—a crisis that's to be the starting-point of an entirely new life—of a communion founded on truth and free from falsehood of any kind——

HIALMAR. Yes yes, I know; I know that quite well.

GREGERS. I confidently expected, when I entered the room, to find the light of transfiguration beaming upon me from both man and wife. And now I see nothing but dulness, oppression, gloom——

GINA. Oh, is that it?

(*Takes off the lamp-shade.*)

GREGERS. You will not understand me, Mrs. Ekdal. Ah well, *you*, I suppose, need time to—— But you, Hialmar? Surely you feel a new consecration after the great crisis.

HIALMAR. Yes, of course I do. That is—in a sort of way.

GREGERS. For I'm sure there's nothing in the world to compare with the joy of forgiving one who has erred, and raising her up to one's self in love.

HIALMAR. Do you think a man can so easily throw off the effects of the bitter cup I have drained?

GREGERS. No, perhaps not a common man. But a man like you!

HIALMAR. Good God! I know that well enough. But you must keep me up to it, Gregers. It takes time, you know.

GREGERS. You have a great deal of the wild duck in you, Hialmar.

(RELLING *has come in at the passage door.*)

RELLING. Oho! is the wild duck to the fore again?

HIALMAR. Yes; Mr. Werle's wing-broken prey.

RELLING. Mr. Werle's——? So you're discussing him?

HIALMAR. Him and—ourselves.

RELLING (*in an undertone to* GREGERS). May the devil take you!

HIALMAR. What's that you're saying?

RELLING. I was uttering a heartfelt wish that this quacksalver would take himself off. If he stops here he's sure to get you both into a mess.

GREGERS. These two won't make a mess of it, Mr. Relling. Of course I won't speak of Hialmar—him we know. But she too, in her innermost heart, has certainly something loyal and sincere——

GINA (*almost crying*). You might have let me pass for what I was, then.

RELLING (*to* GREGERS). Is it rude to ask what you really want in this house?

GREGERS. To lay the foundations of a true marriage.

RELLING. So you don't think Ekdal's marriage is good enough as it is?

GREGERS. No doubt it's as good a marriage as most others, worse luck. But a *true* marriage it has never been.

HIALMAR. You have never had eyes for the claims of the ideal, Relling.

RELLING. All rubbish, my boy! But excuse me, Mr. Werle: how many—in round numbers—how many true marriages have you seen in the course of your life?

GREGERS. Scarcely a single one.

RELLING. Nor I either.

GREGERS. But I've seen innumerable marriages of the opposite kind. And it has been my fate to see at close quarters what ruin such a marriage can work.

HIALMAR. A man's whole moral basis may give way under his feet; that's the terrible part of it.

RELLING. Well, I can't say I've ever been exactly married, so I don't pretend to speak with authority. But this I know, that the child enters into the marriage problem. And you must leave the child in peace.

HIALMAR. Oh—Hedvig! my poor Hedvig!

RELLING. Yes, you must be good enough to keep Hedvig outside of all this. You two are grown-up people; you can, in God's name, mess and muddle with your relations as you please. But you must deal circumspectly with Hedvig, I tell you; or else you may do her a great injury.

HIALMAR. An injury!

RELLING. Yes, or she may do herself an injury—and perhaps others too.

GINA. How can you know that, Relling?

HIALMAR. Her sight is in no immediate danger, is it?

RELLING. I'm not talking about her sight. Hedvig is at a critical age. She'll be taking all sorts of mischief into her head.

GINA. That's true—I've noticed it already! She's taken to carrying on with the fire, out in the kitchen. She calls it playing at house-on-fire. I'm often afraid she'll really set fire to the house.

RELLING. You see; I thought as much.

GREGERS (*to* RELLING). But how do you account for that?

RELLING (*low*). Her constitution's changing, sir.

HIALMAR. So long as the child has me——! So long as I'm above ground——!

(*A knock at the door.*)

GINA. Hush, Ekdal; there's some one in the passage. (*Calls out.*) Come in!

(MRS. SÖRBY, *in walking dress, comes in.*)

MRS. SÖRBY. Good evening.

GINA (*going towards her*). Is that really you, Bertha?

MRS. SÖRBY. Yes, of course it is. But I've come inopportunely, I'm afraid?

HIALMAR. No, not at all; an emissary from *that* house——

MRS. SÖRBY (*to* GINA). To tell the truth, I hoped your men-folk would be out at this time; I just ran up to have a little chat with you, and to say good-bye.

GINA. Indeed? Are you going away, then?

MRS. SÖRBY. Yes, to-morrow morning,—up to Höidal. Mr. Werle has started this afternoon. (*Lightly, to* GREGERS.) He wished me to say good-bye for him.

GINA. Only fancy——!

HIALMAR. So Mr. Werle has gone? And now you're going after him?

MRS. SÖRBY. Yes, what do you say to that, Ekdal?

HIALMAR. I say: beware!

GREGERS. I must explain the situation. My father and Mrs. Sörby are going to be married.

HIALMAR. Going to be married!

GINA. Oh Bertha, so it's come to that at last!

RELLING (*his voice quivering a little*). This is surely not true?

MRS. SÖRBY. Yes, my dear Relling, it's true enough.

RELLING. You're going to marry again?

MRS. SÖRBY. Yes, it looks like it. Werle has got a special licence, and we're going to be married quite quietly, up at the works.

GREGERS. Then I must wish you all happiness, like a dutiful stepson

MRS. SÖRBY. Thank you very much—if you mean what you say. I hope it will lead to happiness, both for Werle and for me.

RELLING. You have every reason to hope that. Mr. Werle never gets drunk, so far as I know; and I don't suppose he's in the habit of thrashing his wives, like the late lamented horse-doctor.

MRS. SÖRBY. Oh now, let Sörby rest in peace. He had his good points too.

RELLING. Mr. Werle has better ones, I should think.

MRS. SÖRBY. He hasn't frittered away all that was good in him, at any rate. The man who does that must take the consequences.

RELLING. I shall go out with Molvik this evening.

MRS. SÖRBY. You mustn't do that, Relling. Don't do it—for my sake.

RELLING. There's nothing else for it. (*To* HIALMAR.) If you're going with us, come along.

GINA. No, thank you. Ekdal doesn't go in for such dispensations.

HIALMAR (*half aloud, in vexation*). Oh, do hold your tongue!

RELLING. Good-bye, Mrs.—Werle.

(*Goes out through the passage-door.*)

GREGERS (*to* MRS. SÖRBY). You seem to be pretty intimate with Dr. Relling.

MRS. SÖRBY. Yes, we've known each other for many years. At one time it seemed as if things might have gone further between us.

GREGERS. It was surely lucky for you that they didn't.

MRS. SÖRBY You may well say that. But I've always been wary of acting on impulse. A woman can't afford absolutely to throw herself away.

GREGERS. Aren't you just the least bit afraid that I may let my father know about this old friendship?

MRS. SÖRBY. Why, of course I've told him all about it myself.

GREGERS. Indeed?

MRS. SÖRBY. Your father knows everything that could, with any truth, be said about me. I've told him all; it was the first thing I did when I became aware of his intentions.

GREGERS. Then you've been franker than most people, I think.

MRS. SÖRBY. I've always been frank. We women get on best that way.

HIALMAR. What do you say to that, Gina?

GINA. Oh, we women are very different. Some get on best one way, some another.

MRS. SÖRBY. Well, for my part, Gina, I believe it's wisest to act as I've done. And Werle has no secrets either, on his side. That's really the bond of union between us, you see. Now he can sit and talk with me as openly as a child. He's never had the chance to do that before. Fancy a man like him, full of health and vitality, passing his whole youth and the prime of his life in listening to nothing but moral homilies! And very often the homilies were called forth by the most imaginary offences—at least so I believe.

GINA. That's true enough.

GREGERS. If you ladies are going to indulge in mutual confidences, I had better retire.

MRS. SÖRBY. You can stay so far as that's concerned. I shan't say a word more. But I wanted you to know that I had done nothing secretly or in any underhand way. It may seem as if I'd come in for a great piece of luck; and that's true in a sense. But after all, I don't think I'm getting any more than I'm giving. I shall stand by him always, and I can tend and care for him as no one else can, now that he's getting helpless.

HIALMAR. Getting helpless?

GREGERS (*to* MRS. SÖRBY). Don't speak of that here.

MRS. SÖRBY. There's no disguising it any longer, however much he would like to. He's going blind.

HIALMAR (*starts*). Going blind? That's strange. He too becoming blind!

GINA. Lots of people do.

MRS. SÖRBY. And you can imagine what that means to a business man. Well, I shall try as well as I can to make my eyes replace his. But I mustn't stay any longer, I'm so busy just now.—Oh, by-the-bye, Ekdal, I was to tell you that if there was anything Werle could do for you, you must just apply to Gråberg.

GREGERS. I'm sure Hialmar will decline that offer with thanks.

MRS. SÖRBY. Indeed? I don't think he used to be so——

GINA. No Bertha, Ekdal doesn't need anything from Mr. Werle now.

HIALMAR (*slowly, and with emphasis*). Will you present my compliments to your future husband, and say that I intend very shortly to pay a visit to Mr. Gråberg——

GREGERS. What! You don't really mean that?

HIALMAR. To pay a visit to Mr. Gråberg, I say, and obtain an account of the sum I owe his principal. I will pay that debt of honour—ha ha ha! a debt of honour, let us call it! In any case I will pay the whole, with five per cent. interest.

GINA. But,my dear Ekdal, God knows we haven't got the money to do it.

HIALMAR. Please tell your future husband that I am working assiduously at my invention. Please tell him that what stimulates me in this laborious task is the wish to free myself from a torturing burden of debt. That is my reason for proceeding with the invention. The entire profits are to be devoted to repaying your future husband's pecuniary advances.

MRS. SÖRBY. Something has happened here.

HIALMAR. Yes, that is so.

MRS. SÖRBY. Well, good-bye. I had something else to speak to you about, Gina; but it must keep till another time. Good-bye.

(HIALMAR *and* GREGERS *bow silently.* GINA *follows* MRS. SÖRBY *to the door.*)

HIALMAR. Not beyond the threshold, Gina!

(MRS. SÖRBY *goes;* GINA *shuts the door after her.*)

HIALMAR. There now, Gregers; I've got that burden of debt off my mind.

GREGERS. You soon will, at all events.

HIALMAR. I think my attitude may be called correct.

GREGERS. You are the man I have always taken you for.

HIALMAR. In certain cases, it's impossible to disregard the claim of the ideal. Yet, as the breadwinner of a family, I cannot but writhe and groan under it. I can tell you it's no joke for a man without capital to attempt the repayment of a long-standing obligation, over which, so to speak, there lies the dust of oblivion. But it can't be helped: the Man in me demands his rights.

GREGERS (*putting his hand on* HIALMAR'S *shoulder*). My dear Hialmar, now wasn't it a good thing I came?

HIALMAR. Yes.

GREGERS. Aren't you glad to have had your true position made clear to you?

HIALMAR (*somewhat impatiently*). Yes, of course I am. But there's one thing that's exasperating to my sense of justice.

GREGERS. And what's that?

HIALMAR. It is that—but I don't know whether I ought to express myself so unreservedly about your father.

GREGERS. Say what you please, so far as I am concerned.

HIALMAR. Well then, isn't it exasperating to think that it's not I, but he, who will realise the true marriage?

GREGERS. How can you say such a thing?

HIALMAR. I say it because it's the case. Isn't the marriage between your father and Mrs. Sörby founded upon complete confidence, upon entire and unreserved candour on both sides. They hide nothing from each other, they keep no secrets in the background; their relation is based, if I may put it so, on mutual confession and absolution.

GREGERS. Well, what then?

HIALMAR. Well, isn't that the whole thing? Didn't you yourself say that these were just the difficulties that had to be overcome in order to found a true marriage?

GREGERS. But this is quite another matter, Hialmar. You surely don't compare either yourself or your wife with those two——? Oh, you understand me well enough.

HIALMAR. Say what you like, there's something in all this that hurts and offends my sense of justice. It really looks as if there were no just providence to rule the world.

GINA. Oh no, Ekdal; you mustn't say such things.

GREGERS. Hm; don't let's get upon those questions.

HIALMAR. And yet, after all, I can't but recognise the guiding finger of fate. He's going blind.

GINA. Oh, you can't be sure of that.

HIALMAR. It's indubitable. At all events we oughtn't to doubt it; for in that very fact lies the just retribution. He has blinded a confiding fellow-creature in days gone by——

GREGERS. Unfortunately he has blinded many.

HIALMAR. And now comes inexorable, mysterious Fate, and demands Werle's own eyes.

GINA. Oh, how dare you say such dreadful things! I'm getting quite frightened.

HIALMAR. It is profitable to dive into the night side of existence now and then.

(HEDVIG, *in her hat and cloak, comes in through the passage door. She is in high spirits, and out of breath.*)

GINA. Are you back already?

HEDVIG. Yes, I didn't care to go any farther. It was a good thing, too, for I met some one at the door.

HIALMAR. It must have been that Mrs. Sörby.

HEDVIG. Yes.

HIALMAR (*walks up and down*). I hope you've seen her for the last time.

(*Silence.* HEDVIG, *discouraged, looks first at one and then at the other, as if to ascertain their frame of mind.*)

HEDVIG (*approaching, coaxingly*). Father.

HIALMAR. Well—what is it, Hedvig?

HEDVIG. Mrs. Sörby had got something for me.

HIALMAR (*stops*). For you?

HEDVIG. Yes. Something for to-morrow.

GINA. Bertha has always given you some little thing on your birthday.

HIALMAR. What is it?

HEDVIG. Oh, I mustn't tell you just now. Mother is to give it to me to-morrow morning before I'm up.

HIALMAR. What's all this nonsense that I'm to be kept in the dark about!

HEDVIG (*quickly*). No, you may see it if you like. It's a big letter.

(*Takes the letter out of her cloak pocket.*)

HIALMAR. A letter, too?

HEDVIG. Yes, it *is* only a letter. The rest will come later, I suppose. But fancy—a letter! I've never had a letter before. And there's "Miss" written upon it. (*Reads.*) "Miss Hedvig Ekdal." Only fancy—that's me!

HIALMAR. Let me see that letter.

HEDVIG (*hands it to him*). There it is.

HIALMAR. That's Mr. Werle's hand.

GINA. Are you sure of that, Ekdal?

HIALMAR. Look for yourself.

GINA. Oh, do you think I know about such like things?

HIALMAR. Hedvig, may I open the letter—and read it?

HEDVIG. Yes, of course you may, if you want to.

GINA. No, not to-night, Ekdal; it's to be kept till to-morrow.

HEDVIG (*softly*). Oh, can't you let him read it!

It's sure to be something good; and then father'll be glad, and it'll all be pleasant again.

HIALMAR. I may open it then?

HEDVIG. Yes do, father. I'm so anxious to know what it is.

HIALMAR. All right. (*Opens the letter, takes out a paper, reads it through, and appears bewildered.*) What's this——?

GINA. What does it say?

HEDVIG. Oh yes, father, tell us!

HIALMAR. Be quiet. (*Reads it through again; he has turned pale, but says with self-control:*) It's a deed of gift, Hedvig.

HEDVIG. Is it? What sort of gift am I to have?

HIALMAR. Read for yourself.

(HEDVIG *goes over and reads for a time by the lamp.*)

HIALMAR (*half-aloud, clenching his hands*). The eyes! The eyes!—and then that letter!

HEDVIG (*leaves off reading*). Yes, but it seems to me that it's grandfather that's to have it.

HIALMAR (*takes the letter from her*). Gina—can you understand this?

GINA. I know nothing whatever about it; tell me what's the matter.

HIALMAR. Mr. Werle writes to Hedvig that her old grandfather needn't trouble himself any longer with the copying, but that he can henceforth draw on the office for a hundred crowns a month.

GREGERS. Aha!

HEDVIG. A hundred crowns, mother! I read that.

GINA. What a good thing for grandfather.

HIALMAR. A hundred crowns a month so long as he needs it—that means, of course, so long as he lives.

GINA. Well, so he's provided for, poor dear.

HIALMAR. But there's more to come. You didn't read that, Hedvig. Afterwards this gift is to pass on to you.

HEDVIG. To me! The whole of it?

HIALMAR. He writes that the same amount is assured to you for the whole of your life. Do you hear that, Gina?

GINA. Yes, I hear.

HEDVIG. Fancy—all that money I'm to get! (*Shakes him.*) Father, father, aren't you glad——?

HIALMAR (*eluding her*). Glad! (*Walks about.*) Oh what vistas—what perspectives open up before me! It's Hedvig, Hedvig that he showers these benefactions upon!

GINA. Yes, because it's Hedvig's birthday——

HEDVIG. And you'll get it all the same, father! You may be sure I shall give all the money to you and mother.

HIALMAR. To mother, yes! There we have it.

GREGERS. Hialmar, this is a trap he's setting for you.

HIALMAR. Do you think it's another trap?

GREGERS. When he was here this morning he said: Hialmar Ekdal is not the man you imagine him to be.

HIALMAR. Not the man——!

GREGERS. You will see that, he said.

HIALMAR. He wanted to show you that I would let myself be put off with money——!

HEDVIG. Oh mother, what does all this mean?

GINA. Go and take off your things.

(HEDVIG *goes out by the kitchen door, half-crying.*)

GREGERS. Yes, Hialmar—now we shall see who was right, he or I.

HIALMAR (*slowly tears the paper across, lays both pieces on the table, and says*). Here is my answer.

GREGERS. Just what I expected.

HIALMAR (*goes over to* GINA, *who stands by the stove, and says in a low voice*). Now please make a clean breast of it. If the connection between you and him was quite over when you—came to care for me, as you call it, why did he put us in a position to marry?

GINA. I suppose he thought our house would be open to him.

HIALMAR. Only that? Wasn't he afraid of a possible contingency?

GINA. I don't know what you mean.

HIALMAR. I want to know whether—your child has the right to live under my roof.

GINA (*draws herself up; her eyes flash*). *You* ask that!

HIALMAR. You shall answer me this one question: Does Hedvig belong to me—or——? Well!

GINA (*looking at him with cold defiance*). I don't know.

HIALMAR (*quivering a little*). You don't know!

GINA. How should *I* know? A creature like *me*——

HIALMAR (*quietly, turning away from her*). Then I have nothing more to do in this house.

GREGERS. Take care, Hialmar! Think what you're doing!

HIALMAR (*puts on his overcoat*). In this case, there's nothing for a man like me to think twice about.

GREGERS. Yes indeed, there are endless things to be considered. You three must be together if you're to attain the true frame of mind for self-sacrificing forgiveness.

HIALMAR. I don't want to attain it. Never, never! My hat! (*Takes his hat.*) My home has fallen in ruins about me. (*Bursts into tears.*) Gregers, I have no child!

HEDVIG (*who has opened the kitchen door*). What is that you're saying? (*Coming to him.*) Father, father!

GINA. There, you see!

HIALMAR. Don't come near me Hedvig! Keep far away. I can't bear to see you. Oh! those eyes——! Good-bye. (*Makes for the door.*)

HEDVIG (*clinging tight to him and screaming loudly*) No, no! Don't leave me!

GINA (*cries out*). Look at the child, Ekdal! Look at the child!

HIALMAR. I won't! I cannot! I must get out—away from all this!

(*He tears himself away from* HEDVIG, *and goes out through the passage door.*)

HEDVIG (*with despairing eyes*). He's going away from us, mother! He's going away from us! He'll never come back again!

GINA. Don't cry, Hedvig. Father's sure to come back again.

HEDVIG (*throws herself sobbing on the sofa*). No, no, he'll never come home to us any more.

GREGERS. Do you believe I meant all for the best, Mrs. Ekdal?

GINA. Yes, I suppose so; but God forgive you, all the same.

HEDVIG (*lying on the sofa*). Oh, this will kill me! What have I done to him? Mother, you must fetch him home again!

GINA. Yes yes yes; only calm yourself, and I'll go out and look for him. (*Puts on her outdoor things.*) Perhaps he's gone in to Relling's. But you mustn't lie there and cry. Promise me!

HEDVIG (*weeping convulsively*). Yes, I'll leave off; if only father comes back!

GREGERS (*to* GINA, *who is going*). After all, hadn't you better leave him to fight out his bitter fight to the end?

GINA. Oh, he can do that afterwards. First and foremost we must pacify the child.

(*Goes out by the passage-door.*)

HEDVIG (*sits up and dries her tears*). Now you must tell me what all this means. Why doesn't father want me any more?

GREGERS. You mustn't ask that until you're a big girl—quite grown-up.

HEDVIG (*sobs*). But I can't go on bearing all this misery till I'm grown-up.—I think I know what it is. —Perhaps I'm not really father's child.

GREGERS (*uneasily*). How could that be?

HEDVIG. Mother might have found me. And perhaps father has just got to know it; I've read of such things.

GREGERS. Well, but if it were so——

HEDVIG. I think he might love me just as well for all that. Yes, even more. We got the wild duck as a present, and I love it so dearly all the same.

GREGERS (*diverting the conversation*). Ah, the wild duck, by-the-bye! Let's talk about the wild duck a little, Hedvig.

HEDVIG. The poor wild duck! He doesn't want to see it any more either. Only think, he wanted to wring its neck!

GREGERS. Oh, he won't do that.

HEDVIG. No; but he said he wanted to. And I think it was horrid of father to say it; for I pray for the wild duck every night, and ask that it may be preserved from death and all that is evil.

GREGERS (*looking at her*). Do you say your prayers every night?

HEDVIG. Yes.

GREGERS. Who taught you to do that?

HEDVIG. I myself; once when father was very ill, and had leeches on his neck, and said that death was staring him in the face.

GREGERS. Well?

HEDVIG. Then I prayed for him as I lay in bed; and since then I've always kept it up.

GREGERS. And now you pray for the wild duck too?

HEDVIG. I thought it was best to bring in the wild duck; for she was so weakly at first.

GREGERS. Do you pray in the morning, too?

HEDVIG. No, of course not.

GREGERS. Why not in the morning?

HEDVIG. In the morning it's light, and there's nothing in particular to be afraid of.

GREGERS. And your father was going to wring the neck of the wild duck that you love so dearly?

HEDVIG. No; he said he would like to wring its neck, but he would spare it for my sake; and that was kind of father.

GREGERS (*coming a little nearer*). But suppose you were to sacrifice the wild duck, of your own free will, for his sake?

HEDVIG (*rising*). The wild duck!

GREGERS. Suppose you were to sacrifice, for his sake, the dearest treasure you have in the world?

HEDVIG. Do you think that would do any good?

GREGERS. Try it, Hedvig.

HEDVIG (*softly, with flashing eyes*). Yes, I will try it.

GREGERS. Have you really the courage for it, do you think?

HEDVIG. I'll ask grandfather to shoot the wild duck for me.

GREGERS. Yes, do. But not a word to your mother about it!

HEDVIG. Why not?

GREGERS. She doesn't understand us.

HEDVIG. The wild duck! I'll try it to-morrow morning! (GINA *comes in by the passage door.*)

HEDVIG (*going towards her*). Did you find him, mother?

GINA. No, but I heard he had called and taken Relling with him.

GREGERS. Are you sure of that?

GINA. Yes, the porter's wife said so. Molvik went with them too, she said.

GREGERS. This evening, when his mind so sorely needs to wrestle in solitude——!

GINA (*takes off her things*). Yes, men are never to be depended on. The Lord only knows where Relling has dragged him to! I ran over to Madam Eriksen's, but they weren't there.

HEDVIG (*struggling to keep back her tears*). Oh, if he should never come home any more!

GREGERS. He *will* come home again. I shall have news to give him to-morrow; and then you'll see *how* he'll come. You may rely upon that, Hedvig, and sleep in peace. Good-night.

(*He goes out through the passage door.*)

HEDVIG (*throws herself sobbing on* GINA'S *neck*). Mother, mother!

GINA (*pats her shoulder and sighs*). Ah yes; Relling was right, he was. That's what happens when crazy people go about presenting the claims of the what-do-you-call-it.

Act Fifth.

(HIALMAR EKDAL'S *studio. Cold, grey, morning light. Wet snow lies upon the large panes of the sloping roof-window.*)

(GINA *comes from the kitchen with an apron and bib on, and carrying a dusting-brush and a duster; she goes towards the sitting-room door. At the same moment* HEDVIG *comes hurriedly in from the passage.*)

GINA (*stops*). Well?

HEDVIG. Oh, mother, I almost think he's down at Relling's——

GINA. There, you see!

HEDVIG. ——because the porter's wife says she could hear that Relling had two people with him when he came home last night.

GINA. That's just what I thought.

HEDVIG. But he might just as well have gone right away, if he won't come up to us.

GINA. I'll go down and speak to him, at all events.

(OLD EKDAL, *in dressing-gown and slippers, and with a lighted pipe, appears at the door of his room.*)

EKDAL. Hialmar—— Isn't Hialmar at home?

GINA. No, he's gone out.

EKDAL. So early? And in such a furious snow-storm? Well well; don't mind me; I can take my morning walk alone.

(*He slides the garret door aside;* HEDVIG *helps him; he goes in; she closes it after him.*)

HEDVIG (*in an undertone*). Only think, mother, when grandfather hears that father's going to leave us.

GINA. Oh nonsense; grandfather mustn't hear anything about it. It was a heaven's mercy that he wasn't at home yesterday in all that hurly-burly.

HEDVIG. Yes, but——

(GREGERS *comes in by the passage door.*)

GREGERS. Well, have you any news of him?

GINA. They say he's down at Relling's.

GREGERS. At Relling's! Has he really been out with those creatures?

GINA. Yes, like enough.

GREGERS. When he should have been yearning for solitude, for earnest self-examination——

GINA. Yes, you may well say so.

(RELLING *enters from the passage.*)

HEDVIG (*going to him*). Is father in your room?

GINA (*at the same time*). Is he there?

RELLING. Yes, of course he is.

HEDVIG. And you never let us know!

RELLING. Yes; I'm a brute. But in the first place I had to look after the other brute; I mean our dæmonic friend, of course; and then I fell asleep, so sound asleep that——

GINA. What does Ekdal say to-day?

RELLING. He says nothing whatever.

HEDVIG. Doesn't he speak?

RELLING. Not a blessed word.

GREGERS. No no; I can understand that very well.

GINA. But what's he doing then?

RELLING. He's lying on the sofa, snoring.

GINA. Oh is he? Yes, Ekdal's a rare one to snore.

HEDVIG. Asleep? Can he sleep?

RELLING. Well, it certainly looks like it.

GREGERS. Very natural, after the spiritual conflict that has rent him——

GINA. And then he's not accustomed to roving about out of doors at night.

HEDVIG. It's perhaps a good thing that he's getting some sleep, mother.

GINA. Of course it is; and we must take care not to rouse him too early. Thank you, Relling. I must get the house cleaned up a bit now, and then—— Come and help me, Hedvig.

(GINA *and* HEDVIG *go into the sitting-room.*)

GREGERS (*turning to* RELLING). What's your theory as to the spiritual tumult that's now going on in Hialmar Ekdal?

RELLING. Upon my word I haven't noticed any spiritual tumult about him.

GREGERS. What! not at such a crisis, when his whole life has been placed on a new foundation——? How can you think that such an individuality as Hialmar's——?

RELLING. Oh, individuality—he! If he ever had any tendency to the abnormal developments you call individuality, it was extirpated, root and fibre, before he was out of his teens.

GREGERS. It would be strange if that were so,

considering the loving care with which he was brought up.

RELLING. By those two affected, hysterical maiden aunts, you mean?

GREGERS. Let me tell you that they were women who never forgot the claim of the ideal—but of course, you'll simply make game of me again.

RELLING. No, I'm in no humour for that. I know all about these ladies; for he has favoured me with floods of rhetoric on the subject of his "two soul-mothers." But I don't think he has much to thank them for. Ekdal's misfortune is that in his own circle he has always been looked upon as a shining light——

GREGERS. Not without reason, surely. Look at the depth of his mind!

RELLING. I've never discovered it. That his father believed in it I don't so much wonder; the old lieutenant has been an ass all his days.

GREGERS. He has had a childlike mind all his days; that's what you don't understand.

RELLING. Well, so be it. But then, when our dear, sweet Hialmar went to college, he immediately passed for the great light of the future amongst his comrades too. He was handsome, the rascal—red and white—a shop-girl's ideal of manly beauty; and with his superficially emotional temperament, and his sympathetic voice, and his talent for declaiming other people's verses and other people's thoughts——

GREGERS (*indignantly*). Is it Hialmar Ekdal you're talking about in that strain?

RELLING. Yes, with your permission; I'm simply showing you the other side of the idol you're grovelling before.

GREGERS. I shouldn't have thought I was so utterly blind.

RELLING. Oh, there's nothing strange in that. You're a sick man, too, you see.

GREGERS. You're right there.

RELLING. Yes. Yours is a complicated case. First of all there's that troublesome integrity-fever; and then—what's worse—you're always in a delirium of hero-worship; you must always have something to adore, outside yourself.

GREGERS. Yes, I must certainly seek it outside myself.

RELLING. But you make such shocking mistakes about every new phœnix you think you have discovered. Here again you've come to a cotter's cabin with your claim of the ideal; the people of the house are insolvent.

GREGERS. If you don't think better than that of Hialmar Ekdal, what pleasure can you find in being everlastingly with him?

RELLING. Well, you see, I'm supposed to be a sort of a doctor—save the mark! I can't but give a hand to the poor sick people who live under the same roof with me.

GREGERS. Oh, indeed! Ekdal is sick too, is he?

RELLING. Most people are, worse luck.

GREGERS. And what remedy are you applying in Hialmar's case?

RELLING. My usual one. I'm fostering the life-illusion[1] in him.

GREGERS. Life—illusion? Is that what you said?

RELLING. Yes, I said illusion. For illusion, you know, is the stimulating principle.

GREGERS. May I ask with what illusion Hialmar is inoculated?

RELLING. No, thanks; I don't betray professional secrets to quacksalvers. You would probably go and make a still worse muddle of him. But my method is infallible. I've applied it to Molvik as well. I've made him "dæmonic." That's the blister I have to put on *his* neck.

GREGERS. Isn't he really dæmonic then?

RELLING. What the devil do you mean by dæmonic? It's only a piece of hocus-pocus I've invented to keep up a spark of life in him. But for that, the poor harmless creature would have succumbed to self-contempt and despair many a long year ago. And then the old lieutenant! But he has hit upon his own cure, you see.

GREGERS. Lieutenant Ekdal? What of him?

RELLING. Just think of the old bear-hunter shutting himself up in that dark garret to shoot rabbits! I tell you there isn't a happier sportsman in the world than that old man pottering about in there among all that rubbish. The four or five withered Christmas-trees he has saved up are the same to him as the whole great fresh Höidal forest;

[1] "Livslögnen," literally "the life-lie." The context sufficiently explains the difference between Relling's "life-illusion" and Schopenhauer's.

the cock and the hens are big game-birds in the fir-tops; and the rabbits that flop about the garret floor are the bears he has to battle with—the mighty hunter of the mountains!

GREGERS. Poor unfortunate old man! Yes; he has had to narrow the ideals of his youth, indeed!

RELLING. While I think of it, Mr. Werle, junior, don't use that foreign word: ideals. We've got the excellent native word: lies.

GREGERS. Do you think the two things are related?

RELLING. Yes, just about as closely as typhus and putrid fever.

GREGERS. Dr. Relling, I shall not give in until I have rescued Hialmar from your clutches!

RELLING. So much the worse for him. Rob the average man of his life-illusion, and you rob him of his happiness at the same time. (*To* HEDVIG, *who comes in from the sitting-room.*) Well, little wild-duck-mother, I'm just going down to see whether papa is still lying meditating upon that wonderful invention of his. (*Goes out by the passage door.*)

GREGERS (*approaches* HEDVIG). I can see by your face that you haven't done it.

HEDVIG. What? Oh, that about the wild duck. No.

GREGERS. Your courage failed when the time for action came, I suppose.

HEDVIG. No, that wasn't it. But when I awoke this morning and remembered what we had been talking about, it seemed so strange.

GREGERS. Strange?

HEDVIG. Yes, I don't know—— Yesterday evening, at the moment, I thought there was something so delightful about it; but since I've slept and thought of it again, it somehow doesn't seem worth while.

GREGERS. Ah, I thought you couldn't have grown up quite unharmed in this house.

HEDVIG. I don't care about that, if only father would come up——

GREGERS. Oh, if only your eyes had been opened to that which gives life its value—if you possessed the true, joyous, fearless spirit of sacrifice, you would soon see *how* he would come up to you.—But I believe in you still, Hedvig.

(*He goes out by the passage door.*)

(HEDVIG *wanders about the room for a time; she is on the point of going into the kitchen when a knock is heard at the garret door.* HEDVIG *goes over and opens it a little; old* EKDAL *comes out; she pushes the door to again.*)

EKDAL. Hm, it's not much fun to take one's morning walk alone.

HEDVIG. Wouldn't you like to go shooting, grandfather?

EKDAL. It's not the weather for it to-day. It's so dark there, you can scarcely see where you're going.

HEDVIG. Do you never want to shoot anything besides the rabbits?

EKDAL. Do you think the rabbits aren't good enough?

HEDVIG. Yes, but what about the wild duck?

EKDAL. Ho-ho! are you afraid I shall shoot your wild duck? Never in the world. Never.

HEDVIG. No, I suppose you couldn't; they say it's very difficult to shoot wild ducks.

EKDAL. Couldn't! Should rather think I could.

HEDVIG. How would you set about it, grandfather?—I don't mean with *my* wild duck, but with others?

EKDAL. I should take care to shoot them in the breast, you know; that's the surest place. And then you must shoot against the feathers, you see—not the way of the feathers.

HEDVIG. Do they die then, grandfather?

EKDAL. Yes, they die right enough—when you shoot properly. Well, I must go in and have a wash. Hm,—understand—hm.

(*Goes into his room.*)

(HEDVIG *waits a little, glances towards the sitting-room door, goes over to the bookcase, stands on tip-toe, takes the double-barrelled pistol down from the shelf, and looks at it.* GINA, *with brush and duster, comes from the sitting-room.* HEDVIG *hastily lays down the pistol, unobserved.*)

GINA. Don't stand raking amongst father's things, Hedvig.

HEDVIG (*goes away from the bookcase*). I was only going to tidy up a bit.

GINA. Go into the kitchen, and see if the coffee's keeping hot; I'll take his breakfast on a tray, when I go down to him.

(HEDVIG *goes out.* GINA *begins to sweep and clean up the studio. Presently the passage door is opened with hesitation, and* HIALMAR EKDAL *looks in. He has on his overcoat, but not his hat; he is unwashed, and his hair is dishevelled and unkempt. His eyes are dull and heavy.*)

GINA (*standing with the brush in her hand, and looking at him*). Oh, there now, Ekdal—so you've come after all?

HIALMAR (*comes in and answers in a toneless voice*). I come—only to depart again immediately.

GINA. Yes yes, I suppose so. But, Lord help us! what a sight you are!

HIALMAR. A sight?

GINA. And your nice winter-coat too! Well, that's done for.

HEDVIG (*at the kitchen door*). Mother, hadn't I better——? (*Sees* HIALMAR, *gives a loud scream of joy, and runs to him.*) Oh father, father!

HIALMAR (*turns away and makes a gesture of repulsion*). Away, away, away! (*To* GINA.) Keep her away from me, I say!

GINA (*in a low tone*). Go into the sitting-room, Hedvig.

(HEDVIG *goes silently in.*)

HIALMAR (*fussily pulls out the table-drawer*). I must have my books with me. Where are my books?

GINA. Which books?

HIALMAR. My scientific books, of course; the technical magazines I use for my invention.

GINA (*searches in the bookcase*). Is it these with paper covers?

HIALMAR. Yes, of course.

GINA (*lays a heap of magazines on the table*). Shan't I get Hedvig to cut them for you?

HIALMAR. I don't require to have them cut for me.

(*Short silence.*)

GINA. Then you're still bent on leaving us, Ekdal?

HIALMAR (*rummaging amongst the books*). Yes, that's a matter of course, I should think.

GINA. Well well.

HIALMAR (*vehemently*). How can I live here, to be stabbed to the heart every hour of the day?

GINA. God forgive you for thinking so vilely of me.

HIALMAR. Prove——!

GINA. I think it's you that have got to prove.

HIALMAR. After a past like yours? There are certain claims—I may almost call them claims of the ideal——

GINA. But what about grandfather? What's to become of him, poor dear?

HIALMAR. I know my duty; my helpless father will come with me. I'm going out into the town to make arrangements—. Hm—(*hesitatingly*) has any one found my hat on the stairs?

GINA. No. Have you lost your hat?

HIALMAR. Of course I had it on when I came in last night; there's no doubt about that; but I couldn't find it this morning.

GINA. Lord help us! where have you been to with those two ne'er-do-wells?

HIALMAR. Oh, don't bother me about trivial things. Do you suppose I'm in the humour to remember details?

GINA. If only you haven't caught cold, Ekdal.

(*Goes out into the kitchen.*)

HIALMAR (*talks to himself in a low tone of irritation, whilst he empties the table-drawer*). You're a scoundrel, Relling!—You're a low fellow!—Ah, you shameless tempter!—I wish I could get some one to murder you!

(*He lays some old letters on one side, finds the torn paper of yesterday, takes it up and looks at the pieces; puts it down hurriedly as* GINA *enters.*)

GINA (*sets a tray with coffee, etc., on the table*). Here's a drop of something warm, if you'd like it. And there's some bread and butter and a snack of salt meat.

HIALMAR (*glancing at the tray*). Salt meat? Never under this roof! It's true I haven't had a mouthful of solid food for nearly twenty-four hours; but no matter.—My memoranda! The commencement of my autobiography! What's become of my diary, and all my important papers? (*Opens the sitting-room door, but draws back.*) She's there too!

GINA. Good Lord! the child must be *somewhere!*

HIALMAR. Come out.

(*He makes room,* HEDVIG *comes, scared, into the studio.*)

HIALMAR (*with his hand upon the door-handle, says to* GINA). In these, the last moments I spend in my former home, I wish to be spared from interlopers.

(*Goes into the room.*)

HEDVIG (*with a bound towards her mother, asks softly, trembling*). Does that mean me?

GINA. Stay out in the kitchen, Hedvig; or, no—

you'd better go into your own room. (*Speaks to* HIALMAR *as she goes in to him.*) Wait a bit, Ekdal; don't rummage so in the drawers; I know where everything is.

HEDVIG (*stands a moment immovable, in terror and perplexity, biting her lips to keep back the tears; then she clenches her hands convulsively, and says softly*). The wild duck!

(*She steals over and takes the pistol from the shelf, opens the garret door a little way, creeps in, and draws the door to after her.*)

(HIALMAR *and* GINA *can be heard disputing in the sitting-room.*)

HIALMAR (*comes in with some manuscript books and old loose papers, which he lays upon the table*). That portmanteau's no good! There are a thousand and one things I must drag with me.

GINA (*following with the portmanteau*). Why not leave all the rest for the present, and only take a shirt and a pair of woollen drawers with you.

HIALMAR. Whew!—all these wearisome preparations——!

(*Pulls off his overcoat and throws it upon the sofa*).

GINA. And there's the coffee getting cold.

HIALMAR. Hm. (*Drinks a mouthful without thinking of it, and then another.*)

GINA (*dusting the backs of the chairs*). Your great difficulty will be to find such a big garret for the rabbits.

HIALMAR. What! Am I to drag all those rabbits with me too?

GINA. I'm sure grandfather can't get on without his rabbits.

HIALMAR. He must just get used to doing without them. Haven't *I* got to sacrifice very much greater things than rabbits!

GINA (*dusting the bookcase*). Shall I put the flute in the portmanteau for you?

HIALMAR. No. No flute for me. But give me the pistol!

GINA. Do you want to take the pigstol with you?

HIALMAR. Yes. My loaded pistol.

GINA (*searching for it*). It's gone. He must have taken it in with him.

HIALMAR. Is he in the garret?

GINA. Yes, of course he's in the garret.

HIALMAR. Hm—poor lonely old man.

(*He takes a piece of bread and butter, eats it, and finishes his cup of coffee.*)

GINA. If we hadn't let that room, you could have moved in there.

HIALMAR. And continued to live under the same roof with——! Never,—never!

GINA. But couldn't you put up with the sitting-room for a day or two? You could have it all to yourself.

HIALMAR. Never within these walls!

GINA. Well then, down with Relling and Molvik.

HIALMAR. Don't mention those creatures' names to me! It takes away my appetite only to think of them—— Oh no, I must go out into the storm and the snow-blast,—go from house to house and seek shelter for my father and myself.

GINA. But you've got no hat, Ekdal! You've lost your hat, you know.

HIALMAR. Oh those two brutes, those slaves of all the vices! A hat must be got for me. (*Takes another piece of bread and butter.*) Something must be done. For I have no mind to throw away my life, either. (*Looks for something on the tray.*)

GINA. What are you looking for?

HIALMAR. Butter.

GINA. I'll get you some at once. (*Goes out into the kitchen.*)

HIALMAR (*calls after her*). Oh it doesn't matter; dry bread is all I require.

GINA (*brings a dish of butter*). Look here; this is fresh churned.

(*She pours out another cup of coffee for him; he seats himself on the sofa, spreads more butter on the already buttered bread, and eats and drinks awhile in silence.*)

HIALMAR. Could I, without being intruded on by any one—by any one at all—could I live in the sitting-room for a day or two?

GINA. Yes, you could quite well, if you only would.

HIALMAR. For I see no possibility of getting all father's things out in such a hurry.

GINA. And besides, you'll have to tell him first that you don't mean to live with us others any longer.

HIALMAR (*pushes away his coffee cup*). Yes, there's that too; I'll have to lay bare the whole complicated history to him—— I must turn matters over; I must have breathing-time; I can't take the whole burden upon my shoulders in a single day.

GINA. No, especially in such horrible weather as it is outside.

HIALMAR (*touching* WERLE'S *letter*). I see that paper is still lying about here.

GINA. Yes, *I* haven't touched it.

HIALMAR. So far as I'm concerned it's mere waste paper——

GINA. Well *I'm* certainly not thinking of making any use of it.

HIALMAR. ——but we'd better not let it get lost all the same;—in all the upset when I move, it might easily——

GINA. I'll take care of it, Ekdal.

HIALMAR. The donation is really made to father, and it rests with him to accept or decline it.

GINA (*sighs*). Yes, poor old father——

HIALMAR. To make quite safe—— Where shall I find some gum?

GINA (*goes to the bookcase*). Here's the gum-pot.

HIALMAR. And a brush?

GINA. Here's the brush too.

(*Brings him the things.*)

HIALMAR (*takes a pair of scissors*). Just a strip of paper at the back——(*clips and gums*). Far be it from me to lay hands upon what is not my own—and least of all upon what belongs to a destitute old man—and to—the other as well.—There now. Let it lie there for a time; and when it's dry, take it away. I wish never to see that document again. Never!

(GREGERS WERLE *enters from the passage.*)

GREGERS (*somewhat surprised*). What,—are you sitting here, Hialmar?

HIALMAR (*rises hurriedly*). I had sunk down from fatigue.

GREGERS. You've been having breakfast, I see.

HIALMAR. The body sometimes makes its claims felt too.

GREGERS. What have you decided to do?

HIALMAR. For a man like me, there's only one way to go. I'm just putting my most important things together. But it takes time, you know.

GINA (*rather impatiently*). Am I to get the room ready for you, or shall I pack your portmanteau?

HIALMAR (*after a glance of annoyance at* GREGERS). Pack—and get the room ready!

GINA (*takes the portmanteau*). Very well; then I'll put in the shirt and the other things. (*Goes into the sitting-room and draws the door to after her.*)

GREGERS (*after a short silence*). I never thought this would be the end of it. Do you really feel it a necessity to leave house and home?

HIALMAR (*wanders about restlessly*). What would you have me do?—I am not fitted to bear unhappiness, Gregers. I must feel secure and at peace in my surroundings.

GREGERS. But can't you feel that here? Just try it. It seems to me you have firm ground to build upon now—if only you start afresh. And remember, you have your invention to live for.

HIALMAR. Oh don't talk about my invention. It's perhaps still in the dim distance.

GREGERS. Indeed!

HIALMAR. Why, great heavens, what would you have me invent? Other people have invented almost everything already. It's more and more difficult every day——

GREGERS. And you've devoted so much work to it.

HIALMAR. It was that blackguard Relling that urged me to it.

GREGERS. Relling?

HIALMAR. Yes, it was he that first led me to notice my aptitude for making some notable discovery in photography.

GREGERS. Aha—it was Relling!

HIALMAR. Oh, I've been so truly happy over it! Not so much for the sake of the invention itself, but because Hedvig believed in it—believed in it with a child's whole earnestness of faith. At least, I've been fool enough to go and imagine that she believed in it.

GREGERS. Can you really think that Hedvig has been false towards you?

HIALMAR. I can think anything now. It's Hedvig that stands in my way. She will blot out the sunlight from my whole life.

GREGERS. Hedvig! Is it Hedvig you're talking of? How should *she* blot out your sunlight?

HIALMAR (*without answering*). I have loved that child so unspeakably. I have felt so unspeakably happy every time I came home to my poor room, and she flew to meet me, with her sweet little short-sighted eyes. Oh, confiding fool that I have been! I loved her unspeakably; and I yielded myself up to the dream, the delusion, that she loved me unspeakably in return.

GREGERS. Do you call that a delusion?

HIALMAR. How should I know? I can't get anything out of Gina; and besides, she's totally blind to the ideal side of these complications. But to you I feel impelled to open my mind, Gregers. I can't shake off this frightful doubt—perhaps Hedvig has never really and honestly loved me.

GREGERS. What would you say if she were to give you a proof of her love? (*Listens.*) What's that? I thought I heard the wild duck——?

HIALMAR. It's the wild duck quacking. Father's in the garret.

GREGERS. Is he? (*His face lights up with joy.*) I say you may yet have proof that your poor misunderstood Hedvig loves you!

HIALMAR. Oh, what proof can she give me? I dare not believe in any assurances from that quarter.

GREGERS. Hedvig does not know what deceit means.

HIALMAR. Oh Gregers, that's just what I can't be certain about. Who knows what Gina and that Mrs. Sörby may many a time have sat here whispering and tattling about? And Hedvig usually has her ears open, I can tell you. Perhaps the deed of gift didn't come so unexpectedly after all. In fact, I'm not sure but that I gathered something of the sort.

GREGERS. What spirit is this that has come over you?

HIALMAR. I've had my eyes opened. Just you notice;—you'll see, the deed of gift is only a beginning. Mrs. Sörby has always been a good deal taken up with Hedvig; and now she has the power to do whatever she likes for the child. They can take her from me whenever they please.

GREGERS. Hedvig will never leave you.

HIALMAR. Don't be so sure of that. If only they beckon to her and throw out a golden bait——! Oh, and I have loved her so unspeakably! I would have counted it my highest happiness to take her tenderly by the hand and lead her, as one leads a timid child through a great dark empty room!—I am cruelly certain now that the poor photographer in his humble attic has never really and truly been anything to her. She has only cunningly contrived to keep on a good footing with him until the time came.

GREGERS. You don't believe that yourself, Hialmar.

HIALMAR. That's just the terrible part of it—I don't know what to believe,—I never can know it. But can you really doubt that it must be as I say? Ho-ho, you rely too much upon the claim of the ideal, my good Gregers! If those others came, with the glory of wealth about them, and called to the child:—"Leave him: come to us: here life awaits you"——!

GREGERS (*quickly*). Well, what then?

HIALMAR. If I then asked her: Hedvig, are you willing to renounce that life for me? (*Laughs scornfully.*) No thank you! You'd soon hear what answer I should get.

(*A pistol shot is heard from within the garret.*)

GREGERS (*loudly and joyfully*). Hialmar!

HIALMAR. There now; he must needs go shooting too.

GINA (*comes in*). Oh Ekdal, I can hear grandfather blazing away in the garret by himself.

HIALMAR. I'll look in.

GREGERS (*eagerly, with emotion*). Wait a bit! Do you know what that was?

HIALMAR. Yes, of course I know.

GREGERS. No you don't know. But *I* do. That was the proof!

HIALMAR. What proof?

GREGERS. It was a child's act of sacrifice. She has got your father to shoot the wild duck.

HIALMAR. To shoot the wild duck!

GINA. Oh, think of that——!

HIALMAR. What was that for?

GREGERS. She wanted to sacrifice to you her most cherished possession; for then she thought you would surely come to love her again.

HIALMAR (*tenderly, with emotion*). Oh, poor child!

GINA. What things she thinks of!

GREGERS. She only wanted your love again, Hialmar. She couldn't live without it.

GINA (*struggling with her tears*). There, you can see for yourself, Ekdal.

HIALMAR. Gina, where is she?

GINA (*sniffs*). Poor dear, she's sitting out in the kitchen, I daresay.

HIALMAR (*goes over, tears open the kitchen door, and says*). Hedvig, come, come in to me! (*Looks round.*) No, she's not here.

GINA. Then she must be in her own little room.

HIALMAR (*without*). No, she's not here either. (*Comes in.*) She must have gone out.

GINA. Yes, you wouldn't have her anywhere in the house.

HIALMAR. Oh, if she would only come home quickly, so that I can tell her—— Everything will come right now, Gregers; now I believe we can begin life afresh.

GREGERS (*quietly*). I knew it; I knew the child would make amends.

(OLD EKDAL *appears at the door of his room; he is in full uniform, and is busy buckling on his sword.*)

HIALMAR (*astonished*). Father! Are you there?

GINA. Have you been firing in your room?

EKDAL (*resentfully, approaching*). So you go shooting alone, Hialmar?

HIALMAR (*excited and confused*). Then it wasn't you that fired that shot in the garret?

EKDAL. *Me* that fired? Hm.

GREGERS (*calls out to* HIALMAR). She has shot the wild duck herself!

HIALMAR. What can it mean? (*Hastens to the garret door, tears it aside, looks in and calls loudly.*) Hedvig!

GINA (*runs to the door*). Good God, what's that!

HIALMAR (*goes in*). She's lying on the floor!

GREGERS. Hedvig! lying on the floor!

(*Goes in to* HIALMAR.)

GINA (*at the same time*) Hedvig! (*inside the garret*). No, no, no!

EKDAL. Ho-ho! does she go shooting too, now?

(HIALMAR, GINA, *and* GREGERS *carry* HEDVIG *into the studio; in her dangling right hand she holds the pistol fast clasped in her fingers.*)

HIALMAR (*distracted*). The pistol has gone off. She has wounded herself. Call for help! Help!

GINA (*runs into the passage and calls down*). Relling! Relling! Doctor Relling; come up as quick as you can!

(HIALMAR *and* GREGERS *lay* HEDVIG *down on the sofa.*)

EKDAL (*quietly*). The woods avenge themselves.

HIALMAR (*on his knees beside* HEDVIG). She'll soon come to now. She's coming to——; yes, yes, yes.

GINA (*who has come in again*). Where has she hurt herself? I can't see anything——

(RELLING *comes hurriedly, and immediately after him* MOLVIK; *the latter without his waistcoat and necktie, and with his coat open.*)

RELLING. What's the matter here?

GINA. They say Hedvig has shot herself.

HIALMAR. Come and help us!

RELLING. Shot herself!

(*He pushes the table aside and begins to examine her.*)

HIALMAR (*kneeling and looking anxiously up at him*). It can't be dangerous? Speak, Relling! She's scarcely bleeding at all. It can't be dangerous?

RELLING. How did it happen?

HIALMAR. Oh, we don't know——!

GINA. She wanted to shoot the wild duck.

RELLING. The wild duck?

HIALMAR. The pistol must have gone off.

RELLING. Hm. Indeed.

EKDAL. The woods avenge themselves. But I'm not afraid, all the same.

(*Goes into the garret and closes the door after him.*)

HIALMAR. Well, Relling,—why do you say nothing?

RELLING. The ball has entered the breast.

HIALMAR. Yes, but she's coming to!

RELLING. Surely you can see that Hedvig is dead.

GINA (*bursts into tears*). Oh my child, my child!

GREGERS (*huskily*). In the depths of the sea——

HIALMAR (*jumps up*). No, no, she must live! Oh, for God's sake, Relling—only a moment—only just till I can tell her how unspeakably I loved her all the time!

RELLING. The bullet has gone through her heart. Internal hemorrhage. Death must have been instantaneous.

HIALMAR. And I! I hunted her from me like an animal! And she crept terrified into the garret and died for love of me! (*Sobbing.*) I can never atone to her! I can never tell her——! (*Clenches his hands and cries, upwards.*) O thou above——! If thou *art* there! Why hast thou done this thing to me!

GINA. Hush, hush, you mustn't speak so wildly. We had no right to keep her, I suppose.

MOLVIK. The child is not dead, but sleepeth.

RELLING. Bosh!

HIALMAR (*becomes calm, goes over to the sofa, folds his arms, and looks at* HEDVIG). There she lies so stiff and still.

RELLING (*tries to loosen the pistol*). It's so tight, so tight.

GINA. No, no, Relling, don't break her fingers; let the pigstol be.

HIALMAR. She shall take it with her.

GINA. Yes, let her. But the child mustn't lie here for a show. She shall go into her own little room. Help me in with her, Ekdal. (HIALMAR *and* GINA *take* HEDVIG *between them.*)

HIALMAR (*as they are carrying her*). Oh Gina, Gina, can you survive this!

GINA. We must help each other to bear it. For now, at least, she belongs to both of us.

MOLVIK (*stretches out his arms and mumbles*). Blessed be the Lord; to earth thou shalt return; to earth thou shalt return——

RELLING (*whispers*). Hold your tongue, you fool; you're drunk.

(HIALMAR *and* GINA *carry the corpse out through the kitchen door.* RELLING *shuts it after them.* MOLVIK *slinks out into the passage.*)

RELLING (*goes over to* GREGERS *and says*). No one shall ever convince me that the pistol went off by accident.

GREGERS (*who has stood terrified, with convulsive twitchings*). Who can say how the dreadful thing happened?

RELLING. The powder has burnt the body of her dress. She must have pressed the pistol right against her breast and fired.

GREGERS. Hedvig has not died in vain. Did you not see how sorrow set free what is noble in him?

RELLING. Most people are ennobled by the actual presence of death. But how long do you suppose this nobility will last?

GREGERS. Will it not endure and increase throughout his life?

RELLING. Before a year is over, little Hedvig will be nothing to him but a pretty theme for declamation.

GREGERS. How dare you say that of Hialmar Ekdal?

RELLING. We shall talk of this again, when the grass has first withered on her grave. Then you'll hear him spout about "the child too early torn from her father's heart;" then you'll see him steep himself in a syrup of sentiment and self-admiration and self-pity. Just you see!

GREGERS. If you're right and I'm wrong, then life is not worth living.

RELLING. Oh, life would be quite tolerable, after all, if only we could be rid of the confounded duns that keep on pestering us, in our poverty, with the claim of the ideal.

GREGERS (*looking straight before him*). In that case, I'm glad that my destiny is what it is.

RELLING. Excuse me,—what *is* your destiny?

GREGERS (*going*). To be the thirteenth at table.

RELLING. The devil it is.

THE END.